BODYWORK & PAINTWORK
Manual

Martynn Randall

The Haynes Manual for automotive bodywork repair and painting

Haynes Publishing
Sparkford, Nr Yeovil, Somerset BA22 7JJ England

Haynes North America, Inc
861 Lawrence Drive, Newbury Park, California 91320 USA

Editions Haynes
4, Rue de l'Abreuvoir
92415 COURBEVOIE CEDEX, France

Haynes Publishing Nordiska AB
Box 1504, 751 45 Uppsala, Sweden

Acknowledgements
Thanks are due to Haynes Inc. for providing most of the text
and illustrations used in this book. Thanks are also due to
Draper Tools Ltd.

This manual is not a direct reproduction of any vehicle
manufacturer's data, and its publication should not be taken
as implying any technical approval by vehicle manufacturers
or importers.

A book in the Haynes Service and Repair Manual Series

Printed in the USA

ISBN 1 84425 198 5

British Library Cataloguing in Publication Data
A catalogue record for this book is available from the British
Library

**While every attempt is made to ensure that the
information in this manual is correct, no liability can be
accepted by the authors or publishers for loss, damage
or injury caused by any errors in, or omissions from,
the information given.**

(4198-160)

Notes

Introduction

Body/chassis and monocoque design

Introduction to replaceable panels

Safety first!

Body/chassis and monocoque design

Terminology

When talking to a body repairman, you'll hear the terms 'chassis,' 'subframe' and 'structure,' as well as pan, floorpan, bulkhead, connector, rail, underbody and a variety of other terms, all of which refer to the basic structure of a vehicle – the parts that give it strength – which used to be known by the all encompassing term 'chassis'.

What can make this especially confusing to the layman is that many of the terms are, to one degree or another, interchangeable, depending on who you are talking to or what kind of vehicle you are talking about. A subframe is a pair of chassis rails at the front or rear of a car, usually attached to a monocoque structure, but the rails that make up the subframe are often referred to as the rail. A structure can be anything from a floorpan that serves as a structural member (monocoque) to a conventional perimeter chassis made of rectangular, 'U' or 'I' section steel. A bulkhead can be the upright front or rear section of a monocoque structure, which makes it one of the principal stiffeners of the chassis structure, or it can be the bolted-on bulkhead (front or rear) sheet metal attached to a chassis. A floorpan (or pan) can be the stamped sheet metal floor between the chassis rails, the main stressed component of a monocoque or the stressed base for a platform type chassis such as the one used on the VW beetle.

Different terms are used by different workshops (or even different manufacturers). This is also true when you're dealing with cars from different countries, especially traditional European terminology and late model Japanese nomenclature. So, for the sake of clarity, we're going to set some terminology standards for use in this book – and at the same time explain a little about the different types of 'chassis' construction you're liable to run across.

Chassis types

Basically, there are six types of chassis or vehicle structure design. They are . . .

- *Monocoque construction chassis (which is probably the most common design in production today)*
- *Monocoque chassis with bolt on subframe structure(s)*
- *Perimeter chassis*
- *X section chassis*
- *Ladder chassis*
- *Platform chassis*

There are a few other designs, such as the central backbone tube chassis used on most Lotus automobiles and the 'spaceframe' made of small diameter tubing used on some German and Italian sports cars, but these are not something you'll run into very often.

Chapter 1

Monocoque construction

Monocoque construction is the most common form of chassis structure used on modern passenger cars. In this type of construction the floor pan, sill panels, front scuttle assembly, inner wing panels, rear bulkhead, boot floor, side pillars and roof all form an integrated structure which carries all the loads and to which the engine and suspension parts are bolted. Even the sections which look like conventional chassis rails, primarily at the front and rear where the engine and suspension components bolt on, are made of bent sheet metal and are part of the overall structure. Since almost everything except the drivetrain, doors, bonnet and boot lid is a stressed load bearing panel, damage to one part of the structure often means misalignment in other, adjacent parts, and straightening the bent structure is both difficult and critically important when repairing crash damage.

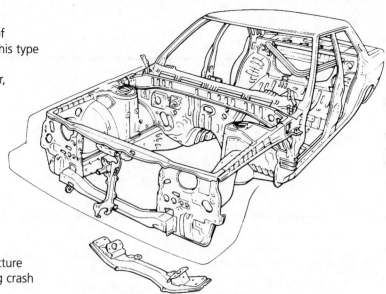

Monocoque construction body/chassis structures such as this are used on the majority of cars built today

Monocoque with subframe

This type of chassis design is popular on vehicles with large and/or heavy front mounted engines, and on many front wheel drive cars. It is, in essence, the monocoque design (see above) from the rear bumper to the bulkhead/scuttle structure, with a conventional box section chassis bolted to this structure and running forward to hold the front suspension components and engine. Since the wings, bonnet, radiator support, etc. are bolted to the subframe, rather than being structural members, front end collision damage is generally easier and/or quicker to repair than with totally monocoque construction vehicles.

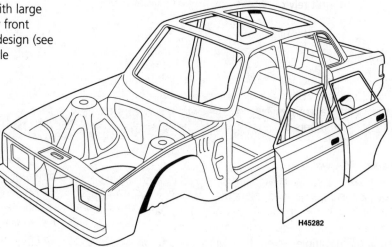

On monocoque structures almost everything except the doors, hood and trunk lid is a load bearing structural member

Perimeter chassis

The perimeter chassis was, for many years, the standard chassis type used on large American cars, and is still the preferred chassis structure for pickup trucks and vans. The chassis rails, generally constructed from box or channel section steel, surround the passenger compartment, with the floor pan adding structural strength (especially resistance to twisting loads) to the chassis. Front and rear crossmembers support the engine, suspension and drivetrain components. Because nearly all body parts are bolted or welded to each other, and bolted to the chassis through insulator mounts, sheet metal damage is much more easily repaired than on monocoque construction vehicles, and chassis damage can usually be remedied on a chassis straightener.

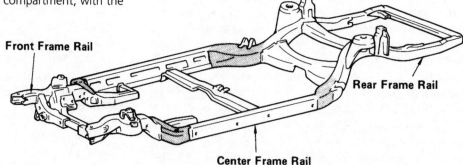

Front Frame Rail

Rear Frame Rail

Center Frame Rail

The perimeter chassis was, for many years, the standard method of chassis construction for large cars, and is still commonly used on pickup trucks and vans

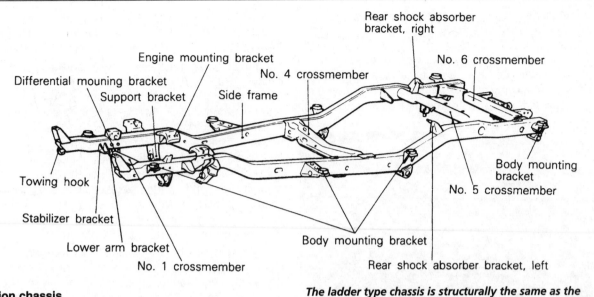

Differential mouning bracket
Engine mounting bracket
Support bracket
No. 4 crossmember
Side frame
Rear shock absorber bracket, right
No. 6 crossmember
Body mounting bracket
No. 5 crossmember
Towing hook
Stabilizer bracket
Lower arm bracket
No. 1 crossmember
Body mounting bracket
Rear shock absorber bracket, left

X section chassis

The X section chassis was also commonly used on large cars. The principle difference between it and the perimeter chassis is that it doesn't rely on the floor pan for torsional rigidity. Instead, increased chassis member size through the centre of the X section and multiple crossmembers give the chassis strength. As with the perimeter chassis, damage to the chassis itself can usually be easily repaired either on a chassis straightening machine or by cutting and welding in a new chassis section. Body panels, since they are not load bearing, can be replaced or repaired much more easily than the structural members of a monocoque type chassis.

Ladder chassis

Structurally, a ladder type chassis is almost identical to a perimeter chassis, except that the chassis rails usually form a straighter section and the use of multiple crossmembers adds stiffness to the chassis. Ladder type chassiss were most common on cars built before and immediately after World War II, but were generally superseded by the perimeter and X type chassis during the 1950's.

Platform chassis

The platform chassis is most commonly seen on the Volkswagen Beetle, where a floor pan and central tunnel provide the majority of the load carrying structure, with the suspension torsion bar housings and engine supports bolted to the front and rear of the platform. The body structure generally adds rigidity to the platform chassis, but only as an incidental fact, with the central tube and outer structure of the floor pan providing the major structure.

The ladder type chassis is structurally the same as the perimeter chassis, although the chassis rails are generally straighter and multiple crossmembers are used (this one is from a sport utility vehicle)

The platform chassis, such as the one used on Volkswagens (shown here), had the virtue of simplicity, but wasn't very stiff or strong

1 Chassis head
2 Floor plan
3 Front cross brace
4 Pedal cluster shaft opening
5 Accelerator pedal mount
6 Seat runners
7 shift lever hole
8 Jacking points
9 Parking brake lever mount
10 Heater control cable tube
11 Spring plate brackets
12 Seatbelt anchors
13 Rear cross brace
14 Chassis fork

Chapter 1

Introduction to replaceable panels

Body repair at a reasonable price is possible because of one design factor – almost every external panel on a car is easily replaceable. The majority of collision damage either does not damage the underlying structure (the chassis or monocoque),

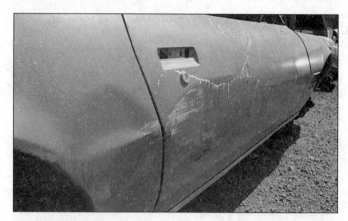

Most collision damage is primarily cosmetic – damage to the outer sheet metal not affecting the underlying structure

Damage such as this is most easily repaired by metal working and filling . . .

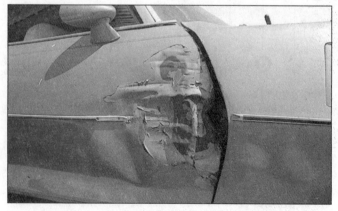

. . . while damage this extreme is usually handled by replacing the entire panel

or does only minor damage to it. This means that the repair of the outer skin of the car (the sheet metal) is the primary form of bodywork.

If a piece of sheet metal is severely damaged it can either be carefully beaten out, or, if it's too severely damaged, a new panel can be fabricated from sheet metal. This is how body repair was done back in the days of the 'classic' automobiles, when every body was a unique, one off creation. Now, however, identical bodies are mass produced by the thousands, and additional thousands of individual replacement panels are also manufactured, both by the original equipment manufacturers and by aftermarket companies. A damaged wing or door skin which might take a body shop worker four hours to straighten can be replaced in one half hour for less than the cost of the professional's labour rate.

This isn't to say that all damage to a car's body should be repaired by replacing the body component. Obviously, small dents and dings are more quickly and cheaply repaired by metal work and filling, especially where access to both sides of the damaged panel is available. But where major damage has been done to the sheet metal, especially tears in the metal or sharp creases which might be impossible to straighten, replacing the entire panel is usually the answer.

Panel replacement generally falls into three categories: Sections that can be replaced simply by unbolting them and bolting a new panel in place, those which must be cut away, requiring that the replacement be welded or riveted in place, and those that are bonded in place. Generally the bolt on panels include the front wings, bonnet and boot lid. In some cases, the doors can also be included in this category. While door 'skins' are widely available, and are virtually the only way a body shop will repair a damaged door, the do-it-yourselfer may find that the cost of an entire door from a breakers yard is a reasonable alternative to cutting off and replacing the door skin.

Panels which must be cut off so replacements can be welded in include the quarter panels, roof section, sill panels and lower rear section. In almost all cases the panels can be obtained from a breakers yard, an aftermarket supplier, or, in the case of many specialty type cars from specialty suppliers. And while traditional straightening and filling bodywork will be required where the new panels attach to the original body, the work required is generally much less than would be needed to repair major damage to the existing panel.

Bonded panels must be carefully cut from place, an all traces of the old bonding removed. Then using the correct bonding agent, the panels must be accurately placed and supported until the bonding is cured.

Deciding whether a panel should be repaired or replaced isn't always an easy decision. In a body workshop, where time and money are interchangeable, the decision will almost always lean towards replacement in all except the most minor damage. The do-it-yourselfer, on the other hand, may elect to 'invest' the time, which doesn't cost him anything, rather than spend the money for a replacement panel. Of course, if the panel is extensively damaged, there may be no choice – replacement may be the only practical answer.

Replacement panel 'skins' are widely available – here the bodyshop worker is checking the fit of the front wing skin

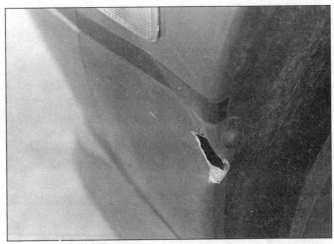

A tear in the sheet metal such as this almost always requires that the panel be replaced

Sometimes buying a complete door from a breaker's yard can be cheaper and faster than repairing a damaged panel or even replacing the door skin

Sharply creased or folded sheet metal is nearly impossible to repair economically – replacement is the best approach

Bolt on components, such as this wing, are easy to replace and cut the bodywork repair time and cost to a fraction of what repairing the original would be

Some damaged panels, such as this quarter panel, must be cut out so a new one can be welded into place

Chapter 1

Safety first!

Regardless of how enthusiastic you may be about jumping into body repair procedures, don't jeopardize your safety in the process! Not paying attention to safety rules or what you are doing at all times can lead to an accident and injury. Accidents do happen, and the following points should not be considered a comprehensive list of all dangers. They are, rather, intended to make you aware of the risks involved in body repair and painting procedures and to encourage a safety conscious approach to all work you do.

Personal safety

Safety rules

DON'T siphon toxic liquids, such as thinners, solvents, paints, petrol, antifreeze or brake fluid by mouth, or allow them to remain on your skin if spilled.

DON'T inhale brake lining dust – it's potentially hazardous (see the asbestos warning below).

DON'T allow spilled paint, thinner, oil or grease to remain on the floor – wipe it up before someone slips on it.

DON'T inhale fumes from paints, thinners, solvents or petrol. Always handle, pour and mix such fluids only in well ventilated areas.

DON'T use loose fitting spanners or other tools that may slip and cause injury.

DON'T push on spanners when loosening or tightening nuts or bolts. Always try to pull the spanner toward you. If the situation requires pushing on a spanner, push with an open hand to avoid scraped knuckles if the spanner slips.

DON'T attempt to lift heavy components alone – get someone to help you.

DON'T rush or take unsafe shortcuts to finish a job.

DON'T allow children or animals in or around the vehicle while you are working on it.

DON'T work with electrical tools if the floor is wet or if you have just sprayed volatile chemicals or paint, which could be ignited by sparks from the electrical tools.

DON'T weld, smoke or allow open flames in any area where volatile chemicals, solvents, cleaners or paints have just been used or where petrol has been spilled.

DON'T, under any circumstances, use petrol to clean parts or tools. Use only an approved safety solvent.

DO wear eye protection when working with power tools such as a grinder, sander, drill, etc. and when working under a vehicle.

DO keep loose clothing well out of the way of moving parts and tools.

DO make sure that pulling and pushing tools such as chassis/structure pullers and body jacks are properly anchored before using them.

DO keep oxygen and acetylene lines away from oil and grease. Oxygen and oil can ignite spontaneously!

DO turn off the oxygen and acetylene valves when your welding and cutting equipment is not in use.

DO wear a safety mask of the correct type when spraying paint, sanding or cutting plastics or fibreglass, especially when toxic or fibrous materials are involved.

DO mix paints, resins, fillers, etc. in a well ventilated area.

DO read the label, especially safety warnings, before using any paints, thinners, solvents or cleaning fluids.

DO keep the work area neat and clean – it's easy to trip over forgotten tools or parts.

DO pick up cut pieces of metal and dispose of them properly. Metal cut with a torch can burn if touched accidentally, and all cut metal has sharp edges which can cut if tripped over or run into.

DO match electrical tools to the electrical current available (120V to 120V, 220V to 220V) and make sure the tool is properly earthed if a three pin plug is used.

DO take the time to get the right tool for whatever job you are doing, not just the closest tool that might work.

DO get someone to check on you periodically when working alone on a vehicle.

DO carry out work in a logical sequence and make sure that everything is correctly assembled and tightened.

DO keep paints, thinners, chemicals and fluids tightly capped and out of the reach of children and pets.

DO remember that your vehicle's safety affects that of yourself and others. If in doubt on any point, get professional advice.

Special asbestos warning

Certain insulating and sealing materials, as well as other products – such as brake linings, brake bands, clutch linings, torque converters, gaskets, etc. – may contain asbestos. Extreme care must be taken to avoid inhalation of dust from such products since it is extremely hazardous to your health! If in doubt, assume that the components do contain asbestos and avoid handling them.

Environmental safety

At the time this manual was being written, several EEC regulations governing the use and disposal of paints, thinners, solvents and other volatile substances normally used during body repair and painting procedures were pending (contact the appropriate government agency or your local supply store for the latest information). It could very well be that many of the materials needed for bodywork and painting will eventually be limited to use by licensed professionals only. Be sure to check with local government agencies and suppliers of materials used for body repair to be certain that all materials are properly stored, handled and disposed of. Never pour used or leftover materials down the drain or dump them on the ground. Also, don't allow volatile liquids to evaporate – keep them in sealed containers.

Maintenance

Paintwork care

Restoration

Rustproofing and undercoating

Paintwork care

Whether you want to preserve the original finish on your car, or you've just sprayed on a new paint job and you want to protect it so it will last (and look good) as long as possible, the key is to keep the finish clean. Wash it before it gets so dirty kids start writing 'wash me' on it, polish it before the oils dry out to the point where the pavement in front of your house has a better shine than your car, then wax it to keep that shine glowing for as long as possible.

Take a trip down to your local car accessory shop and you will probably find dozens (perhaps even hundreds if it's a large store) of liquids, creams, blends, formulations, and preparations, all of which are alleged to be the very thing you need to make your car look better, longer. And while many of them will do just that, some of them will make your car look better – but only for a short while – and then it's time for a new paint job.

The important thing here is to read the label, then stop and think for a while about what you really need. Some of those products are like the engine additives that promise to cure smoking, knocking bearings, collapsed cam followers and rattling pistons. They sometimes work – for a while. But if you've got that kind of wear in your engine, only an overhaul will really cure the problem.

The same is true for the car's finish. If the paint is thin maybe one of those miracle finish products is what you need – to give it one last gasp of life while it's waiting for a date with the spray gun. But if the paint is in reasonably good shape, or even brand new, then you need an entirely different type of product to either restore a missing shine or protect the one already there.

Whichever way you're going, trying to get one last shine out of that dead but not buried paint job, working to restore a basically good but somewhat faded/oxidized paint job, or protecting a new paint job, the first, and most important, step is to get the surface clean before you try to do any kind of work on it.

Washing

Washing a car is easy, right? Wrong! Ten minutes with a hose, rags and soap can do more damage to a car's paint than six months of sun and road dirt. Remember, dirt is an abrasive, just like that stuff they glue to paper to make sandpaper, and rubbing on it, even with water and soap, will put scratches in the paint that you'll have to remove if you're going to get the surface to shine again. Also, keep in mind that paint never really dries. If paint becomes completely dry,

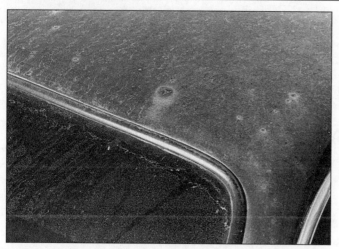

Don't let your car get this dirty if you want the paint job to last

Your local car accessory shop can supply a wide range of cleaners, polishes and waxes – pick up a good quality natural chamois as well

If the finish is this far gone, polishes and waxes are a waste of time and money – only a new coat of paint will do the job

it will have no shine left to it. So any soap that removes the oils that make paint shine serves to drastically shorten the lifespan of the paint job.

Let's take a look at some of the ways you should, and shouldn't, wash a car.

DON'T use clothes washing detergent to wash your car. It's too strong and will remove the oils which give the paint its shine.

DO use soap made especially for washing cars, or, if that isn't available, the liquid soaps made for hand washing dishes (not 'spot free' automatic dishwasher soap).

DO use baking soda as a scrubbing abrasive if you have to remove hard or caked on dirt.

DO use a sponge or a specially designed washing mitt to wash your car, not whatever old rags might be handy, and rinse it often in clean water. Remember that the dirt you are taking off can act just like sandpaper if you rub it into the paint rather than removing it.

If the paint is this badly faded, it can usually still be saved, but only after a lot of work

Baking soda makes an excellent cleaner for getting off stubborn dirt – just be careful the dirt doesn't act like sandpaper while you're trying to get it off, cutting into the paint

A soft, long-nap washing mitt is the best thing for the car's surface, but be sure to rinse it out often

A high-grade chamois or a very soft long-nap towel should be used for drying

DON'T use either hot or cold water to wash your car – only warm, preferably ambient temperature, water.

DON'T wash your car in the hot sun, or when the surface is hot to the touch.

DO use specially designed cleaners to remove road tar and bugs from the finish.

DO make sure the finish is completely clean before you start drying it. Rubbing in missed dirt with the drying cloth can do even more damage than rubbing it in with an unrinsed washing mitt or cloth while you're washing the car.

DO dry the car immediately after washing it to prevent water spotting.

DO use a very soft towel with a deep nap or a high grade chamois to dry your car – not an old T-shirt or an artificial chamois (they are too hard and will scratch the surface).

Cleaning

You're probably ready to start waxing about now, but you're a couple of steps early if you want a really sharp shine that will last. Before you wax, you need to polish.

If the paint's a real mess, turn to the **Restoration** section, where we've compiled all the secrets of restoring the shine to old, badly oxidized paint. Here we're assuming the paint is in fairly good shape, with maybe a light layer of oxidation.

The first thing you'll need is a very fine polishing compound. It usually comes as either a liquid or a paste, and since any abrasive compound, even one as fine as polishing compound, leaves scratches in the paint, it should be used sparingly and rubbed very lightly. A word of warning . . . be sure to use polishing compound, not rubbing compound. Rubbing compound has a much coarser abrasive (although both feel very fine to the touch), which will cut through the paint rather than just removing the oxidized top layer.

The secret of using polishing compound is to apply it to only a small area at a time, rubbing it in lightly and turning

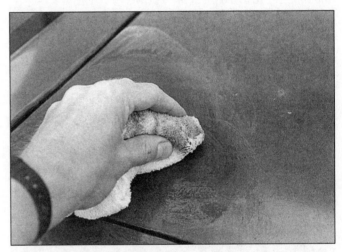

Use the polishing compound sparingly to avoid taking off paint along with the oxidation

the cloth often. Most polishing compound is designed to be applied with a damp cloth, so rinse the cloth often, then wring it almost dry before applying more compound. Rub the compound in just hard enough to remove the oxidized layer, and be especially careful around the edges of panels and on sharp ridges or curves in the sheet metal, since the paint is usually thinner there and you could rub right through it. Power applicator/buffing devices are available and will certainly help make the polishing chores much easier, but they should be used with extreme caution to avoid damage to the paint. Follow the instructions with the buffer to the letter if you use one!

Don't try to rub the compound off with the application cloth. Work on it while it's damp, then let it dry thoroughly and wipe off the residue with a dry polishing cloth or old towel. Again, keep changing the wiping surface so you don't begin wiping with a cloth so dirty it acts like a piece of sandpaper. One of the best ways to remove the polishing

A power applicator/buffer can help relieve the tedious nature of polishing the vehicle, but it MUST BE USED WITH CARE to avoid damage to the paint. (Note how the cord is draped over the shoulder to avoid dragging it across the paint)

Be careful working around the edges of panels and on sharp curves where the paint is usually thinner than on the flat surfaces

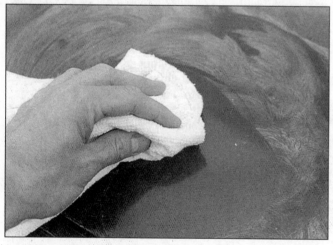

Use a soft cloth in a 'buffing' motion to remove the polishing compound residue

residue is with a buffing motion, like you would use when polishing a pair of shoes, rather than a rubbing motion.

Once you've gone over the entire car with polishing compound, removing all the oxidation, WASH THE CAR AGAIN, but don't use any soap this time. Just warm water and a very soft cloth. As soon as you've finished washing it, dry it thoroughly with a soft towel or high grade chamois.

Sealing and waxing

After polishing, the car should be shining like a mirror – unfortunately, that shine will last only a couple of hours, at most, unless you do something to protect it. And in most cases that protection comes in the form of wax.

Years ago applying a good grade of wax was the next, and final, step in protecting the paint. The wax would last for anywhere from a month to three months, depending on the weather in the area, and then you'd have to go through the whole thing again. Now, however, there's an intermediate step between the polishing and waxing that can protect a car's paint for up to a year, making the polishing step unnecessary for a while. You'll still have to wash the car often and rewax it every three months or so, but you can leave out the polishing step (which will make the paint last just that much longer) for quite a while.

The secret is using a polymer sealant to protect the finish. The polymer (often called resin glaze or polyresin protectant), usually comes as a liquid, and is applied either with a rag or by spraying it on. Don't try to rub it in or polish it while it's wet. Let it dry thoroughly, until it has formed a haze over the finish, then buff it with a soft polishing cloth. Polymer sealants dry very hard, so don't worry about applying too much pressure when you're getting rid of that haze – but don't wear yourself out rubbing on it, either. Just get rid of the haze, and you're done with this step.

Now it's time for the wax. Your local car accessory shop has a wide assortment of cleaner/wax and wax/polishes – all of which should be avoided at this point. A cleaner/wax (or a wax/polish) contains either a mild abrasive cleaner or a chemical cleaner. These things are designed to do in one step what you did with the polishing compound. Unfortunately, while almost all of them do a fairly good (and quick) job, they just can't do the professional job that hand polishing with polishing compound can do, and to apply one of them at this point would only scratch up the coating of polymer sealant you just applied.

Also on the market are a variety of synthetic waxes, most of which are silicone based. They work very well, but have a couple of drawbacks. They tend to dull if you put too much on (or apply second coats without thoroughly washing off the first coat), and they can make any future repainting, touch up or spot painting a repaired area a real hassle, since the new paint will not stick to a surface which has any trace of silicone on it. And the silicone penetrates all the paint layers, even the primer, right down to bare metal! The silicone based waxes are, though, harder than organic waxes, giving the paint more protection, and last somewhat longer, allowing longer intervals between rewaxing.

Restoration

Washing your car will remove the dirt and grime that has built up on the paint, but it will do nothing to remove oxidation, chemical (pollutant) film and 'dead' paint. The paint on your car never completely dries. It contains oils which give the paint its shine. The oils evaporate, though, and as they do, the surface oxidizes, the oxidized paint eventually covering the still oil saturated paint underneath with a dull white coating. When this has happened, the only recourse is to remove the top layer of dead (oxidized) paint, exposing the healthy paint underneath.

There are two kinds of cleaners normally used to remove the top layer of oxidized paint. One is the abrasive cleaner, which removes the oxidized layer essentially by 'sanding' it away. These cleaners come in grades all the way from the very mild polishes to the various grades of rubbing compounds. Just remember that, in sanding off the oxidation, they all leave the surface covered with scratches, which will have to be polished out before applying wax.

Also used for removing oxidation are chemical cleaners, which dissolve the layer of dead pigment, exposing the good paint underneath. It's essential that this type of cleaner, as opposed to an abrasive cleaner, be used on the newer acrylic finishes, since the gloss in these paints comes from the clear coating which has been sprayed over the colour coat. (Note that this does not refer to acrylic enamel or acrylic lacquer, which are 'conventional' paints.) If an abrasive cleaner is used, the clear coat will lose its gloss, and the only way to restore it is to apply more clear coat. Where conventional painted surfaces (lacquer or enamel) are concerned, though, the chemical cleaners are generally not as effective at removing oxidation as the abrasive cleaners, and can prevent getting a really top shine by cutting into the layer of oily 'good' paint below the oxidation.

Types of abrasive cleaners

Cleaner polishes

These are the mildest of the abrasive cleaners, and, when applied by hand, they will remove a top layer of oxidized paint. Don't confuse them with 'polish', which contains no abrasives. Polish (technically) simply adds oils to the existing paint, increasing the paint's gloss. The polish is then sealed in with wax.

Polishing compound

Very fine abrasive for removing a more severe type of oxidation than a cleaner polish will handle, or for getting through a 'gone' coat of dead paint. On large flat surfaces, polishing compound can be applied with a power buffer, but extreme care must be exercised to avoid damage to the paint (follow the instructions included with the tool). Don't use a power buffer on sharp edges or ridges, as the paint is usually much thinner there and you can polish right through it and expose the primer or even bare metal.

Rubbing compound

For heavy duty industrial strength removal of thoroughly dead paint only. Use with caution, or you can go right through to bare metal with this stuff. Use by hand only. Even if you don't polish through the paint, using a buffer with rubbing compound will often burn the underlying paint. Work only a small area at a time and don't allow the compound to dry out.

Chemical cleaners

Several different companies produce chemical cleaners for restoring old paint. The important thing to remember with these cleaners is to read the label carefully and follow the instructions to the letter when using them!

Rustproofing and undercoating

In Chapter 5 we show you how to repair minor rust damage with a fibreglass repair kit. The repair procedure is fairly simple and straightforward, and if it's done right it will restore the original appearance of the car. But there is one way of taking care of the rust problem that is even easier than using a repair kit – stop the rust before it starts!

Before we get started on the how's and why's of rustproofing and undercoating, let's make it clear that, despite what many people think, they are not the same thing. Rustproofing involves spraying a rust preventive chemical, usually wax based but sometimes a silicone compound, inside various body panels where water can collect and rust can start. Just getting a panel wet usually won't cause rust problems, by the way. It's places where water gets to and stays that rust sets in.

Undercoating, on the other hand, is a petroleum based, tar like coating that's applied to the outside (normally the under side) surfaces of a vehicle, usually for sound deadening purposes and not necessarily to protect a metal surface from rust.

The application of undercoating is often a 'gimmick' used by used (and sometimes new) car dealers to add a little extra profit to a car sales deal. The fee charged for undercoating is generally 'gravy,' since the cost of undercoating materials is very low and it can be applied in less than an hour with no special equipment.

Most rustproofing kits will include rustproofing compound, nozzles to let you spray into hidden areas and rubber plugs to fill the holes you will have to drill in body panels

Chapter 2

This isn't to say that undercoating is without value. As stated earlier, it's excellent for sound deadening, making the car quieter on the inside, and it does have some rust preventing qualities. But if you want undercoating, simply purchase several aerosol cans of undercoating at a parts store and spray it on yourself. Follow the directions on the can (they usually consist of nothing more than 'take the vehicle to a car wash, clean the inside of the wheelarches and the underside of the body as thoroughly as possible, let it dry completely, then spray on the undercoating') and you've got yourself as good an undercoating job as you're likely to get. Just remember to keep the undercoating off suspension, steering and drivetrain parts.

Rustproofing, on the other hand, is much more involved and usually requires drilling a series of holes in hidden portions of the body, then plugging the holes after the rustproofing material has been injected into the body cavities.

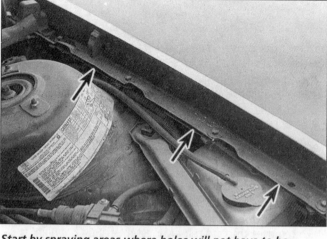

Start by spraying areas where holes will not have to be drilled, such as where the wing panel bolts to the inner wing panel inside the engine compartment

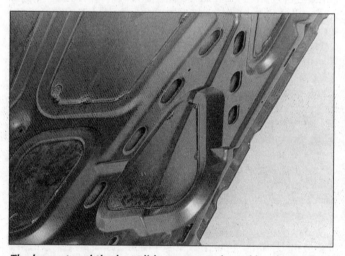

The bonnet and the boot lids are strengthened by sheet metal cross braces. Inside these braces is where rust starts, so get in and around them with a heavy coating of rustproofing

Inside the wheelarch is another critical area. If it has been covered with undercoating, spray right over it. The really important area is where the wheelarch bolts to the wing (arrowed), as this is where water can be trapped and rust will start

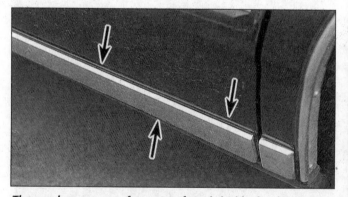

The number one area for rust to form is inside the door panel. Water runs down the outside of the glass, collects in the bottom of the door either because the drain holes are blocked or because the design allows small pockets of water to stand, and soon rust begins to eat through the door along the lower edge (arrowed)

To prevent door rust-out, the first step is to locate and clear the drain holes

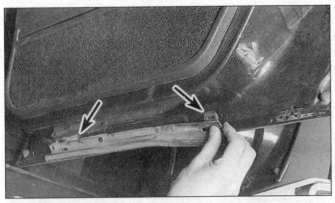

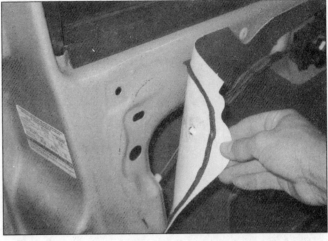

Roll the window all the way up, then carefully drill a 10 to 12 mm hole in the lower part of the door – make sure the drill doesn't hit the door latch or window winding mechanism. (This particular vehicle has holes [arrows] with rubber plugs, so drilling wasn't necessary, but the lower weatherstrip had to be removed)

If you're in doubt about where the mechanisms are inside the door, or if you really want to thoroughly rustproof the inside of the door, remove the door panel weatherproof membrane

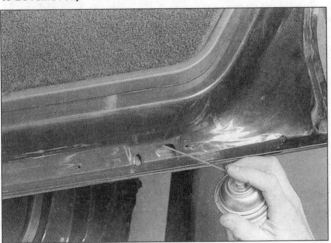

Attach the spray nozzle to the can of rustproofing and thoroughly spray the inside of the door, moving the nozzle around to make sure you get complete coverage

When you've finished spraying, install the rubber plug that came with the rustproofing kit in the hole you drilled. You might even want to add a coat of RTV sealant to make sure the plug is water tight

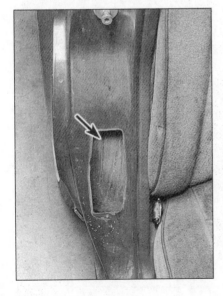

Repeat the procedure inside the rear quarter panels. In this example, a piece of trim was removed for access to the inside of the panel. Don't be stingy with the rustproofing – it costs a lot less than repairing a rusted out panel

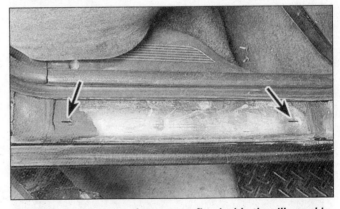

The easiest way to get the rustproofing inside the sill panel is to remove the sill trim, drill holes, then spray the rustproofing in from the top. In this example, the sill panel has slots (arrowed) for the sill trim screws – the rustproofing material can be injected through the slots

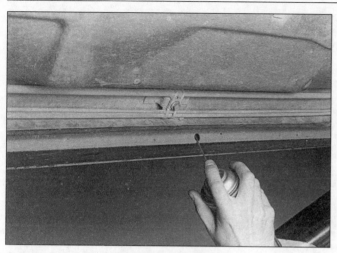

An alternative is to drill up from underneath into the sill panels, but chances are the coverage won't be as complete as injecting the rustproofing from the top

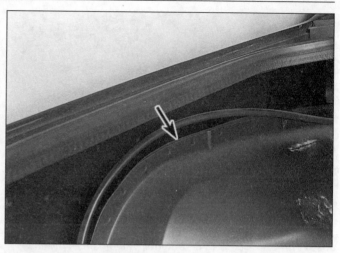

Don't forget the inside of the rear wing panels (inside the boot) and the rear wheelarches

Damage assessment and repair

3

Determining the extent of the damage

Repair or replace?

Determining the extent of the damage

Deciding how to deal with body damage, whether it's caused by a collision or corrosion, is a process that should always begin with a careful determination of the extent of the damage – don't rush into repairs without doing this first.

Since modern automobile bodies, particularly monocoque designs, are made to deform at the front and rear in the event of an impact, to protect the passenger compartment and, obviously, the vehicle occupants, most accident damage caused by front or rear collisions is difficult to repair correctly. The reason is that the monocoque structural components (particularly the chassis rails) usually end up distorted. Due to the fact that they're difficult to straighten or replace, the job should be done by a professional with the necessary equipment and expertise to handle such involved repairs.

On the other hand, the decision to repair other types of body damage, rather than replace body components, depends on several factors that must be assessed individually before arriving at a decision. Once the damage is carefully noted, it's very important to devise a plan for repair, whether it involves panel replacement or not, prior to beginning any work.

As a general rule, if major damage to the vehicle's chassis and/or structural components has occurred, and extensive cutting and rewelding of body components is indicated, the repairs probably should be left to a professional. If the damage is relatively minor, requiring the repair of small dents or creases in large flat panels, fixing small, isolated rusted out areas or replacing items such as doors, the bonnet, wings, sills or quarter panels, it may be a good idea to consider doing it yourself.

At any rate, it can't hurt to conduct a thorough inspection of any type of damage yourself. Then, even if you decide to let a body repair workshop handle the repairs, you'll know in advance what to expect and be able to communicate intelligently with the repairman handling the job.

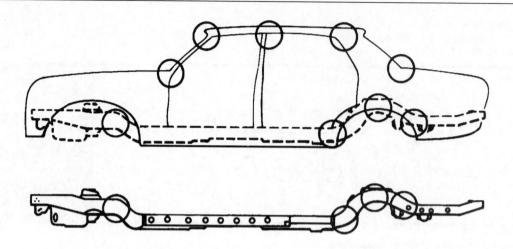

Collision damage

A vehicle with a perimeter chassis has built in collapsible sections. Portions of the chassis are designed to absorb the major impact of a front or rear end collision. The body is normally attached to the chassis with rubber mounts which reduce the effects of shocks transferred from the chassis to the body. If the impact is great, the mounting bolts may bend, producing a gap between the chassis and the body. Also, depending on the size and direction of the shock, the chassis may be damaged while the body isn't – an important difference between perimeter and monocoque type designs.

Chassis Deformation

Chassis deformation is broken down into four categories or simple examples: vertical bends; horizontal bends; crushing and twisting. In reality, most collisions result in a complicated mixture of many types of damage, depending on the magnitude and direction of the shock and the point of impact.

1 *Vertical bends* – Vertical bends occur when a vehicle is involved in an indirect front or rear collision. If the impact occurs at the front of the vehicle, the shock is absorbed by the front chassis box sections. The fronts of the box sections rise up and the portions just behind them drop down. As this happens, the clearances between the wings and the doors change due to distortion. In addition, since the wheelbase is changed by the chassis distortion, it must be measured before beginning repair operations.

2 *Horizontal (side) bends* – This type of bending occurs when the vehicle sustains an impact from the side. Most cars involved in collisions suffer both bending and twisting deformation. If the front wheels are involved in the impact, the suspension arms and mounting brackets are often deformed.

Perimeter chassis and most bodies have sections designed into them to absorb impacts during a collision – when checking for damage, start with the areas indicated by the circles

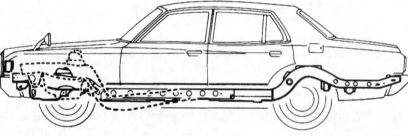

Vertical bends from front impacts normally occur at the front chassis box sections (the dotted lines indicate the shape of the door frame after the impact)

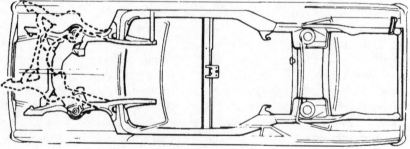

Side bends (indicated by the dotted lines) are normally accompanied by twisting of the chassis as well

The front and rear chassis box sections are designed to crush as impact occurs – this absorbs much of the shock that would normally be transferred to the body and ultimately the occupants of that vehicle. If the vehicle has been involved in a front or rear collision, check the box sections for distortion

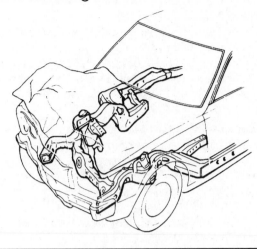

3 Crushing – Crushing usually occurs during direct head on and rear end collisions. Substantial damage is done to the front chassis box sections and the areas near the rear chassis rails/floor pan. Longitudinal damage is almost always involved as well. In the case of a head on collision where the front box sections don't absorb the energy, bending can occur as far back as the centre chassis crossmember.

4 Twisting – Two distinct types of twisting can happen to a vehicle's chassis. One type occurs around the imaginary end to end centreline of the vehicle (sort of like the twisting action used when wringing out a washcloth). The second type, also known as diagonal twisting or 'racking', occurs around the imaginary vertical centreline of the vehicle.

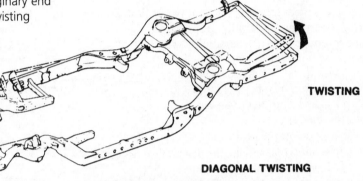

End to end twists develop when one corner of a vehicle is suddenly pushed up (running over a curb or traffic island at high speed, for example). Twisting of a perimeter chassis is usually limited to the front box sections or the rear chassis rails/floor pan. Partial vertical and side bending may also occur.

Diagonal twisting occurs when the vehicle is struck off centre at the front or rear (front or rear impact at one corner). Perimeter chassis almost never experience deformation involving the whole. Diagonal twisting usually occurs along with vertical and crushing type damage.

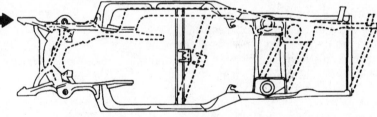

Twisting can occur around the end-to-end centerline of the chassis and diagonally (diagonal twisting is also known as 'racking')

Chassis inspection

The chassis should be inspected by comparing the size of the spaces between the body sill panels and the front and rear of the chassis and by comparing the spaces between the front wings and the front and rear edges of the wheel hubs. To check front chassis deformation, compare the distances from the right and left side rear holes of the front bumper mounts to the front chassis rails.

Monocoque distortion

Since monocoques are manufactured by welding together large sections of sheet metal, the shock of a collision is absorbed by nearly the entire body. The effect of a collision

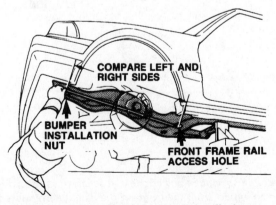

Chassis deformation can be determined visually, but measurements should be taken to avoid missing anything

Chapter 3

shock is reduced as it travels through and is absorbed by the body structure. Front shocks are absorbed by the front body, rear shocks are absorbed by the rear body and side shocks are absorbed by the sill panel, roof side chassis, centre pillar and door (side impact bars). Certain parts of the monocoque structure are designed to collapse or distort in order to absorb the energy of the shock wave.

1 Front impact – The impact from a collision depends on the vehicle's weight, speed, area of impact and the object that's hit. In the case of a minor impact, the bumper is pushed back, bending the front side members (chassis rails), bumper stay, front wing, radiator support, radiator upper support and bonnet slam panel.

If the impact is increased, the front wing will contact the front door, the bonnet hinge will bend up to the scuttle and the front side members will buckle into the front suspension crossmember, causing it to bend.

If the shock is great enough, the front wing apron and front body A-pillar (particularly the front door hinge upper mount area) will be bent, which will cause the front door to drop down. In addition, the front side members will buckle, the front suspension member will bend and the dash panel and front floor pan will bend to absorb the shock.

If a vehicle is hit from the front at an angle, the mounting point of the front side member becomes a turning axis and lateral as well as vertical bending occurs. Since the left and right front side members are connected by the front crossmember, the shock from the impact is transferred from the point of impact to the front side member on the opposite side of the vehicle and causes deformation.

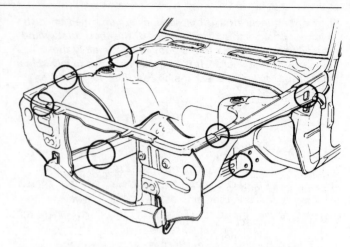

Monocoque structures are also designed to distort under load . . .

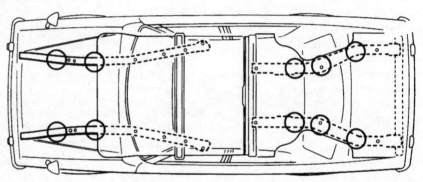

. . . at the areas that are circled – check them carefully for damage after a collision

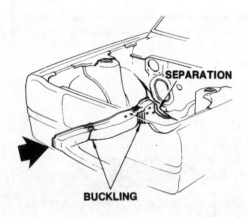

Monocoque structures will buckle and separate as shown here during an impact from the front – if the damage isn't noted, repair may be started that you aren't capable of or equipped to handle

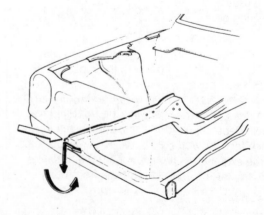

If the front impact occurs at an angle at one corner, look for side bends and twisting as well

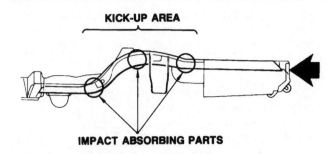

KICK-UP AREA

IMPACT ABSORBING PARTS

If the impact occurs at the rear of the vehicle, monocoque structures will tend to distort at the rear chassis 'kick-up' area

2 Rear end impact – The amount of damage from a rear end collision will depend on factors such as the impact surface area, the speed, the object hit and the vehicle's weight. When the impact is comparatively small, the rear bumper, rear panel, boot lid/tailgate and floor pan will be deformed and the quarter panels will bulge out.

If the impact is severe enough, the quarter panels will collapse to the base of the roof panel and, on 4 door vehicles, the centre body (B) pillar may bend.

Energy is absorbed by the distortion of the above parts and by the deformation of the kick ups in the rear side members.

3 Side impact – When determining the damage from side impacts, vehicle structure is particularly important. Generally, in severe collisions, the door, front section, centre body (B) pillar and even the floor pan will distort. When the front wing or quarter panel receives an impact, the shock travels to the opposite side of the vehicle. When the centre area of the front wing receives an impact, the front wheel is pushed in and the shock is transferred from the front suspension crossmember to the front side member. In this case, the suspension components are damaged and the front wheel alignment and wheelbase is changed. Since the steering components are usually affected by a side impact, the linkage and steering gear or rack and pinion may also be damaged.

4 Top impacts – When damage is caused by falling objects, it not only affects the roof panel but also the roof side rails, the quarter panels and possibly the windows as well. When a rollover has occurred and the body pillars and roof panels have been bent, the opposite ends of the pillars will be damaged as well. Depending on how the rollover happened, the front or back sections of the body will be damaged too. In such cases, the extent of the damage can be determined by deformation around the windows and doors.

Damage assessment

If damage isn't carefully and accurately diagnosed, the repair quality will suffer and it will take a lot longer than necessary. When diagnosing damage, consider the direction and force of the impact (how fast was the vehicle travelling?), where the vehicle was hit and the type of body structure involved (monocoque, separate chassis, etc.).

If possible, the inspection should be done in a well lit shop equipped with a lift. If the damage involves mechanical parts, a detailed inspection of the under body, on a lift, is essential. If a lift isn't available, use axle stands positioned on a level concrete surface to support the vehicle during the inspection.

Generally, obvious physical damage is rarely missed during an inspection. However, the effects of the damage on unrelated parts and damage that took place next to the impacted part are frequently overlooked. A visual inspection alone is often inadequate – accident damage should be assessed by taking measurements with the proper tools and equipment between the specified points (you should have a factory service manual available so the chassis and under body measurements can be looked up). Have a metal tape measure and a torch available. A helper may be needed for some of the measurements.

The following steps are involved in a typical collision damage assessment procedure:

1 Visually locate the point of impact.

2 Visually determine the direction and force of the impact and check for possible damage.

3 Determine if the damage is confined to the body, or if it involves mechanical parts (wheels, suspension, engine, drivetrain parts, etc.).

4 Systematically check for damage to the components along the path of the shock and find the point where there is no longer any evidence of damage.

5 Measure the major components and check body height by comparing the actual measurements with the values in the factory service manual.

The three most important things to remember when trying to determine the extent of damage from a collision are . . .

- *Base the determination on the type of chassis/body structure and the type of impact involved.*
- *Look for hidden damage and try to determine where it ends.*
- *Check the operation/installation of the doors, bonnet, wings and boot lid or tailgate to help decide how severe the damage is.*

Corrosion damage

Because of its insidious nature and the fact that you can't always see what's involved, rust damage can be quite difficult to assess.

Since rust can be hidden behind paint, trim components and outer body panels, tracking it down usually involves removing parts, crawling under the vehicle, scraping away flakes of paint, probing with an awl or other sharp tool and tapping with a hammer on suspected parts. If a hoist isn't available, support the vehicle on axle stands and use a creeper board to examine the lower parts of the body. Areas where rust usually occurs include the lower door and quarter panels, the sill panels, the upper edges of the front wings, particularly where they attach to the inner wing panels, around the headlight and taillight openings and along body side mouldings, where holes are drilled for the fasteners. Have a powerful torch available to check dark, hidden areas of the body. A sharp tool or hammer should be used to probe or tap the borders of rusted areas to determine how far out the rust damage extends.

If possible, try to determine if the rust is on the surface of the body only, isolated and confined to small areas. If it is, pat yourself on the back for noticing it now, because repairs usually can be made fairly easily (see Chapter 5). However, if the rust damage is extensive, and has penetrated the metal of the body, repair may involve unbolting or removing body components with a cutting torch or an air chisel – a very laborious and difficult procedure, especially if large areas of the body are involved. If the latter is true, the repairs may cost more than the vehicle is worth.

Keep in mind that the rusted area on the inner surface of a body panel is always more extensive than it appears on the outside. If rust is concentrated near seams, folds, complex body curves and sharp edges (which it almost always is), repair can be very difficult. Even after repairs are made, the inner areas of the body, where dirt and water collect, are still going to be unprotected and new rust will eventually form.

Repair or replace?

Which way should I go?
If you haven't already read Introduction to replaceable panels in Chapter 1, you may want to do so now. Once the body damage assessment has been made, the best way to approach a repair can be determined. The decision whether to repair a part of the body that's been damaged or simply replace the component depends on several factors . . .

- *Where is the damage located (in the centre of the panel or near the edges or seams)?*
- *How extensive is the damage? Is the panel – and the adjacent parts – severely torn or deformed or is it just dented or creased?*
- *How deep is the dent or crease? Will the metal have to be worked extensively to return it to its original contour or shape?*
- *Can the part be unbolted or is cutting and welding involved?*
- *Have structural parts of the body, chassis or monocoque structure been damaged? Will straightening or strengthening be required?*
- *How much time is available to complete the repair?*

All of the above questions have to be answered when deciding how to approach a particular job. If the damage is concentrated near the centre of a panel or component (such as a door) and relatively small dents, creases or rust areas are

involved, repair of the existing panel would probably be the best approach. On the other hand, if the parts are severely deformed or the metal is torn, replacement of the entire panel or component would be preferred. If extensive straightening of structural components, metal work or welding is required, have a professional do the work – the end result will be easier to live with.

Remember, time is money. If you elect to try to straighten and repair a damaged component, it can certainly be done, but it may take so much time and effort that you would've come out ahead by purchasing a replacement part or even taking the vehicle to a body repair workshop for repair.

Types of replacement parts
As mentioned in Chapter 1, replacement body parts can be classified into two major categories: Those that can be unbolted and those that require cutting and welding for replacement.

Bolt on components usually include the doors, bonnet, boot lid/tailgate, front wings, various front end braces, brackets and mountings.

Weld in components include door skins, quarter panels, roof sections, pillars, floor pan sections, sill panels, wheel arches, rear wings and virtually every pre formed part that the manufacturer welds together to form the body or monocoque structure.

In addition, weld in parts can be fabricated from sheet metal to replace small sections of the body that are cut out, particularly to repair rusted areas. They don't have any effect on the structural integrity of the body and are used simply to replace relatively small areas of the body outer skin.

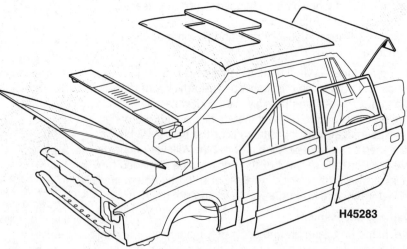

H45283

Replacement bolt-on parts such as the bonnet, scuttle, doors and front wings are usually available from breakers yards or the can be obtained from dealers parts department, or good motor factors

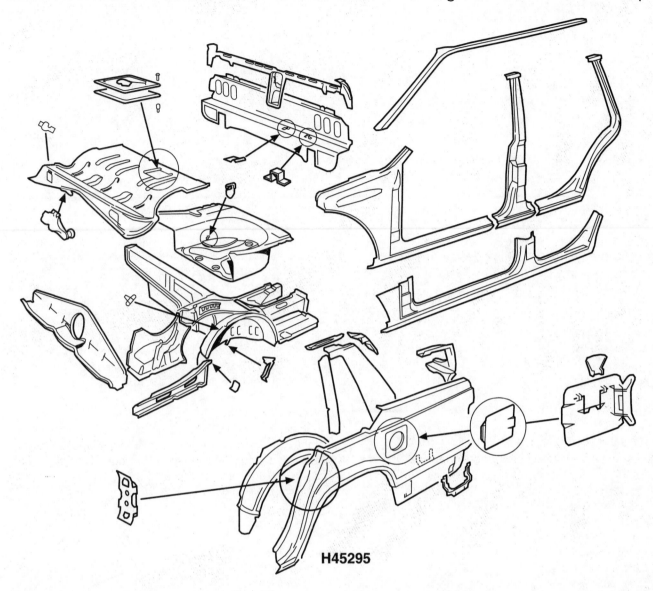

H45295

Replacement parts sources

The first place to look for replacement parts, if you have the time and need such items as a door, bonnet, boot lid, front wing or bumper (primarily bolt on parts), is a local breakers yard. Most bolt on parts can be obtained for a reasonable price, but you may have to do your own searching and possibly even remove the part you need from a wrecked car yourself. Be sure to compare the original part with the replacement part before purchasing anything – details that may be important can easily go unnoticed when you're in a hurry to get home and get to work. Obviously, it's a good idea to try to colour match any replacement parts with the paint on the vehicle's body, but don't count on being able to find parts that are the right colour. Concern yourself with the general condition of the part and plan to repaint as needed.

New bolt on components are also available through car accessory shops, motor factors and dealer parts

Rear wings . . . sills, door pillars . . . and even bulkheads, floor pan parts and wheel arches can be welded in to replace severely damaged or rusted out body sections

departments, but they'll cost a lot more than used parts. If you purchase them from a dealer, and you get original equipment parts, they'll be very high quality and will fit very well. However, if you buy parts from an car accessory shop or motor factors, you may get cheap, imported components that don't fit very well, so make sure you understand the conditions of any purchase before laying out any cash.

Pre-formed body panels, door skins and structural parts that must be welded in place are also available from dealers and car accessory shops/motor factors, but the preferred source is the dealer – you'll be assured of getting high quality components that will be the exact same size and shape as the original and they'll fit right into place.

Notes

Tools and working facilities

Tools and equipment

Working facilities

Tools and equipment

In addition to the tools normally found in any mechanic's toolbox, such as sockets, ratchets, open-ended and ring spanners, screwdrivers, pliers, etc., there are many tools specifically designed for body work that will be needed to properly repair distorted metal parts, apply and work fillers and sand and grind body panels in preparation for welding or painting. They range from simple cast iron dollies to sophisticated (and expensive) hydraulic monocoque/chassis aligners.

The two basic tools needed for bodywork are the body hammer and the dolly. In general, the hammer is used to stress (and shape) the metal, while the dolly keeps it from moving too far. There are dozens of different hammer and dolly designs, each with a different shape to handle a different type of dent or curvature in a metal body panel, but only four or five of each are really necessary for most bodywork.

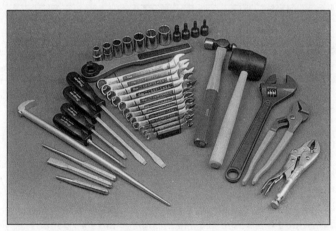

Many of the tools used for mechanical repairs are also needed for body work – spanners, sockets, ratchets, screwdrivers and pliers should all be available

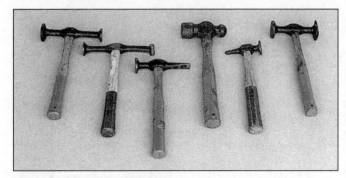

Body hammers are needed to align and shape sheet metal panels. They have a wide almost flat smooth surface on one end that ranges from about 19 mm to 37 mm in diameter. The edges are rounded to prevent the formation of sharp dents if the sheet metal is struck with the hammer held at a slight angle – if the edges on the hammers you have are sharp, round them over with progressively finer grades of wet or dry sandpaper. The opposite end of the hammer head is usually pointed or tapered and is used to flatten bumps and high spots

Here, a body hammer is being used to reshape a portion of a rear quarter panel

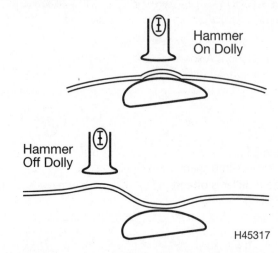

Dollies are used to back up the wide, flat end of the body hammer when shaping panels . . .

. . . and can be used directly behind the area being struck by the hammer or off to one side – as the hammer strikes the sheet metal, the dolly is bumped off and then returns, shaping the panel from the back side in the process

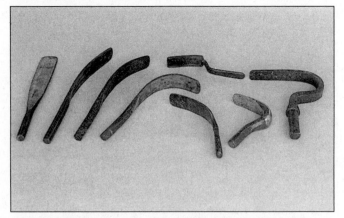

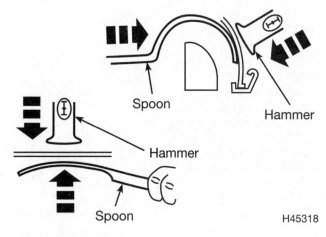

Body spoons are used just like the dollies, but they'll reach into tight spots where dollies can't fit. Since they come in many shapes and sizes, it's easy to find one that matches the shape of the panel

Body spoons in use

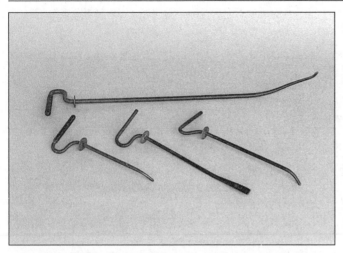

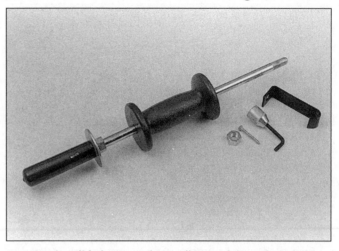

Pry tools are used to pry body panels back into shape. They're preferable to dent pullers if the distorted area is within reach and there's something to pry against. They can be inserted through drain holes and small openings in the back side of panels

Inexpensive slide hammer dent pullers with interchangeable tips are widely available at car accessory shops and motor factors

One other basic tool belongs in any bodyworkers tool box – the body spoon. A spoon is basically another form of dolly, designed with a handle so you can reach areas you can't reach with a conventional dolly. Spoons can also be used as a large surface hammer to knock out dents.

Pry bars specially designed for body repair are available in several sizes. They're made to be inserted through holes along the edge of a panel (such as door drain holes) to pry the panel back into shape from the backside.

The dent puller is often the first tool used when you begin straightening a damaged area. Most dent pullers are a slide hammer design and the better ones have replaceable tips so you can use screws or L shaped hooks to attach the slide hammer to the metal to be straightened. Just remember when using a slide hammer – all those holes you make to attach the slide hammer to the sheet metal will have to be filled later.

A more sophisticated type of dent puller is also available. It uses metal pins spot welded to the sheet metal to pull on and doesn't require holes to be drilled in the body. This type of tool is generally used only by professional body repair workshops, since you would have to do a lot of body work to justify its cost, but it's capable of doing a much cleaner job of pulling out sheet metal than the screw tip slide hammer dent puller.

One other type of dent puller that can sometimes be used to straighten body panels is the suction cup puller. They're primarily used where the metal hasn't been creased or stretched, such as when a door panel has just been pushed in. The suction cup type dent puller can, in this case, often pull the panel out again, leaving only minor sheet metal damage to be repaired. They're also useful for holding the glass when removing and installing windows.

Once the sheet metal is straightened, the two most often used tools for body work are the metal file and the Surform or 'cheese grater' file. The metal file is used to clean, shape

A slide hammer dent puller is essential for pulling panels back into place before reshaping them

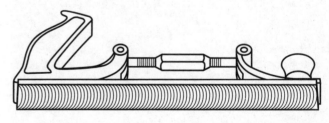

H45319

The flexible file can be adjusted to conform to the general shape of curved body sections and is used to shape and form metal particularly

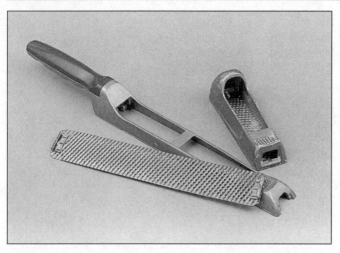

Surform tools come in several sizes, have replaceable blades . . .

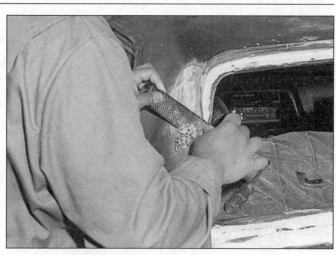

. . . and are excellent for rough shaping of body filler because they cut quickly and don't clog

Electric sanders, polishers and grinders are available from many manufacturers – be sure to buy a heavy duty model

and surface metal panels. It usually consists of two pieces – the curved tooth file itself and the handle it's attached to. The handle (or holder) is usually adjustable, so the file can be curved to match the metal surface being worked (it's because of this feature that it's sometimes called a flexible file). The Surform file is not used to work metal, but to shape plastic body filler material. It's a very open tooth design to allow the cut off filler material to escape, with hundreds of small, very sharp teeth that quickly work the plastic material before it completely hardens.

Air or electric sanders are an absolute must for doing bodywork. Several types are available, including disc sanders, double action (DA) sanders, orbital action sanders, straight line sanders and belt sanders. Air disc sanders are used for light duty jobs such as paint removal. They're light and compact and produce low rpm and high torque, so there's little heat produced. Double action sanders have a dual rotation feature that prevents scratches from forming.

The air disc sander is ideal for light work . . .

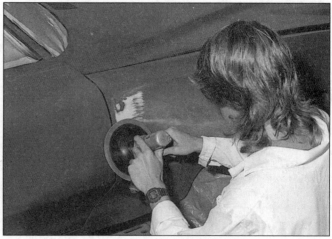

. . . like feathering out paint and body filler

They're also useful for buffing, since their low speed makes it difficult to burn the paint

The dual action sander is used for rapid shaping of body filler, as well as fine finishing work, and leaves a swirl free finish

The orbital sander is great for quick removal of body fillers on both vertical and horizontal surfaces

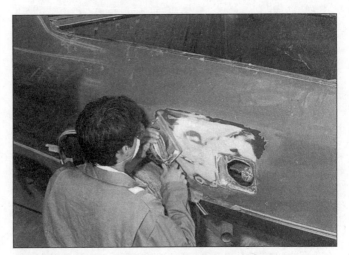

Since it has a large sanding pad, the orbital sander is very useful on large flat surfaces

The straight line sander has an unusually long pad so it can bridge filled areas . . .

. . . and is particularly well suited for rapid sanding of body filler on long flat surfaces

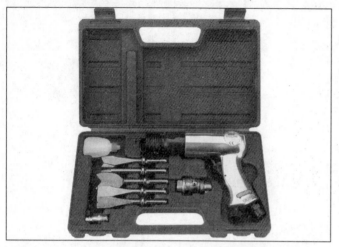

Air hammers accept many different types of chisels, are quite inexpensive . . .

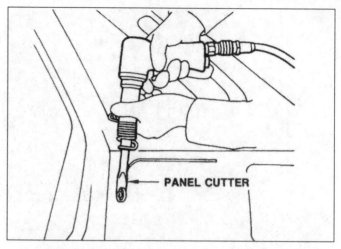

. . . and are very useful for cutting out sheet metal sections such as this quarter panel

They're used primarily for rough sanding of metal and plastic fillers. Orbital action sanders have a large, flat sanding pad that makes them useful for removing small surface imperfections. They're usually used for rough and medium sanding of plastic fillers. The straight line sander is excellent for removing paint or working down a large plastic filled surface, but it leaves definite scratch marks which will later have to be sanded out before painting. Recently, air powered belt sanders that are priced within the reach of any do-it-yourselfer have become available. They can be used in narrow or deep recesses that can't be reached with a disc sander and are very useful for removing paint from welds.

An air hammer with a selection of chisel heads is a required tool for any body repairs requiring panel replacement. It's almost impossible to remove a panel with a cutting torch without either warping the surrounding panels or setting fire to flammable components, such as headliners, door trim panels, etc. The air chisel can be used to make clean cuts and, if care is taken, cuts that will have a

minimum of stretched metal along the edges, making the welding on of a new panel easier. Electric and air powered panel saws are also available. They work very well for cutting out door pillars, sill panels and other structural components.

Grinders come in two types – air and electric – each with advantages and disadvantages. The air grinders are usually much lighter and are generally more powerful, making them easier to use on big jobs such as large panels or grinding down welds. However, they generally can't be used for light sanding or buffing, simply because they turn too fast. Electric grinders, on the other hand, can often be used for buffing and polishing as well as grinding. However, electric grinders must be used with caution, since some of them are too powerful (and turn too fast) to use for either sanding or buffing on painted surfaces.

One of the most indispensable tools around is the common electric drill. One with a 10 mm capacity chuck should be sufficient for most body repair jobs. Collect several different types of wire brushes to use in the drill and make

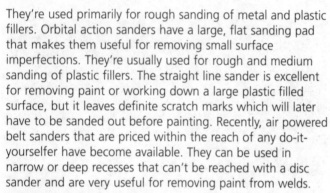

Electric grinders come in many different sizes – one of the most useful types is this compact design that can also be used for sanding simply by substituting a sanding disc for the grinding wheel

A wire brush mounted in an electric drill can be used for rust removal prior to the application of body filler or primer

Buy a compressor that can handle the demands of your largest air tool and maintain it diligently!

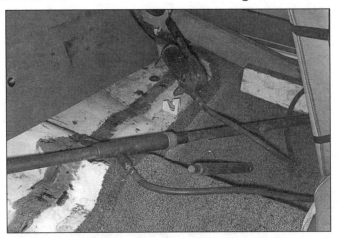

Body jacks are used to push structural members back into shape prior to finishing work

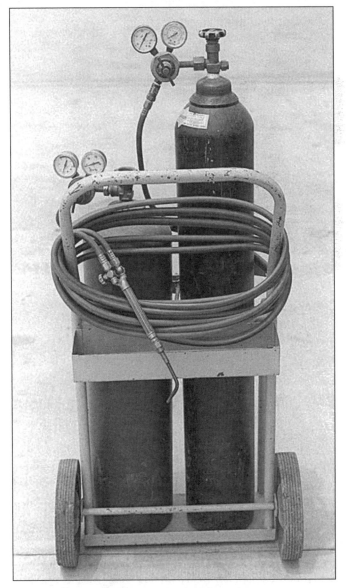

A typical oxy acetylene welding outfit

sure you have a complete set of sharp bits (for drilling metal, not wood).

Keep in mind that air tools also require a power source – in this case a compressor. If you plan on spraying primer or paint, a compressor will be needed anyway, so buy one that has a large enough output to keep up with the demands of a spray gun and any air tools you'll be using. Don't buy a compressor that's too small for the job. You'll also need hoses and quick disconnect fittings to adapt the various air powered sanders, grinders and spray guns used for body work.

If you intend to do any major straightening of automotive structures, a selection of hydraulic body jacks is an absolute must. Hydraulic power supplied through a body jack is often the only way sufficient force can be applied to a component to get it straight again. This is especially true of the roof and door pillars. Body jacks can also be used to a limited extent for chassis straightening and, of course, are very useful for straightening bent monocoque components.

If you're going to get involved in major body repair procedures, welding and cutting equipment is an absolute must. The most common and familiar type of welding equipment is the oxy acetylene set – also known as a gas welder – which can be used for flame cutting, welding steel and brazing. It consists of two tanks, or cylinders (one containing oxygen and one containing acetylene), a regulator for each tank, hoses, torches and tips for different applications, eye protection, a spark lighter to ignite the gases and usually a trolley for storage and movement of the gas cylinders. Compact, relatively inexpensive oxy acetylene outfits

Gas welding is used to attach sheet metal panels and patches, not for welding structural members

A typical MIG welder

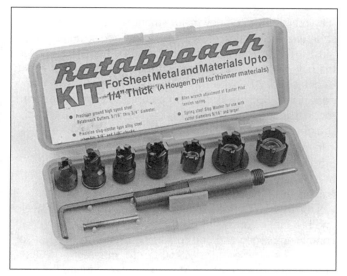

When mounted in an electric drill, a tool like this is great for drilling out spot welds to remove panels

are available from several sources – they should be adequate for the types of welding associated with body repairs.

Several types of electric arc welding machines are also suited for use in body repair procedures. They include the conventional arc welder (both AC and DC versions are available), MIG and TIG welders, which are arc welders that use inert gases to shield the weld (which produces a superior weld joint) and electric arc spot welders.

Gas welding is used for attaching relatively thin gauge sheet metal parts such as door skins, quarter panels, rocker panels, etc. and for welding in small patches used to repair rusted out areas. If the repair requires welding of heavy gauge steel, such as chassis members and body reinforcements, arc welding, preferably MIG or TIG, is better than gas welding. Since it operates at low voltage and current, MIG welding equipment can also be used for welding thin panels without fear of warping them. Although TIG welders can be used on a wide range of materials, they haven't enjoyed widespread acceptance in the car body repair field. Electric arc spot welding is used mainly in the factory production of welded sheet metal parts. Although it's widely used in professional body shops, it really isn't a necessary piece of equipment for the do-it-yourselfer. However, special cutters (spot drills and hole saws) that can be used with an electric drill are available for cutting out spot welds when removing components. They're very useful because they prevent damage to and distortion of surrounding panels.

Some of the most useful tools you can have, especially when welding of sheet metal panels is being done, are Self Grip clamping pliers. They are available in several configurations for clamping and holding sheet metal during body repairs. They're quickly and infinitely adjustable and can be attached and removed with one hand.

MIG welders are capable of handling virtually all welding jobs associated with body repairs – they're comparatively easy to use, produce a superior weld joint and won't warp the sheet metal

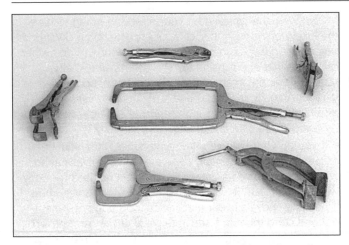

Self-grip clamping tools, which come in a wide variety of shapes and sizes . . .

. . . are indispensable when attaching body panels

Not to be overlooked when discussing tools required for sheet metal work are the various types of snips needed to cut and fabricate sheet metal patches. Commonly known as 'tin snips', the best ones for the job are actually 'compound leverage snips' (although they're also labelled 'aviation snips'). You'll need a set of three – one cuts in a straight line, one cuts curves to the left and one cuts curves to the right.

For those on a limited budget, pop rivets can be used to fasten body panels and sheet metal patches in place as a substitute for welding. However, keep in mind that the rivet heads should be recessed to avoid having to use excess amounts of body filler to hide them. Buy a good quality pop rivet tool and steel rivets if this method is used.

One very helpful piece of equipment to have on hand is a vacuum cleaner. Don't steal the house one – use an industrial type vacuum cleaner to keep dust and debris under control. If you keep the car and the work area clean, the final results, especially if you are doing the painting, will be much better.

Compound leverage snips (tin snips) are great for cutting sheet metal (they come in straight, left and right hand cut versions)

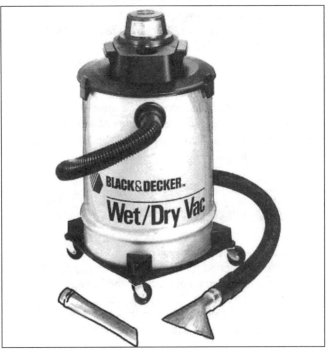

A good workshop vacuum cleaner is one of most valuable pieces of equipment you can have around, particularly if you intend to do any painting and need to control the dust produced by sanding

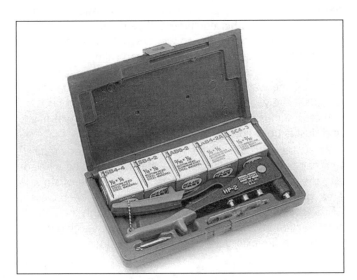

Pop rivets, which require a special installation tool, can be used for fastening body panels in place

Have a dry powder extinguisher handy and know how to use it!

Safety equipment – perhaps the most important items needed – is usually overlooked during any discussion of tools. Since safety is actually a matter of simple common sense . . .

- *be sure to purchase and use a good quality dust mask when sanding*
- *if painting is done, use an air-fed mask for keeping paint out of your lungs*
- *when grinding and sanding, wear a face shield or safety goggles, not just safety glasses*
- *when grinding on metal for extended periods, wear ear plugs (you'll be glad you did!)*
- *never do any type of welding without adequate face and eye protection (arc welding is especially harmful to the eyes)*
- *buy a fire extinguisher that can be used on flammable liquid fueled fires and keep it handy at all times!*

Additional important safety related information can be found in Chapter 1.

Working facilities

Body and paint workshops usually have large, elaborate facilities (at least the good ones do), with areas specifically set apart and designed for body work, chassis straightening, masking, paint spraying, paint drying and storage of tools, equipment and materials. They're also equipped with elaborate dust control systems and they have plenty of fluorescent lights and air outlets strategically placed around the shop.

Obviously, the typical do-it-yourselfer isn't going to have the luxury of working in such a facility. He/she's lucky if one side of the garage can be taken over for working on his/her car. And what about painting? Well, that's almost always done outside on a calm day or in a cramped, poorly lit garage. Actually, it's not as bad as it sounds – very good results (nearly as good as a professional can do) can be achieved if you plan ahead and work carefully.

If you do your own vehicle maintenance, then you probably have a reasonably large area already available to work in, probably in a garage. If so, it can be used for body work as well, but be forewarned – body work is very messy! If possible, move all your mechanic's tools and equipment out and store them in a separate place. If that isn't possible, get some large plastic sheets to cover tools, workbenches and storage shelves. Keeping things covered will save you from having to do a massive clean up job afterwards.

If you plan to do any painting, even if it's just the application of primer, you'll need to wet down the floor of the garage before doing any spraying (this minimizes airborne dust that inevitably will end up embedded in the paint), so move everything off the floor, onto shelving or to another location, before starting any work on the body. Moving things out of the way will not only keep them from getting wet, but will also make it much easier to work around the car. Unless the garage has several fluorescent lights overhead, it's a good idea to make a portable light unit out of a four foot fluorescent fixture (the type commonly available at hardware and home stores) to provide adequate light when spray painting. You can move the light around as you paint different sections of the car – just be sure to protect the light tubes with a stiff plastic cover or wire mesh shield.

Because of its messy nature, doing body work outside is a very good idea, as long as the weather cooperates. Just make sure there's a large enough concrete or asphalt surface to work on and don't use too many long extension cords to plug in tools and other equipment. If painting is done outside, it's still a good idea to wet down the area around the vehicle and wait for a day that's dead calm, overcast and slightly humid. Even under the best conditions, there's absolutely no way to guarantee good results when painting outside – the wind can come up suddenly, trees and birds can drop things on the car, insects can fly into the wet paint and dust is unavoidable.

Be aware that many of the materials used for body repair and painting are very dangerous – they shouldn't be inhaled and they are definitely a fire hazard, so some type of storage area, preferably a metal cabinet, will be needed, regardless of the size of the job you're doing. Read through the Safety first! Section in Chapter 1 immediately before starting work. And have a fire extinguisher on hand at all times!

Minor body repairs

Repair of scratches in paint

Body damage can generally be divided into four categories: minor scratches which do not penetrate all the way to the metal, small dings and dents which can be filled without reworking the metal, major dents which will require metal work before filling, and 'where do we start on this mess?'

In this Chapter we're going to take a look at the repair of scratches and minor dents – both of which can be repaired quite easily, but only if you're willing to invest the time to do the job right.

Repairing major damage is, in many ways, easier than fixing a minor scratch or dent, simply because you're almost starting from scratch and building a new body part. When you're dealing with a minor repair, though, it's easy to pay a little less attention than you normally would, and when the repair is finished you find that, because you didn't sand it quite as well as you should have, or paid a little less attention to fogging the paint on, the repair looks almost as bad as the original damage.

The secret to minor scratch and dent repair is to take your time, do the work carefully (especially since you'll usually be working with a very small area) and DON'T DO ANY MORE WORK THAN NECESSARY. Many minor repair jobs turn into major projects simply because the person doing the job didn't know where to stop sanding, grinding or banging away at the metal.

Let's start by looking at the best way to get scratches out of paint.

Minor scratches

Minor scratches, that don't penetrate through the paint, can be repaired by simply cleaning the scratched area with a wax/silicone remover and filling the scratch with touch up paint. If the paint container includes an applicator, use it – otherwise, use a toothpick or matchstick to carefully dab the paint into the scratch (application of several thin layers is better than one thick one). After the paint has dried for several days, use a new double edge razor blade to trim the paint bead down even with the surrounding paint. Polishing compound or a very fine rubbing compound can be used next to blend the new paint into the old. Apply a coat of wax and you're finished. **Note:** *If the vehicle has a clearcoat over the paint, apply one or two VERY THIN coats of touch up clearcoat to the repaired area. If you don't do this, the colour of the repaired area may not match the rest of the body.*

Apply wax/silicone remover to the scratched area . . .

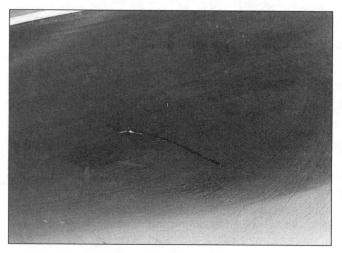

. . . then fill the scratch with paint (build up several thin layers rather than one thick one)

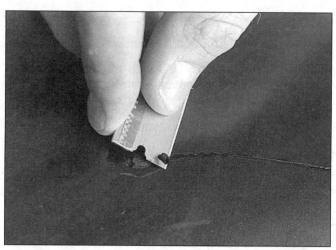

Use a razor blade to trim off the excess paint and make the filled area even with the paint surrounding it

Deep scratches

Severe scratches, resulting in chipped paint, exposed sheet metal and perhaps even a crease or dent in the metal, are more difficult and time consuming to repair. You'll need the following materials for this job . . .

- *Lint free cloths*
- *Wax/silicone remover (eg. 3M General Purpose Adhesive Cleaner and Wax Remover)*
- *A tack cloth*
- *Chemical metal conditioner (if bare metal is visible)*
- *Primer and touch up paint (available in aerosol cans)*
- *320, 400 and 1000 grit wet or dry sandpaper*
- *Stopper (filler)*
- *Masking materials (paper and tape)*
- *Rubbing compound*
- *Automotive wax*
- *If rust is involved, a chemical rust remover*
- *If a clearcoat is used, some touch up clearcoat*

Note: *The following photos are keyed to the step by step procedure with a number in the upper left corner of each illustration. The number corresponds to the step number of the procedure.*

1 The first step in repairing any paint scratch is to get it, and the area around it, completely clean, so wash the surface with mild soap and water, rinse it well and dry it with a lint free cloth. You absolutely have to get off all traces of old wax, which will keep the new paint from adhering properly. Automotive paint shops sell special cleaners designed to remove all traces of wax, grease, silicone and other sealers from the paint – buy and use one!

2 Remove all traces of rust with 400 grit wet or dry sandpaper, then use a chemical rust remover (follow the directions on the container). Apply the wax/silicone remover again.

3 Sand over the area to be repaired with medium fine (320) grit sandpaper, but don't sand so hard you go right through the paint. All you want to do is clean off the top layer and start feathering down the edges of the scratch.

4 Follow up by wet sanding with 400 or 600 grit sandpaper, using a hose or a bucket of water to keep the paper clean. After sanding, you should have a finish as smooth as the original painted surface.

5 When you've finished sanding, the area should 'feather' (blend very gradually) into the surrounding paint. If you can feel a ridge as you run your hand over the area, sand some more.

6 Spray on a light coat of primer, let it dry, and follow with another light coat. Don't spray the primer so heavy you get runs or sags and be sure to let the first coat dry before spraying on the second coat.

7 Let the primer dry COMPLETELY, then get out the hose or bucket and wet sand the primer with 400 or 600 grit wet or dry sandpaper. Work the paper over the area very lightly. The idea is to get the primer smooth.

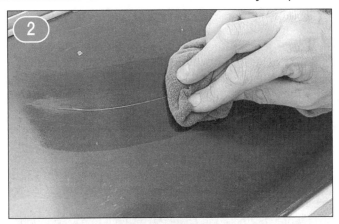

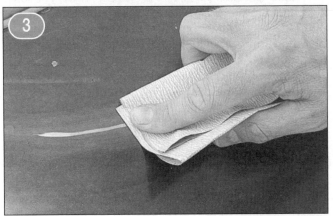

8 If you sand completely through the primer, don't worry about it. Just spray on another light coat, let it dry, and sand some more. Remember- if you leave the primer coat rough, or a ridge is present where it blends into the existing paint, the roughness or ridge will still be there after you spray the paint.

9 Wait for the primered area to dry completely, then wipe it clean with a tack cloth to make sure there's no dust left on the surface.

10 Spray a very light 'fog' coat of paint onto the repaired area. The paint coat should be so thin you can still see the repaired area. This fog coat is just to give a tack base for the following coats of paint to adhere to.

11 Spray on the finish coat. Make sure it's heavy enough to cover the repair, but not so heavy that the paint runs or sags. Several thin coats are better than one heavy coat. Let each coat dry to the tack free stage before applying the next one.

12 Let the paint dry for several days (a week would be best), then use a very fine rubbing compound very gently to blend the new paint into the existing finish. If it's done right, and followed with a thorough cleaning of the old paint and a fresh coat of wax over the whole area, you won't be able to tell where the repair was made.

Scratches accompanied by minor dents or creases

Note: *The following photos are keyed to the step by step procedure with a number in the upper left corner of each illustration. The number corresponds to the step number of the procedure.*

If the scratch is deeper, and there's a minor dent or crease associated with it, then the repair technique is a little different . . .

1 Sand thoroughly along the edge of the scratch, feather edging back into the good paint.

2 Fill the depression with stopper (filler). Spreading on several light coats rather than one heavy one will usually give a better result.

3 After the stopper has dried thoroughly, sand it with very fine (400) grit sandpaper.

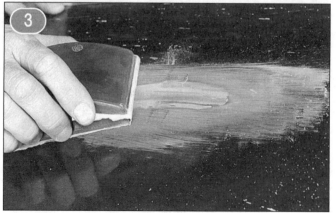

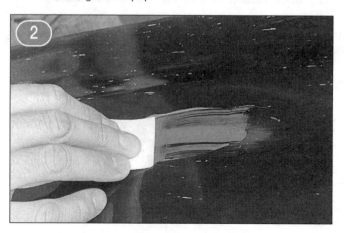

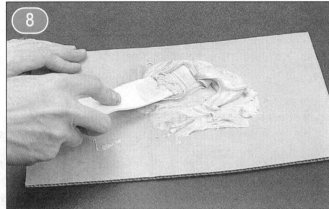

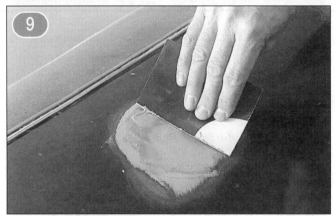

4 Clean the area thoroughly with a tack rag to make sure the surface is free of dust and sanding debris.

5 Spray on several light coats of primer. Wait for each coat to dry thoroughly before spraying on the next coat.

6 If you have a dent which isn't deep enough to justify pounding out, but is too deep for filling with stopper (see Chapter 6 for more information), use a number 80 grit sanding disc and an electric drill to take the paint down to bare metal for two inches around the dent or ding.

7 Purchase a small can of plastic body filler – don't forget to buy the tube of hardener, which should come with it. Many stores keep the hardener separate from the filler, so you may have to ask for it specifically. Tell the parts man what you're using the filler for so he can help you choose the right type.

8 On a mixing palate (or a piece of cardboard if that's all you have), mix up a batch of plastic filler and hardener. Be careful to follow the directions on the container and get the filler and hardener mixed thoroughly (streaks in the filler mean that more mixing is necessary). If you don't, the filler won't harden properly and you'll end up having to grind it off and start over.

9 Spread the plastic filler evenly over the damaged area. Don't worry about getting it on the unsanded paint – you'll be sanding it off and feathering it out as soon as it cures.

10 Let the filler dry until it can be just scratched with your fingernail (not until it's completely hardened), then work it down to match the body contours with a surform file. **Note:** *Follow the instructions with the plastic filler – some newer fillers can be worked with an 80 grit sanding disc mounted in an electric drill.*

11 If you end up with a low spot, or a place where a bubble formed, simply mix up some more plastic filler and apply another layer.

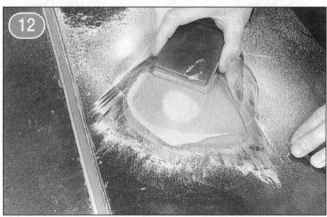

12 Use a sanding block and 320 grit sandpaper to go over the entire area, smoothing the filler and feathering it into the surrounding area. Finish off the sanding and featheredging with 400 grit sandpaper.

13 Refer to Steps 6 through 12 in the previous section to complete the repair.

Chapter 5

Repair of minor dents

The great majority of body repairs come under the heading of 'minor' damage. They're dents that may be too big to simply fill with plastic filler, but not major enough to require replacement of the panel.

Even in this minor repair category, there are several different degrees of repair that might be necessary. Dents that require a puller to get the metal out to a reasonable approximation of the original contour, dents that only need some hammer work from behind, and dents that can't be reached from behind so they have to be worked with a puller. Bear in mind that many dents that don't involve the sheet metal being creased or torn can often be repaired without disturbing the paintwork, by specialists such as 'Dent Devils, Smart Repair, Dent Wizards' etc. Here, trained operatives using specialised tools can carefully repair seemingly major dents, without the need for paint repairs. Well worth a phone call before you get the sander out!

If the dent you're trying to fix is big enough, deep enough or has deformed the metal to the point where simple banging or pulling won't bring it back into close enough shape for filling, go on to Chapter 6 (the Section on **Metal working**) for information on using specialised bodywork tools, especially the hammers and dollies necessary to straighten sheet metal.

Here, though, what we're dealing with is metal which can easily be returned to near original contour. Depending on the nature and depth of the dent, you'll need the following tools and materials for this procedure . . .

• *Slide hammer dent puller*
• *Electric or air powered disc sander*
• *Body hammer and dolly*
• *Surform file*
• *Sanding block/sanding board*
• *Sandpaper (various grits)*
• *Plastic body filler and hardener*
• *Body filler applicator*
• *Stopper (also called glazing compound)*
• *Primer*
• *Paint (use lacquer for spot repairs such as this)*

1 If the dent's in an inaccessible area, or too deep or creased to simply bang out from behind, punch a series of 3.0 mm diameter holes along the crease line or in the deepest portion of the dent. Use an awl or center punch and hammer to make the holes.

2 Screw the slide hammer tip into the hole in the SHALLOWEST portion of the dent and pull the dent out. Be careful, you don't want to end up with a 'reverse dent' where the surface is raised higher than it was originally. It helps to tap along the edge of the dent as you operate the slide hammer – this will help 'pop' the sheet metal back into its original shape.

3 Once you've pulled the dented area up near the original body contour with a slide hammer, use a 'pull rod' to make more precise changes in the shape of the metal. If you can get behind the panel with a hammer, keep your hand on the outside of the dented area while tapping on the back side to make sure you're getting the metal where you want it. In this case, what you feel with your palm and fingers about the dent will usually be a lot more accurate than what your eyes may tell you.

4 When you think you have the sheet metal out near the original contour, use a body grinder or sander with an 80 grit disc to remove the paint right down to bare metal. When sanding away the paint, the disc will probably reveal any major high or low spots in the metal.

5 Switch to a 100 grit sanding disc and go over the area again. Featheredge the paint out at least 25 mm around the dented area.

6 With all the paint gone, run your hand over the damaged area. Again, touch will probably be more helpful than sight for telling you if the metal is straight or not. A little more work with the hammer, on both sides of the panel, **may** be necessary to get things ready for the plastic filler. Clean the repair area one more time with wax/silicone remover – you can't get it too clean!

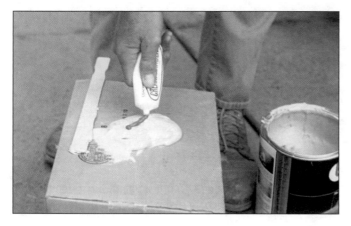

7 On a mixing palate (or a piece of cardboard if that's all you have), mix up a batch of plastic filler and hardener. Be careful to follow the directions on the container and get the filler and hardener mixed thoroughly (streaks in the filler mean that more mixing is necessary). If you don't, the filler won't harden properly and you'll end up having to grind it off and start over.

8 Working quickly so the filler doesn't harden, spread a layer over the repair area with a plastic applicator, using long, smooth strokes. Don't be afraid to press firmly to ensure that the filler bonds to the metal. As soon as the filler starts to ball up under the tool, stop trying to make it smoother.

9 Let the filler harden until you can just dent it with your fingernail, then use a Surform file to work the material down to the proper contour. **Note:** *Follow the instructions with the plastic filler – some newer fillers can be worked with an 80 grit sanding disc mounted in an electric drill or power sander.*

10 Use a sanding board or block that will bridge the undamaged areas on either side of the filled area and 80 grit sandpaper to work the filler down until it's smooth and even. If you end up with low spots, or if the edges of the filler flake away, apply another thin layer of plastic filler. When it dries, repeat the file and 80 grit sandpaper work.

11 Use medium fine (320) grit sandpaper to work the filler down to the desired final contour. Note that the filler feather edges down to bare metal, not existing paint. Again check the repair area with the palm of your hand, feeling for uneven spots in the filler. Highs and lows your eye can't see at this stage, but which your palm can feel, will show up clearly after the panel is painted.

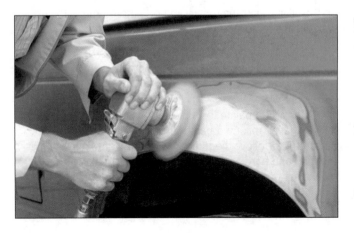

12 Use a medium fine (320) grit sanding disc to feather the old paint into the bare metal all around the repair area.

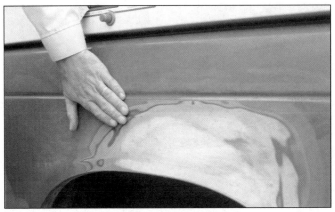

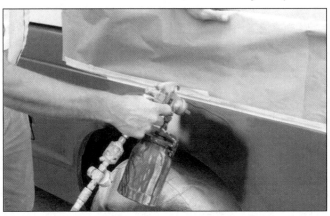

13 Use the palm of your hand to check the transition from bare metal to the old paint. You shouldn't be able to feel any kind of a ridge where the paint stops. As soon as you're satisfied the repair is flat and uniform, blow away the dust with compressed air and mask off the adjacent panels or trim pieces.

14 Apply several layers of primer to the area. Don't spray the primer on too heavy, so it sags or runs, and make sure each coat is dry before you spray on the next one.

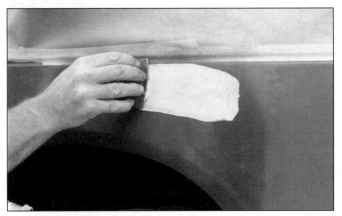

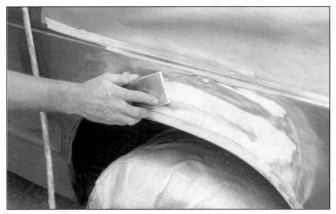

15 Use stopper to fill any scratches or other imperfections in the primer.

16 Sand the area with 360 or 400 grit sandpaper to remove the excess glazing compound, then apply more primer.

17 Remove the masking materials, then apply a thin layer of rubbing compound to the area around the repair that was sprayed with primer overspray.

18 Use a buffer to remove the rubbing compound and the primer overspray.

19 Finish sand the primer with very fine sandpaper (1000 grit), then mask off the repair area again.

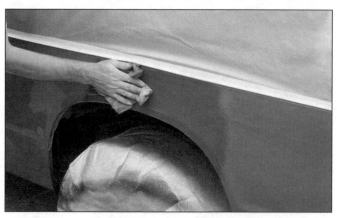

20 Use a tack rag to remove the dust from the repair area.

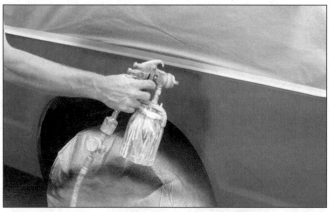

21 Apply the finish coat. Touch up paint in aerosol cans can be used, but the preferred approach, especially after all the work you've done to this point, is to use a spray gun and a good quality paint intended for spot repairs. If you're using touch up paint, apply several light coats rather than one heavy one and let each coat dry until tacky before applying the next one. If you're using a gun, follow the instructions with the paint regarding time between coats, etc.

22 Stand back and admire the end result! Don't attempt to rub out or wax the repair area until the paint has dried for the recommended time (read the paint container for instructions).

Repair of minor rust damage

Where older cars are concerned, and in some parts of the country, even newer cars, rust is the number one body killer. Whether it's from water that's run down into the door and trapped there by plugged drain holes, or wings rusted out because of salt applications to the roads, eventually rust is going to form, and when it does it can make any car look terrible.

The most common way of fixing rust damage is the same way a minor dent would be fixed. Cut out the rusted area, put some sort of backing in place and lay on a coat of plastic filler. Unfortunately, where rust is concerned, this is the absolute worst way to fix the problem.

The rust started because, for whatever reason, water got to the metal and stayed there. Filling a rusted away section of a body with plastic filler will look fine – for about a week, or until the first time it rains real hard. Some fillers, even when fully cured and hard as a rock, act just like a sponge where water is concerned. Get some water behind the repair, where the rust originally started, and before long either the plastic filler simply falls off or, at the very least, the paint will begin to bubble because of the water underneath it.

The best way to fix rust damage is by welding a new panel into place, be it a sill panel, door panel or an entire wing. But this can also be the most expensive way to go about the job, and if there are lots of rusted areas, the repairs can end up costing more than the car is worth.

Cutting out the rusted area and welding a 'patch' in place is a better solution, but usually the patch will have to be moulded in with plastic filler, leading to the potential for the same problems you would've encountered using plastic filler for the whole repair, or in areas where there are lots of curves to contend with, getting the patch shaped right can be more trouble than it's worth (although special pre formed patches that match certain body contours are available for some vehicles).

Fiberglass rust repair kits – which include nearly everything you'll need for the job – are widely available at car accessory shops/motor factors

All things considered, the ideal method of fixing a minor rusted out area is to use a fibreglass repair kit. Fiberglass is a little harder to use than plastic filler, but it's well within the ability of the average do-it-yourselfer. This type of repair should only be used where the damaged area is 50 mm or less in diameter – for larger areas, refer to Chapter 6, **Major rust repair**.

The easiest way to use fibreglass for this sort of repair work is to buy a complete fibreglass repair kit, available at most car accessory shops/motor factors. Many kits come with everything you need except the paint to finish the job off, along with complete instructions. If you purchase one of the kits which only contains the actual fibreglass materials (fibreglass cloth, liquid or jelly epoxy, release film and cream or liquid hardener), you'll also need assorted grinding discs for your electric drill, sandpaper, stopper and primer.

Note: *The following photos are keyed to the step by step procedure with a number in the upper left corner of each illustration. The number corresponds to the step number of the procedure.*

1 Using a hacksaw, air chisel or snips, cut out the rusted portion. An air powered grinder equipped with an abrasive cut off wheel was used in the example in the photographs included in this Section. It produced a very clean cut. Make sure you get all the rusted metal, or you'll be doing the repair all over again in a couple of months.

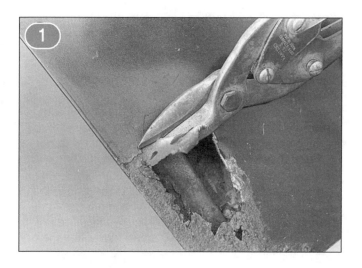

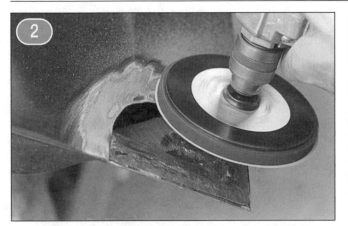

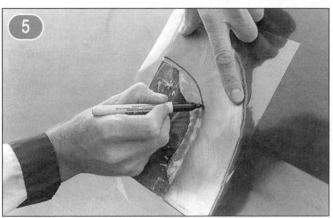

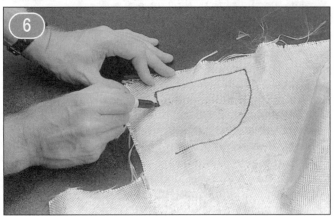

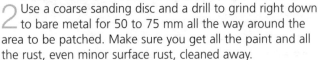

2 Use a coarse sanding disc and a drill to grind right down to bare metal for 50 to 75 mm all the way around the area to be patched. Make sure you get all the paint and all the rust, even minor surface rust, cleaned away.

3 Apply a rust arresting chemical to the surrounding metal, particularly on the inside of the panel. **Note:** *Rust arresting chemicals are made by several manufacturers. They react with rust and transform it into a substance called 'black rust', which is chemically stable and won't continue to eat away at the metal.*

4 Use a self-grip pliers and a body hammer to form a recessed flange around the edge of the opening – the opening itself and the surrounding good metal must form a depression extending about 18 mm beyond the hole.

5 Cut a piece of release film about 50 to 75 mm larger than the repair area, then lay it over the opening. Use a grease pencil or felt tip marker to outline the depressed repair area on the release film. Lay the film aside until you're ready to mix up the fibreglass resin.

6 Cut a piece of fibreglass cloth the same size and shape as the outline on the release film. Use a sharp pair of scissors to make the cut – not a razor blade – to ensure that the fibreglass cloth threads won't be 'pulled.'

7 Cut a second piece of fibreglass cloth the same shape as the first one, but about 25 mm smaller all the way around.

8 You'll need some form of backing for the fibreglass in the hole. Stuffing the area with wire mesh or coarse steel wool will give you a flexible yet firm base to work on. However, after the repair is complete, remove the steel wool from the back side of the panel or it'll promote the formation of new rust.

9 Open the container of epoxy resin (liquid or jelly) and pour a substantial amount into a plastic container. It's easier to go buy more resin if you run out than it is to mix up a fresh batch halfway through a job when you find out you didn't make up enough.

10 Add the cream or liquid hardener to the resin in the proportions specified with the kit and mix it in thoroughly, until you can no longer see any difference in texture or colour in the resin (the hardener will cause the resin to change colour).

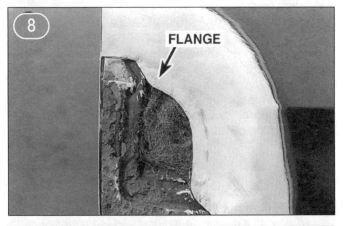

FLANGE

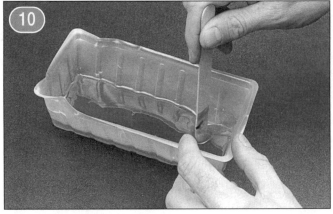

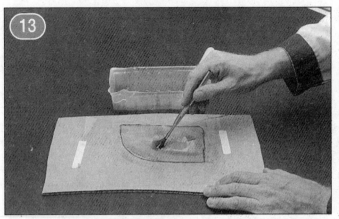

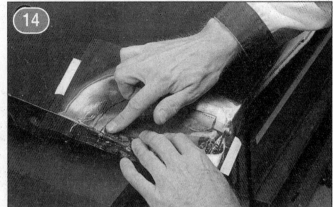

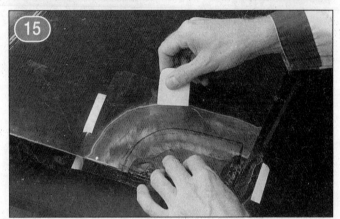

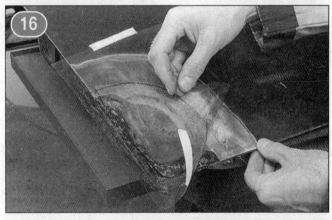

11 Lay the release film on a clean, flat surface (a piece of cardboard is fine), then spread an even layer of the mixed epoxy resin and hardener on the release film until it covers the outlined area.

12 Lay the smaller of the two pieces of fibreglass cloth in the center of the layer of resin and work another layer into the cloth. Be aware that as you're working, the resin is setting up (hardening), so don't take any breaks during the process.

13 Lay the larger of the two pieces of fibreglass cloth over the smaller piece and again work a layer of resin into the second layer of cloth.

14 Pick up the release film by the top edge and place it over the area to be repaired, with the release film facing OUT. Press it into place with your fingertips, moving it only as much as necessary to get the fibreglass cloth over the area to be repaired. The outer edges of the fibreglass should overlap the flange around the opening.

15 Slide a spreader over the release film to press the fibreglass cloth firmly against the bare metal. Make sure that all air bubbles are worked out. The release film will allow you to use the spreader to form the fibreglass to the metal without having it bunch up or stick. Don't worry if you get epoxy into the unsanded area – it will sand off.

16 Every so often, check the exposed resin to see how it's drying. When it's tack free, peel off the release film.

17 You'll want to give the fibreglass plenty of time to cure before starting to work on it. A heat lamp or even a couple of ordinary light bulbs can be used to speed up the curing process on a cool day.

18 As soon as the repair has cured to the point where it's hard to the touch, you can use an electric drill and sanding disc to start working the fibreglass patch down to match the body contour.

19 Finish the sanding, including feather edging the resin and fibreglass down to the metal surface with a sanding block and progressively finer grades of sandpaper.

20 When you have the repair down to a smooth surface, use body filler or stopper over the top to get it ready to paint smooth and to cover any 'weave' that may be showing through from the fibreglass cloth.

21 Finish sand the body filler/glazing compound until the surface is perfectly smooth.

22 The repaired area is now ready for priming and painting. Refer to Steps 6 through 12 in the first part of the ***Repair of scratches in paint*** Section of this Chapter. If necessary, be sure to mask off adjoining areas to prevent overspray.

Once you've finished the job, there's one final step that's absolutely necessary. The reason rust formed originally was because, for whatever reason, water and/or a water salt mixture was able to get in behind the panel and stay there long enough to start the rust eating away at the metal. And, despite your fancy fibreglass repair, the same thing is going to happen again if you don't take the necessary steps to prevent it. Turn to the Section on ***Rustproofing and undersealing*** in Chapter 2 and make sure this will be the last rust repair job you'll have to do on this car.

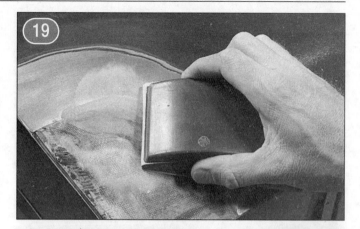

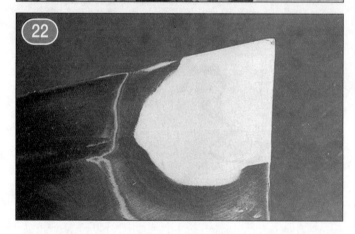

Plastic repair

In many cases, flexible body parts (bumper covers or extensions, etc.) can be repaired without removing the part from the car, but it's usually easier to do the work with it off. Generally speaking, removing a few screws or bolts is all that's necessary to detach the component.

The following procedure is general in nature, but it should be sufficient for repair of most plastic bumper components. Check with your local automotive paint shop for the correct type of primer and paint, as well as any special paint additives, to use on specific plastic parts. Many car accessory shops/motor factors sell kits specifically for the repair of plastic bumpers etc.

1 Use a wax/silicone remover solvent to thoroughly clean the area to be repaired. This step is an absolute must! Clean both the inside and outside of the part in the area to be repaired.

2 After cleaning, the inside and outside will have to be sanded with a coarse (about 50 grit) sanding disc, at least 50 mm beyond the area to be repaired on the inside and 25 mm beyond on the outside.

3 Cut two pieces of fibreglass cloth about 50 mm larger than the damaged area.

4 Mix equal amounts of both flexible repair material components on a sheet of glass or metal, then apply a 3.0 mm thick layer of the material to the back of the part to be repaired.

5 Place one of the pieces of fibreglass cloth over the material, pressing it gently but evenly into place, then cover the fibreglass with another layer of the flexible repair material.

6 Lay the second piece of fibreglass cloth in place, pressing it firmly into the repair material, then apply a final coat of the flexible repair material thick enough to fill the weave of the fibreglass cloth. Allow the flexible repair material to cure for approximately 1/2-hour.

7 Move to the outside of the part and use 180 grit sandpaper to remove all paint from the area to be repaired. The flexible repair material must not be applied over paint.

8 Use 5 grit sandpaper or an electric drill and rotary file to cut a 12 mm wide 'V' along the break in the material.

9 Mix more of the flexible repair material and spread a light coat of it into the area to be repaired. Wait a few minutes, then apply more material, until the level is slightly above the original panel contour. Allow it to cure for 1/2-hour.

10 Block sand the repair with 220 grit sandpaper to establish the proper contour, then finish sanding it with 320 or 400 grit sandpaper.

⚠ *Warning: Most flexible paints contain isocyanates – wear a high quality air fed mask respirator whenever these paints are sprayed!*

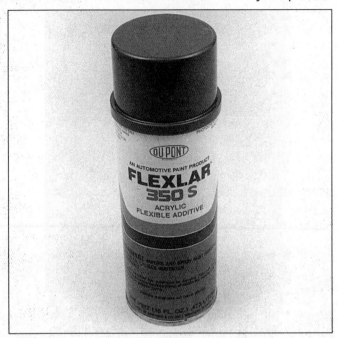

Additives for making paint flexible are available from automotive paint shops – be sure to read the label on the container

11 The entire part should be repainted, not just the area that's been repaired.

12 Clean the part with wax/silicone remover solvent – this is essential!

13 Clean the area with a tack cloth, then apply four medium dry coats of flexible primer/surfacer. Use a fast evaporating thinner and don't apply 'wet' coats of primer/surfacer, since the repair material will absorb excess thinner and swell, leaving a highly visible repaired area after painting.

14 Allow the primer to dry for at least an hour, then sand with 400 grit sandpaper. Follow with a rub down with a Scotch-Brite pad to remove any gloss from the surface.

15 Mix the base colour paint (enamel, lacquer, acrylic, etc.), then add the flexcoat additive and thinner, following the manufacturer's recommendations. Allowing flash time between them, apply a sufficient number of coats to achieve complete coverage of the repaired area and obtain a good colour match to the rest of the body.

16 If a clearcoat is used, allow the base colour coat to dry for at least one hour. Mix the clearcoat with the flex additive, then apply three coats of clear at 2.4 to 2.7 bar gun pressure, allowing each coat to flash dry before applying the next. Allow to dry for at least four hours before reinstalling the part.

Note: *Do not apply rubbing compound or an abrasive polish to clearcoat with a flexible additive. Use non abrasive polish to clean and wax only.*

Notes

Major body repair

Metal working techniques

Body fillers

Major rust repair

Fibreglass body repair techniques

Pulling bent monocoque structures

Metal working techniques

Panel shapes

While in many cases a damaged area can either be pulled out and then filled with plastic filler, or the panel can be completely replaced either by bolting on a new component or welding in a new panel section, there are times when the most expedient way to repair a damaged area is to work the metal back into shape. The basic tools for doing this sort of work are hydraulic jacks and/or pullers, hammers and dollies (see Chapter 4).

Before getting into how a metal panel can be worked into shape, let's examine some of the shapes panels are formed into for automotive uses. Almost all panels have one or more curves to them – the curvature is referred to as the crown. A panel that has a smooth, gentle curve to it, like most roof panels, is called a low crown panel. A panel with a sharp curve, like the area where a wing wraps over to meet the bonnet, is called a high crown panel. Some panels combine high and low crown, like a boot lid which curves gently from the rear window line to near the rear edge of the car (low crown), then curves down sharply (high crown) to meet the rear bumper. Occasionally you'll also run into reverse crown panels, where the panel curves in.

Most body panels are a low crown type and because there is very little panel curvature, are structurally very weak. Because of this, most low crown panels are reinforced, either with flanged edges to add strength or with welded on reinforcements on the back of the panel. Most wings have flanged edges to add strength to the panel, while the roof, doors, etc. have welded in reinforcements. The bonnet and boot lids of most cars combine the two types of reinforcement, with a flanged edge and welded on inner panels to add strength to what would otherwise be a large, unsupported structure which would be prone to vibration and flexing.

Chapter 6

Types of sheet metal damage

When a car is involved in a collision, there will be highly visible damage at the point of impact, but the force of that impact will also be transferred to the surrounding sheet metal. The type of damage can be separated into four distinct types: Displaced areas, simple bends, rolled buckles and stretches. Each one requires a different repair procedure and specialized tools.

Displaced area

Where a section of sheet metal has been moved, but not otherwise damaged, it's referred to as a displaced area. For example, a hit in the rear quarter panel will cause damage where the impact occurred, but the entire panel may be pushed in. In most displaced areas, the panel can be pushed back out with the only actual damage being to the point of impact.

Simple bend

When a piece of sheet metal is hit hard enough to take on an 'S' shape, usually in conjunction with a sharp crease in the metal, it's referred to as a simple bend. In a simple bend there is usually very little stretching of the metal.

Rolled buckle

A rolled buckle is the usual result of a severe impact like most front and rear collisions. The rolled buckle is much like a simple bend, but with extensive stretching of the metal, which usually results in the sheet metal trying to tuck under.

Stretches

Almost all body damage you're liable to run into will involve some form of stretching. A gouge in the metal is typical of stretch damage, where the metal has both been pushed in and the surface area enlarged. Although some stretches can be shrunk through the use of body tools and heat, most often stretch damage is repaired by filling with plastic filler.

Tools

The two primary tools used for working damaged sheet metal are pulling and pushing devices (slide hammer pullers, hydraulic jacks, body jacks, hydraulic pullers, etc.) and body hammers and dollies.

Hydraulic jacks and body jacks can often be rented from tool hire shops, and can prove invaluable to the do-it-yourselfer for restoring body panel alignment. However, it should be kept in mind that it's much better to PULL a panel back into position than to push it, primarily because there will be less damage to the metal while it's being forced back into position. Hydraulic jacks, during the course of pushing a panel, tend to stretch it, and while you can usually easily push a structure or panel back into place, you may find afterwards that restoring the contour of the panel is impossible because of the amount of stretching that occurred when pushing. Some areas, though (especially

those that are strongly reinforced, such as door and windshield pillars), require a hydraulic jack or body jack for realignment if care is taken in determining where the unit is mounted.

Pulling, on the other hand, can be done without stretching the metal, since the pull can be either concentrated in a reinforced area or spread over a wide non-reinforced panel. In addition, when pulling sheet metal it's easier to control the amount of movement of the panel, so you can stop pulling just at the point where the panel is returned to the original position.

Body hammers come in a wide variety of styles and sizes (see Chapter 4 for additional information and an illustration of the various hammer types), with specialised hammers available for the many different shaping jobs that might be necessary for a professional body worker. For the do-it-yourselfer, though, only two or three different types of hammers will be needed to cover almost any job you might run into.

Body hammers are designed expressly for working sheet metal – YOU SHOULD NOT TRY TO REPAIR SHEET METAL DAMAGE WITH ANY OTHER TYPE OF HAMMER! Using a ball peen hammer or a carpenter's claw hammer to work sheet metal will usually end up doing more damage than the original collision. The large, essentially flat face of the body hammer spreads the blow over a large area, reducing the possibility of accidentally stretching the metal being worked on. The large face also gives you a better chance of hitting the metal in line with the dolly being held underneath the damaged panel.

Most body hammers come with two heads – one large, nearly flat round or square head, and at the opposite end, a picking head. The flat head is used for working the metal against a dolly, lowering a high spot, while the picking head is usually used for raising low spots, working from the back side of a panel.

Almost all forms of sheet metal work can be accomplished with a body hammer and one of four dollies. There are many different dollies available for body work, some very specialised, but for general applications (and especially for the do-it-yourselfer), **general purpose**, **low crown** and **heel and toe** dollies will be sufficient (see Chapter 4 for more information and an illustration of several types of dollies).

The general purpose dolly is often called a railroad dolly because it's shaped like a section cut from a piece of railroad track. The low crown dolly is shaped a lot like the railroad dolly, but with less curvature across the top face for working on flat panels. Heel and toe dollies are smaller, with sharper curves, for working in confined areas and on high crown panels. Remember that a dolly is not an anvil. It isn't used as something to pound metal down onto. Instead, by properly using it in conjunction with a body hammer, the dolly is used to raise metal from underneath as it's being struck from above by the body hammer.

Techniques

Working sheet metal can be divided into three general techniques: *Roughing* the metal into shape, *hammer and dolly work* to bring the contour back to the original shape of the panel, then *grinding and filing* to prepare the surface for filling, sanding and painting. Hammer and dolly work is usually called bumping and the grinding and filing is termed finish work. Quite often pulling the structure straight is required before the metal can be reworked.

The first step, roughing, is where the metal is brought back into general contour. It's generally accomplished either by pushing the metal out with a hydraulic jack or body jack, or by pulling it out on a sophisticated body alignment rack. Quite often a body hammer will be used in conjunction with the pushing or pulling tools to provide localised pressure, such as to a creased area that's being pulled straight. Where low crown panels are involved, quite often the roughing can be done with a slide hammer type puller. A series of small holes are punched or drilled in the panel, then the slide hammer tip is screwed into the holes, one at a time starting at the edge of the damaged area, and the sheet metal is pulled back into shape. Slide hammer tips that hook onto the sheet metal are also available – they're used primarily along the edges of panels and eliminate the need for holes. Remember, it's essential that the underlying structure is properly aligned first, or the finished panels won't line up with the rest of the vehicle.

Once the damaged area has been returned to rough shape, the 'bumping' with the body hammer and dolly begins. Hammers and dollies are used in two ways – the *hammer-on* technique and the *hammer-off* technique. Chapter 4 contains general illustrations of the two approaches.

When doing hammer-on work, the kind the do-it-yourselfer will find himself doing most often, the dolly is placed behind the damaged panel and the body hammer is brought down on the sheet metal directly above the dolly. The hammer hits 'on' the dolly, with the sheet metal in between. At first you'll find the dolly rebounding away from the blow, which is exactly the opposite of what you want to happen. You want the body hammer to bounce up after striking the sheet metal, with the dolly staying in contact with the under side of the metal, or bouncing away only slightly. The dolly, because it weighs more than the hammer, will be pushing up in response to the hammer blow, rather than the hammer head pushing down. This causes the metal to be raised where it was hit with the hammer, rather than being lowered. The less bounce there is to the dolly (controlled by the pressure you put on the dolly and how much you 'snap' the hammer with your wrist, causing it to rebound), the more the metal will be raised.

Hammer-off sheet metal work also uses the body hammer and dolly, with the dolly behind the panel being worked and the hammer hitting the outer surface, but the hammer doesn't hit right over the dolly. Instead, it hits just off to one side. However, for the hammer off technique to be effective,

A body hammer is often used in conjunction with a slide hammer puller, especially where a crease in the metal is involved

Special hook attachments are often used with slide hammer pullers to straighten body parts – here the hook is used to grip the edge of the wing opening so it can be pulled back into shape

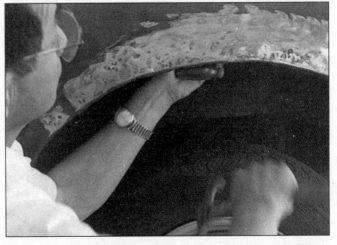

Using a body hammer and dolly to reshape the rear wing lip

the hammer must hit just barely off the location of the dolly, since it's important that a portion of the force from the hammer blow be imparted to the dolly.

This technique is used when you have an area where the sheet metal is raised in one spot and pushed in adjacent to the raised area – common to most gouge type damage. Almost any blow which causes metal to be pushed in will raise the surrounding metal to a degree, and if the blow was a glancing one, rather than a direct hit, it's likely the metal adjacent to the gouge will be raised considerably above the original panel contour. To work the metal back into shape, the spot struck by the hammer drives the sheet metal down, since it's not being supported by the dolly. Movement of the sheet metal is transferred to the dolly, though, which is placed right next to the high area, and the dolly rebounds, forcing the low area up. Again, the harder the dolly is held against the back of the sheet metal, the more displacement there will be, and the less the hammer is 'snapped,' causing it to bounce away from the metal, the more the high area will be forced down.

The hammer-on and hammer-off body hammer and dolly work is used to bring the damaged panel back to near normal contour, at which point the metal finishing techniques are brought into play. In metal finishing you'll not only be preparing the surface for finishing, but eliminating fine high or low areas through picking and grinding.

The primary tools for metal finishing are the body grinder, body file and pick hammer. The first step is to work the metal over with the grinder or file to locate high and low areas. A professional bodyworker will start right in with the body grinder, but the do-it-yourselfer should start with the body file, since it will more easily reveal areas that need additional work.

When the body file is passed over a repaired area it'll cut the top off any high spots and leave low areas untouched. It's essential that a body file be used for this work, since it's specially designed to cut sheet metal. It should be used with sufficient force to work the metal without distorting the panel. After going over the repaired area with the file, you may see areas that are excessively high and need more hammer and dolly work. It's much more likely, though, that you'll find many low spots in the repaired area, showing up as un-filed metal.

The pick hammer is often used behind the sheet metal being worked to raise low spots. This is a difficult technique to master, since you're hitting an area you can't see, but practice will quickly bring about the ability to strike in just the right area. Put the palm of your hand over the low spot, then gently strike the panel from behind with the pick end of the hammer. You should be able to feel where the blow lands and adjust your aim accordingly. Use a blunt face pick to raise the low spot with a series of light blows. After the area has been raised slightly, use the file again to determine whether the metal has been raised enough. Repeat the pick and file operation until the surface is smooth. The pick hammer can also be used to flatten small raised areas from

Use a pick hammer to flatten small raised areas – don't strike the metal too hard or a reversed dent will form

The palm of your hand will tell you when to stop reshaping the panel

the outside of the panel. Don't strike the sheet metal too hard or it'll be dented in. Use the palm of your free hand to determine when to stop hammering.

Although the beginner body worker should learn to work sheet metal with a body file first, the body grinder is an absolutely essential piece of equipment that will make many repair procedures go much faster. The body grinder is not just a bigger electric drill with a sanding disc on it. A body grinder is much more powerful than any electric drill and it turns much faster. If you aren't careful with it, it's very easy to quickly cut completely through a piece of sheet metal with a body grinder.

Discs for a body grinder are available in a wide variety of grits and in open and closed coat types. Closed coat discs are most often used for finishing body work, while open coat discs are used for paint removal. A 24 grit disc is most often used for working a panel that has been repaired.

Using a body grinder can appear difficult at first, especially since they're relatively heavy and because the speed they turn makes them hard to hold onto, but practice, and using both handles, will soon enable you to master the technique. When using the body grinder, run it across the panel at an angle that produces swirl marks which will bridge the low spots. You don't want the disc to lay flat on the surface to be worked, since this will make the grinder almost impossible to hold onto. Also, you don't want it to hit the metal at too sharp an angle, which would cause it to cut into the surface. A very slight angle is best, and you should apply just enough pressure to cause the disc to flex slightly. The low spots which show up after a pass with the grinder should be worked out with a pick, just as they were with the body file.

Once you've picked up all the low spots and the contour is right, change to a 60 grit disc on the body grinder and use it to buff the surface in preparation for priming. This buffing should remove the deeper scratches left by the grinding disc and body file. If you're using the body grinder in a reverse crown area, cut the disc into a star shape with six to eight points. A round disc will tend to cut into the metal in a reverse crown area, while the cut points of a star shaped disc will flex and follow the contour of the crown.

Do-it-yourself structure pulling

If damage is minimal, pulling/pushing structural components back into place can be accomplished with such commonly available tools as bottle jacks, a hand operated cable winch and chains. Also, tool hire shops may have body jacks available for rent. You'll also need several blocks of wood in 2x4 (50x100mm), 4x4 (100x100mm) and 4x6 (100x150mm) sizes to use for padding and filling gaps when using the jacks.

The main thing to keep in mind when attempting to remedy structural damage, even minimal damage, is that pulling and pushing on car body parts can be very unsafe! If a jack slips or a chain comes off, things can happen very quickly and injury can occur. Always wear eye protection and leather work gloves (to avoid cuts from sharp pieces of metal) and THINK ABOUT WHAT YOU ARE DOING BEFORE APPLYING ANY FORCE WITH A JACK OR WINCH!

If the job you're faced with involves anything but minimal damage or deformation of a structural member, get professional help. Remember, even if you manage to get a section of a monocoque structure back into place, there may still be cracks and other hidden damage that will affect the integrity of the structure and make it unsafe. Body components that can usually be pulled/pushed back into shape by a do-it-yourselfer include inner wing panels and braces and door and window pillars – DO NOT attempt to straighten other monocoque components. Have it done by a professional.

When positioning a jack, make sure it's supported so it won't slip – use wood blocks to protect the metal structure – and work very slowly when applying force. You may have to use a hammer or heat from a torch in conjunction with the jack to get the structural member to move back into place. If

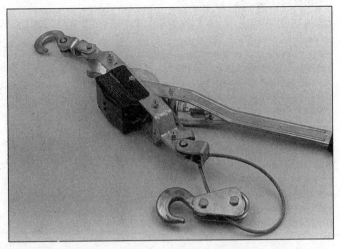

A hand operated winch can be used to pull body parts into position, but make sure the car is securely anchored (don't attach the cable to a building and don't exceed the rated capability of the winch)

Commonly available, inexpensive bottle jacks can be used in conjunction with wood blocks and timbers to push body parts back into place

so, be very careful not to start a fire and don't overheat anything.

When using a hand operated cable winch, make sure the hooks are secured to the car body with a good quality chain or bolts and washers. Don't use slipshod techniques and materials here – your safety will be jeopardised! Also, don't exceed the capabilities of the equipment being used or an accident could occur. If a winch is used, the car body will have to be anchored on two sides – the one being straightened and the opposite one. Don't anchor a winch to a building – try to use a large tree or some other object that will not move when force is applied!

Before doing any actual work, read the **Determining the extent of the damage** and **Repair or replace?** Sections in Chapter 3. Also, read the **Tools and equipment** Section in Chapter 4 and the last Section in this Chapter – **Pulling bent monocoque structures**.

Before plastic body fillers that could take the heat from paint baking ovens were invented, lead was used extensively to fill dents during body repairs. It was also used by the manufacturers to fix imperfections in auto bodies at the factory, particularly at joints between body panels. Although it's no longer used, you may run into it when repairing an older vehicle. If so, the following procedure may prove helpful; even though it's for filling a dent, the lead application techniques also apply to the repair of existing filler. Be aware that lead is much more difficult then plastic to work with and it's also very toxic!

Some specialised materials and tools, as well as a torch, will be required for working with lead. Ads for lead filler materials and tools are generally published in antique and classic car magazines – if you're going to work with the stuff, send for one of the tool kits (which also include very comprehensive instructions)

Body repair using lead filler

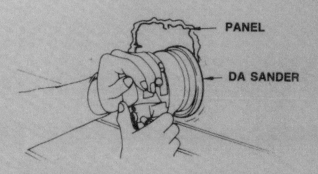

STEP 1 Remove all paint and rust from the dent and the surrounding area (about two inches beyond it) with sandpaper.

STEP 2 Use compressed air to remove all dust, then wipe the repair area with an oil-free cloth.

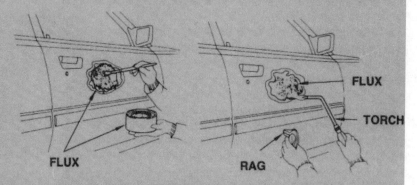

STEP 3 Apply flux to the area to be filled, then heat it and melt a thin layer of the lead over the surface (let the heat from the panel melt the lead, not the torch flame). If the repair area is relatively large, heat small areas at a time and apply the lead until the entire area is covered.

Note: If too much heat is applied, the lead won't adhere properly. Use a rag to wipe off slag that rises to the surface of the lead filler — don't wait until it's cool.

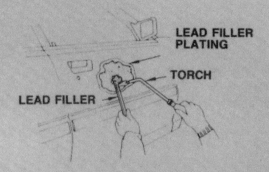

STEP 4 Apply continuous, even heat with the torch to the panel and leaded area and melt more lead into the dent until the level is slightly higher than the surrounding metal.

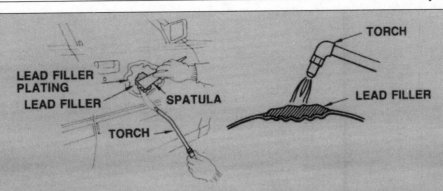

STEP 5 Continue to heat the lead so it flows easily but not so much that it runs off the panel, then press it down and shape it with a spatula (spatulas and a special wax that keeps the lead from sticking to the spatula will be included in any lead filler tool kit).

Note: *The entire repair area must be heated uniformly, but if too much heat is used, the panel will warp. In order to prevent the lead from solidifying, keep the base metal and the lead hot while shaping the filler.*

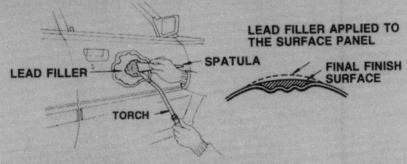

STEP 6 *While still applying heat, use a spatula to smooth out bumps and ridges and to fill low spots. Try to match the contour of the panel at this point.*

Note: *If too much lead is used, the finishing process will take a long time. If too little lead is used, low spots will occur and releading will be required. Build up the repair area until the lead is slightly higher than the body panel itself.*

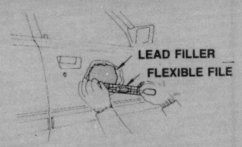

STEP 7 *After the lead is solidified, use a flexible body file to shape it to match the height and surface contour of the panel.*

CORRECT   **INCORRECT**

STEP 8 *Adjust the file so the center is slightly crowned. File in a diagonal pattern to avoid setting up ridges in the lead filler.*

Chapter 6

Body fillers

In Chapter 5 we explained how to repair small dents using plastic body filler. If you're going to get involved in more extensive repairs of major damage, you need to know more about body fillers – the types available, which one(s) to use, how to mix them and how to apply and work them after they're dry.

Plastic body fillers are lightweight, adhere well to the steel used in auto bodies and fill voids very well. However, there are many different types of fillers, specifically designed for use in different situations. They include metal fillers, intermediate fillers, plastic fillers (also called poly putty) and spot fillers (also called stopper and glazing compound). Refer to the accompanying tables for a detailed explanation of the characteristics of each type, their uses and the allowable thicknesses that can be built up.

	Metal filler	Intermediate filler	Fine filler (Poly Putty)		Lacquer putty (Glazing compound – Stopper)
Film thickness for one application	10 mm	10 mm	Spatula application: 3.0 mm	Spray application: 2.0 mm	1.0 mm

Plastic body filler – general allowable 1-layer thickness

	TYPE	MAIN USE	CHARACTERISTICS
METAL FILLER	Waxy surface type	Repair of large dents or scratches	• Wax works up to the surface of the filler as it dries, making it necessary to shape the surface with a surform tool (if sandpaper is used directly on the waxy surface it will gum up quickly) • Thickness building characteristics are extremely good • After drying, compared to other fillers, it's harder and its sanding characteristics are inferior
	Light type		• It contains hollow beads, making it crunch when applied with a spatula • Thickness building characteristics are extremely good • Extremely good sanding characteristics • Very porous
	Fiberglass or Aluminum type		• Thickness building characteristics are extremely good • Superior anti-rust and durability characteristics • Can be used to repair small holes in panels
INTERMEDIATE FILLER			• Good sanding characteristics • It's difficult for fine grain pores to form in it so poly putty can be eliminated and lacquer putty can be applied directly over intermediate filler
FINE FILLER	Spatula type	Fills the pores and sand scratches in metal putty; fills flaws up to 0.080-inch deep in panels	• Not very much thickness can be built up • It has fine grain and good flexibility • Since no volatile content remains, there is no depletion after baking • Sanding characteristics are good
	Spray type		• Not very much thickness can be built up • Since a spray gun is used, it can be applied easily to any location • Drying time is about twice as long as putty applied with a spatula
LACQUER PUTTY (GLAZING COMPOUND)		Fills pores in poly putty, small flaws remaining in primer surfacer and small flaws in old paint	• It's soft and flexibility is good • It cannot be used to build up low areas • Standing characteristics are extremely good • The thicker the build-up, the longer the drying time
		Typical plastic body filler types, uses and characteristics	

Plastic body fillers come in several different types and must be used with a special hardener – be sure to purchase the right type for the particular repair you're doing

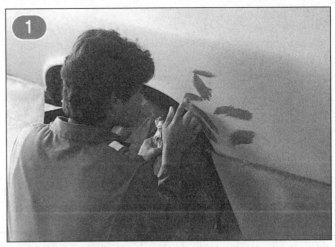

Note: *The following photos are keyed to the step by step procedure with a number in the upper left corner of each illustration. The number corresponds to the step number of the procedure.*

A typical repair procedure that requires the extensive use of body filler should be approached as follows ...

1 Select the type of filler to use. You have to know when and where to use the different types of fillers if you want the best possible results when doing body repairs. Dents that are deeper than 3.0 mm (or if more than 3.0 mm of filler must be used) after the metal has been worked with a puller and hammer should be filled with metal or intermediate type filler first, then topped off with finer filler. Once the finer filler has been sanded, minor imperfections can be filled with stopper or a coat of filler/primer.

If metal filler, intermediate filler or plastic filler is used on top of lacquer, acrylic lacquer, acrylic urethane, acrylic urethane lacquer or baked on paint (most new cars have baked on paint), problems will result (the paint layers may start to separate), so don't use them on top of these types of paints. In these cases, the old paint must be removed before applying body filler to the repair area.

2 Grind or sand off the paint and 'feather edge' the area where body filler will be applied. Use 60 grit sandpaper, except when sanding acrylic lacquer – use 24 grit on acrylic lacquer and follow up with 60 grit to remove the sanding marks left by the 24 grit paper. Remove the paint from an area about 75 mm beyond the edge of the dent, all the way around.

Note: *If large areas are involved, it may be a good idea to sand blast the paint rather than trying to grind it all off (sand blasting equipment for use by do-it- yourselfers is available). If sand blasting is done, wear eye protection and be sure to clean the metal thoroughly when the job is complete. Another alternative is a chemical paint stripper – just be sure to follow the directions on the container carefully and clean the bare metal thoroughly before proceeding with the application of filler material.*

3 Use compressed air to remove all dust from the repair area, then clean it with a wax/silicone remover. If it's raining or extremely humid, the panel should be warmed with a heater (make sure it's safe for use around a car body that's being repaired) after cleaning to avoid problems with body filler adhesion and drying.

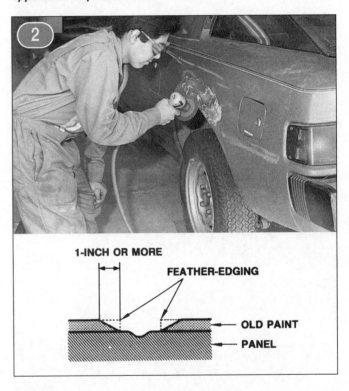

Stopper (also called glazing compound) is used to fill minor scratches and other imperfections noticed after the application of primer

1-INCH OR MORE

FEATHER-EDGING

OLD PAINT

PANEL

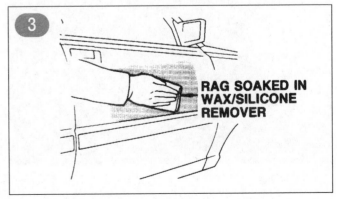

RAG SOAKED IN WAX/SILICONE REMOVER

4 Mix the filler material and the hardener. Be sure to follow the instructions on the container. Use a spatula type applicator to do the mixing and try not to create air bubbles in the material – it will begin to harden as soon as the hardener is mixed in, so work quickly. Note: If large amounts of filler are needed, mix it in small batches that can be applied before it begins to harden too much.

5 **General filler application** – Move the applicator in long strokes and press lightly to ensure good adhesion. It's much better to build up the filler in several layers rather than applying one thick layer – this will help reduce the formation of bubbles and voids. To reduce ridges formed by the applicator, start at the centre of the repair area and gradually widen the contact with the filler material as you sweep the applicator out toward the edge. Fill dents and lower high spots in the filler by tilting the applicator. Apply additional layers of filler before the previous one is completely dry.

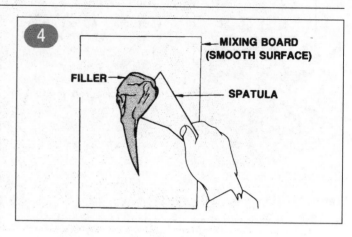

MIXING BOARD (SMOOTH SURFACE)

FILLER

SPATULA

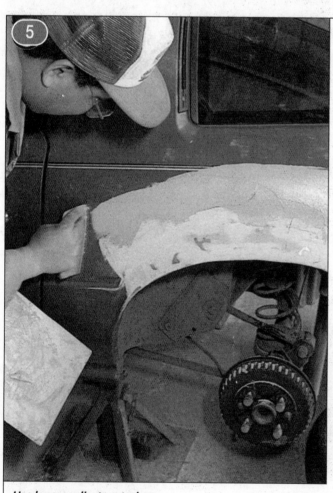

Use long applicator strokes . . .

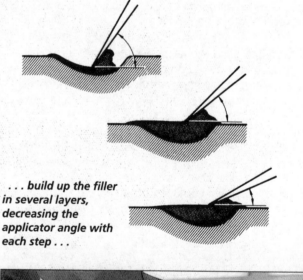

. . . build up the filler in several layers, decreasing the applicator angle with each step . . .

. . . and work from the centre out toward the edge of the dent

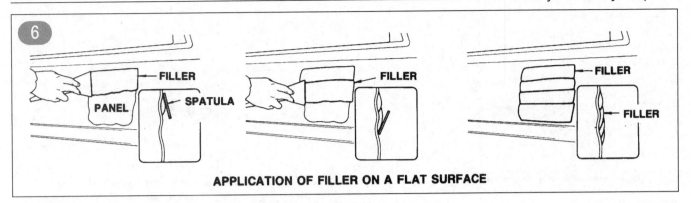

APPLICATION OF FILLER ON A FLAT SURFACE

6 **Applying filler to flat surfaces** – The layer of filler should be thin next to the edge(s) of the repair area. Overlap the first strip of filler 1/3 to 2/3 of its width with the second strip and continue applying applicator width strips until the entire area is covered. The thickness of the filler should be greatest near the centre of the repair and taper out to the edges so there's very little difference between the filler height and the surrounding panel.

7 **Applying filler to curved surfaces** – Use a soft applicator (plastic or rubber) so the filler can be shaped to conform to the surface as it's applied. When applying it to areas that include body lines (slight creases formed intentionally in the sheet metal), apply a couple layers of masking tape to one edge of the body line and apply the filler up to the tape. Let the filler dry for several minutes, then remove the tape and stick new tape to the edge of the new filler (don't press too hard). Apply filler to the remaining side, up to the filler covered with tape.

8 Applying filler to an area that has a combination of flat and curved surfaces is difficult. If the contour of the panel isn't followed, lots of filing and sanding will be required. To get close to the original panel shape, refer to the accompanying sequence of illustrations . . .

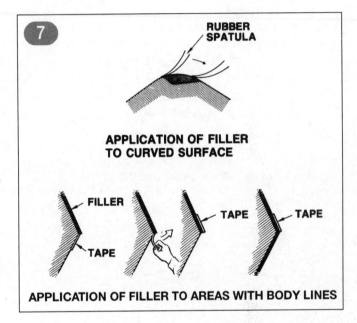

APPLICATION OF FILLER TO CURVED SURFACE

APPLICATION OF FILLER TO AREAS WITH BODY LINES

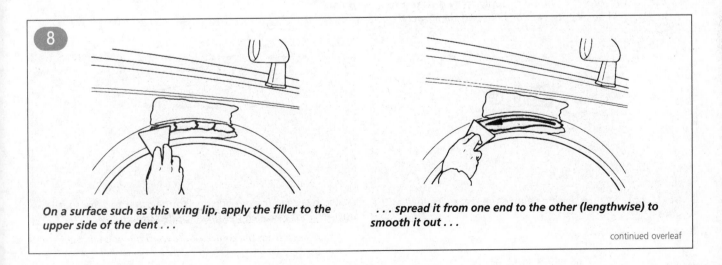

On a surface such as this wing lip, apply the filler to the upper side of the dent . . .

. . . spread it from one end to the other (lengthwise) to smooth it out . . .

continued overleaf

8 continued

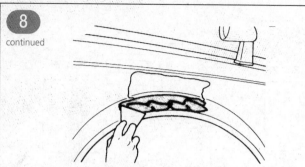

. . . then apply more filler to the lower edge of the dent . . .

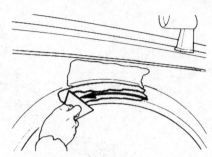

. . . and spread it lengthwise so there's very little height difference between the previously applied filler and the surface is smooth

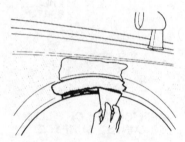

Apply filler to the edge in several small dabs . . .

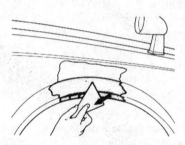

. . . then rub the applicator along it from one end toward the middle . . .

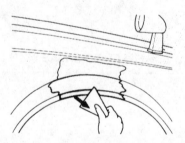

. . . followed by the other end toward the middle to smooth it out – don't be afraid to apply some pressure to ensure a good bond between the filler and sheet metal

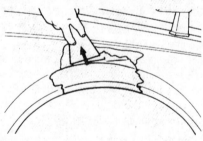

Sweep the applicator up away from the crease at several points

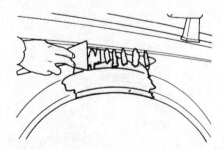

Next, apply filler to the area above the crease in small dabs . . .

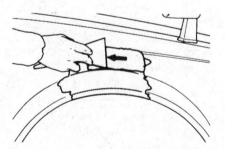

. . . and spread it from one end to the other to smooth it out – try not to touch the filler applied previously

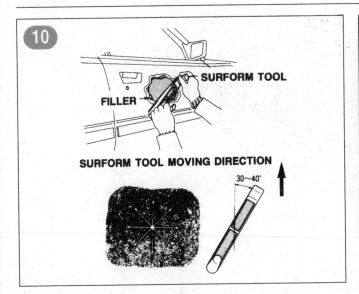

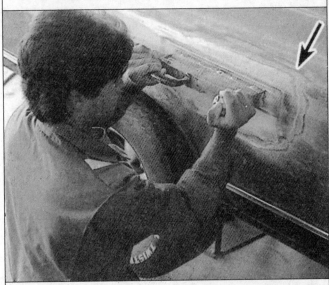

Depending on the size and shape of the repair area, use a DA, an orbital sander (shown here) . . .

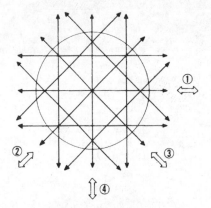

. . . or a straight line sander to shape the filler and feather edge the paint (arrowed)

9 Allow the filler to dry before sanding or shaping it. Normally, 20 to 30 minutes of drying time is sufficient, although low temperatures or high humidity mean more time will be needed.

10 If a wax surface type metal filler was used, it can be rough shaped with a surform file when it's about half dry and still pliable. You have to leave enough material to ensure that the finished surface, after sanding, won't have file marks in it, so don't try to do finish work with the surform file. If the filler gets too hard, the surform tool won't cut it very well. Hold the file at about a 30- to 40-degree angle away from the direction of movement and work from the centre of the repair area out in several directions. Try to match the shape of the panel as the material is worked.

11 To effectively sand the filled area, use a double action (DA), straight line or orbital sander (depending on the shape and contour of the panel area and other factors, one type of sander will be better than the other). The DA sander cuts fast and facilitates feather edging the repair area, but the pad is small and will make the surface wavy if you aren't careful. The straight line sander will ensure a flat repair surface, but they're heavy and vibrate a lot. The orbital action sander is smaller and lighter than the straight line sander and is normally the best choice for simple flat surfaces. Move the sander up and down, diagonally and back and forth across the repaired area until the surface is smooth and flat.

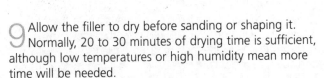

SANDING PATTERN

Move the sander back and forth (1), diagonally (2 and 3) and up and down (4) over the entire repair area and into the surrounding paint

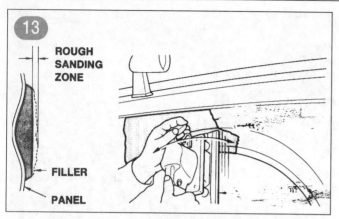

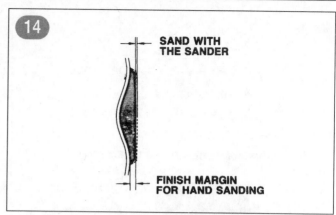

If you're careful, a power sander can be used on surfaces other than flat ones

12 Begin by putting on an approved dust filtering mask – DO NOT sand filler materials without one! If possible, use a dust collection attachment on the sander.

13 Rough sand the entire filled area with a sander and 80 grit sandpaper until the surface is smooth and matches the panel contour – leave enough material to allow for finish sanding. If the surface isn't flat, the sander can still be used to shape it if you're careful.

14 Finish sand the entire surface with 180 grit sandpaper until the filler material is ever so slightly higher than the surrounding body panel. Leave enough material to allow for hand sanding the deep scratches in the filler.

15 Put away the sander and finish by hand. Use 180 grit sandpaper on a sanding block (preferably one made of wood) and feather edge the repair area (taper the filler material into the surrounding panel). For rounded, dished and creased areas, special sanding blocks can be made to follow the contour of the panel.

16 After the edges have been feathered, go over the entire area and sand off a VERY THIN layer to remove any scratches left by the sander and match the filled surface with the body panel. Follow the same pattern that you used with the sander (Step 11). Use the palm of your hand and your fingertips to feel for a step where the filler blends into the panel and for high and low spots. If too much filler is removed, more will have to be applied and the sanding process will have to be repeated.

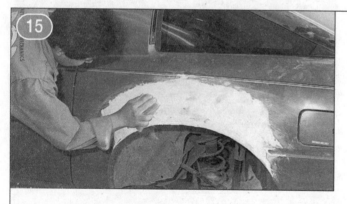

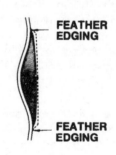

Concentrate your efforts near the edge of the filled area to taper or 'feather edge' the filler into the surrounding panel

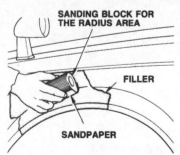

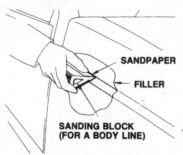

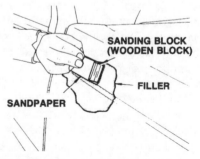

Use a sanding block that's shaped like the part being sanded so the surface will be uniform

Sanding blocks with sharp edges will help keep body lines sharp and straight

A small wood sanding block is very effective for sanding the edge of a narrow line

Major rust repair

Minor rust repair (of holes 50 mm in diameter or less) was covered in detail in Chapter 5. For rusted out areas that are larger, two approaches to repair are possible. If the rust damage is extreme or widespread, it probably would be best to replace the entire panel or, in the case of doors, front wings, the bonnet and boot lid, the body component (see Chapter 7). If the rusted out area is relatively large, but generally confined to that area alone, it can be cut out and a sheet metal patch can be welded or riveted into place or attached with screws. Proceed as follows . . .

Note: *The following photos are keyed to the step by step procedure with a number in the upper left corner of each illustration. The number corresponds to the step number of the procedure.*

1 Remove the paint from a 25 to 50 mm wide area surrounding the rust damage. Use a sander and coarse grit sanding disc.

2 Cut out the rusted metal with snips, an air chisel or a hacksaw.

3 Apply a rust arresting chemical to the surrounding metal, particularly on the inside of the panel. **Note:** *Rust arresting chemicals are made by several manufacturers. They react with rust and transform it into a substance called 'black rust', which is chemically stable and won't continue to eat away at the metal.*

4 Use a body hammer to tap around the edge of the opening – the opening itself and the surrounding good metal must form a depression extending about 25 mm beyond the hole.

5 Use compressed air to get rid of all dust and dirt, then clean the area with a wax/silicone remover.

6 Cut a sheet metal patch that will just fit into the depression and rest on the good metal – it should overlap about 20 mm. The upper surface of the patch should be slightly lower than the surrounding panel. **Note:** *Special pre-formed metal patches, that match certain body contours, are available for some vehicles – check with a car accessory shop or motor factor.*

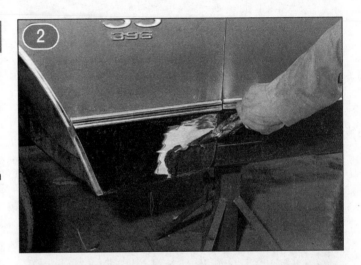

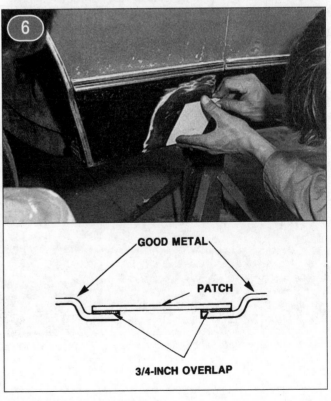

GOOD METAL

PATCH

3/4-INCH OVERLAP

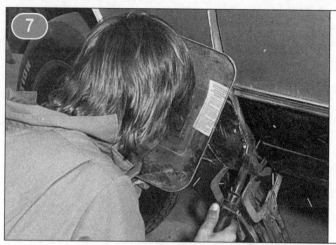

7 The patch can be plug welded, bead welded, riveted in place or attached with screws. If sheet metal screws are used, try to find ones made of stainless steel and be sure to grind down the heads after the patch is secured in place so the filler will cover them adequately. If a welder is used, grind down the bead – the joint between the patch and the panel should be as smooth as possible.

8 Refer to the Plastic fillers Section in this Chapter and use a fibreglass or aluminum type metal body filler to complete the repair.

9 After the body filler has been finish sanded, apply primer and paint as described in Chapters 8 and 9.

10 It's very important to prevent water from reaching the back side of the repair area or rust will soon reappear. Apply rust proofing compound to the back side of the panel and make sure all drain holes are open (if applicable). Also, seal off any openings that could allow water in. If the rear of the repair is accessible, apply a bead of body sealer to the seam between the patch and the original panel.

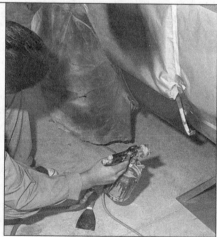

After the filler material has been finish sanded, . . .

. . . mask off the surrounding body panels . . .

. . . and apply primer and paint (aerosol touch up paint can be used, although spray gun applicator is preferred)

Fibreglass body repair techniques

Repairing a fibreglass body or panel is really no more difficult than working on sheet metal – it's just that different techniques and materials are required. And, just as with sheet metal, you have to learn to use the materials correctly if the repair is going to be effective.

Working with fibreglass and fibreglass repair materials can cause some problems, especially skin irritation caused by resins or finely ground fibreglass particles. Because of this, certain precautions must be taken when working with fibreglass . . .

1 Use a protective cream on your hands, wrists and forearms. Apply the cream evenly, work it into the skin, apply a second coat, then hold your hands and arms under cold water for a minute to set the cream.

2 Remove resin mixtures from your skin as quickly as possible – definitely before it begins to set. Lacquer thinner or soap and water can be used to remove the resin.

3 Whenever you're grinding or sanding fibreglass, wear a respirator to keep the fibreglass particles out of your lungs.

4 If skin irritation from fibreglass dust begins to appear, wash the affected area with soap and cold water.

5 Some resin mixtures produce toxic fumes and should be used only in a well ventilated area or outdoors.

6 Vacuum up sanding and grinding residue immediately after finishing the job.

Fibreglass repairs generally fall into one of four categories:
- *Minor cosmetic repair (scratches, etc.)*
- *Build up cosmetic repair*
- *External patch repair*
- *Internal patch repair*

The first two, minor cosmetic repair and build up cosmetic repair, are much like the repair of minor scratches and dents in sheet metal, although some special techniques are required. The final two repair procedures, external and internal patch repairs, are for major damage where there's actually a hole or crack all the way through the fibreglass.

Minor cosmetic repair

1 Where the paint has been scratched down to the fibreglass surface, but the fibreglass itself hasn't been penetrated, the repair is essentially just to the paint. Start by using lacquer thinner to thoroughly clean the area of the scratch.

2 Feather edge the paint in the area of the scratch with 220 grit wet or dry sandpaper, working out approximately 50 mm around the scratch. Don't sand deeply into the fibreglass itself. Finish by wet sanding with 400 grit sandpaper until you have a smooth, completely feather edged surface. Use a wax/silicone remover to thoroughly clean the area, then finish by going over the surface with a tack cloth.

3 Spray on a light coat of primer, let it dry thoroughly, then spray on another coat. Three or four coats should be sprayed on, letting each coat dry completely before applying the next one. Then the primer should be allowed to dry for at least an hour.

4 Once the primer is completely dry, it should be lightly wet sanded with 1000 grit sandpaper. The idea is to get the surface very smooth, but not to sand through the primer. If you do sand through the primer, dry the area thoroughly, apply more primer, let it dry, then start sanding again.

5 Let the sanded area dry completely, wipe it down with a tack cloth to make sure there's no sanded primer residue left, then fog on a coat of paint from an aerosol 'touch up' can (available from most dealers and car accessory shops). Let the fog coat dry for ten minutes or so, then spray on a series of thin finish coats, letting each coat dry before applying the next one.

6 Let the paint dry for at least a week, then use a very fine rubbing compound to blend the new paint into the surrounding finish.

Build-up cosmetic repair

Build up cosmetic repair refers to fixing a damaged area where the damage is deep enough to require the use of a filler, but the fibreglass has not been penetrated completely. Usually this type of damage is in the form of a deep gouge through the paint and into the fibreglass.

The key to repairing this kind of damage is getting a clean surface for the filler . . .

1 To start with, the area should be thoroughly washed down with wax/silicone remover, then a hand grinder should be used to take the top layer off the fibreglass in the repair area. The ideal surface preparation would have the fibreglass cut down in a shallow 'V', starting from the undamaged surface and angling down to the deepest part of the damaged area, like an enlarged version of feather edged paint. Be sure to wear a face mask or respirator when grinding the fibreglass.

2 Clean the repair area with a wax/silicone remover, then wipe it with a tack cloth to remove any sanding residue.

3 For the filler material you'll need to purchase an epoxy adhesive resin specially made for fibreglass body repair. Generally the epoxy is mixed with hardener in a one to one ratio (rather than the fifty to one ratio common with plastic body fillers), but be sure to check the instructions with the product you bought for the exact mixture ratio.

4 Spread the filler material over the damaged area with a putty knife or body filler applicator, using enough material to produce a new surface higher than the original surface. Be sure to use the putty knife or applicator to work all the bubbles out of the filler.

Note: *Epoxy filler takes considerably longer than plastic filler to cure. Use heat lamps, placed 30 to 45 cm away from the repair area, to speed it up. With heat lamps the filler will usually cure in approximately one hour. If heat lamps aren't*

Chapter 6

Special epoxy solder/adhesive, applied with a putty knife or a plastic squeegee, is used for repairs to the fibreglass body

available, the filler can be cured at room temperature, but the curing time will be approximately twelve hours.

5 Once the filler has cured, you'll need a grinder and body file to work the contour down to approximate the panel being repaired. Work carefully so you don't take off too much material. When you have it down to near the original panel, finish the contouring with 320 grit sandpaper and a sanding block, smoothing the filler and blending it into the original fibreglass surface. Switch to 400 grit paper and featheredge the paint down to the fibreglass.

6 Spray on several coats of primer, letting each coat dry before applying the next, then wet sand the primer with 1000 grit wet or dry sandpaper to get a glass smooth surface. When you've finished sanding, let the area dry completely, wipe it down with a tack cloth, then fog on a coat of paint from an aerosol 'touch up' can (available from most dealers and automotive parts stores). Let the fog coat dry for ten minutes or so, then spray on a series of thin finish coats, letting each coat dry before applying the next one.

7 Let the paint dry for at least a week, then use a very fine rubbing compound to blend the new paint into the surrounding finish.

External patch repair

External patch repair is most often used on cracked areas, such as around the wheel arches of fibreglass bodied vehicles, or on fibreglass front spoilers. Cracks generally develop in high vibration areas – it's important that the repair cover the entire crack or the damage could recur.

1 The first step in external patch repair is to grind all the paint off the fibreglass for 50 – 75 mm around the area to be repaired. In the area of the crack itself you should grind down into the fibreglass (without grinding all the way through it), until a shallow 'V' is formed.

2 Cut a small strip of fibreglass cloth, slightly longer than the crack and approximately 20 mm wide. If the crack isn't straight, cut the cloth to match the curvature of the crack.

3 Cut a second piece of fibreglass cloth which will extend for approximately 50 mm on each side of the crack. This cloth should not extend beyond the area that's been sanded down to bare fibreglass. If you can't fit a piece of cloth this size into the sanded area, sand more paint off down to the fibreglass. Don't reduce the size of the patch.

4 Following the directions on the can, mix a small amount of resin and hardener together, then use a brush to apply the resin to the entire sanded area of the panel to be repaired, especially down inside the crack.

5 Before the resin cures, lay the small piece of fibreglass in the crack and coat it liberally with resin. Lay the second (larger) piece of fibreglass cloth over the area and saturate it thoroughly with resin, especially right at the edges.

6 Let the fibreglass cure completely, then use a mechanical sander (not a body grinder) to sand the repaired area down until it roughly matches the original panel contour. Switch to 280 grit sandpaper and a sanding block and smooth the surface some more. Don't worry about sanding down too far, or the appearance of small bubbles in the fibreglass, since you'll be putting a layer of epoxy filler on over the repair.

7 Clean the repair with a wax/silicone remover, then wipe it with a tack cloth to remove any sanding residue.

8 Purchase a can of epoxy filler made for fibreglass body repair and mix it with the hardener in the ratio specified in the instructions. This will usually be one to one.

9 Spread the epoxy filler over the damaged area with a body filler applicator, applying enough material to produce a new surface just slightly higher than the original surface. You'll want to apply only a very thin film of the filler – just enough for sanding. Be sure to work all the bubbles out of the filler.

10 Set up heat lamps 30 to 45 cm from the repair area and allow the epoxy to cure for at least one hour. If heat lamps aren't available, allow the epoxy to cure overnight (at least twelve hours) at room temperature.

11 Once the filler has cured, contour it with 320 grit sandpaper and a sanding block, smoothing the filler and blending it into the original fibreglass surface. Switch to 400 grit sandpaper and feather edge the paint down to the fibreglass.

12 Spray on several coats of primer, letting each coat dry before applying the next, then wet sand the primer with 1000 grit wet or dry sandpaper.

13 When you've finished sanding, let the area dry completely, wipe it down with a tack cloth, then fog on a coat of paint from an aerosol 'touch up' can (available from most dealers and car accessory shops).

14 Let the fog coat dry for ten minutes or so, then spray on a series of thin finish coats, letting each coat dry before applying the next.

15 Let the paint dry for at least a week, then use a very fine rubbing compound to blend the new paint into the surrounding finish.

Internal patch repair

An internal patch repair is used when you have a hole or crack completely through a fibreglass panel.

1 As with other types of fibreglass repairs, the first thing that must be done is to thoroughly clean the area to be repaired. In this case, that means not only removing all the paint and sanding the fibreglass surface, but also sanding the inside of the panel to be repaired and cutting away all loose or shredded fibreglass from the damaged area.

2 Grind the fibreglass down at a shallow angle extending at least 25 to 40 mm out from the break, so the fibreglass at the break area itself is paper thin.

3 Sand the paint back at least 50 mm on all sides around the area to be repaired, then clean the repair area with a wax/silicone remover.

4 Cut a piece of release film large enough to overlap the entire sanded area and extend onto the painted surface. If release film isn't available, the polyethylene film used for wrapping food can be used. Use masking tape to attach the film to the body panel, stretching it tight so it roughly conforms to the original shape of the panel.

5 Cut four or five pieces of fibreglass cloth, each approximately 50 mm larger in all directions than the area to be repaired.

6 Mix the liquid resin and hardener in the proportions specified on the can, then soak the first piece of fibreglass cloth in the resin and lay it over the sheet of release film, smoothing out all the wrinkles and bubbles with a paint brush. Repeat the process with the other sheets of fibreglass, then use heat lamps placed 30 to 45 cm away to speed the curing of the resin. With heat lamps the resin should cure for at least one hour. If heat lamps aren't available, allow the resin to cure overnight (at least twelve hours).

7 When the resin has cured, remove the tape and the release film will allow the fibreglass patch to be separated from the panel.

8 Peel the sheet of release film off the back of the patch, then sand the outside surface with rough (80 grit) sandpaper to provide a good bonding surface.

9 Drill two 3 mm holes through the centre of the patch, in an area that will be exposed through the damaged area.

10 Mix a quantity of epoxy filler adhesive with hardener and apply it liberally to the outside 50 mm of the entire edge of the patch.

11 Thread a piece of wire or strong string through the two holes with the ends protruding through the upper surface of the patch, put the patch in place on the inner surface of the damaged area and use the string or wire to pull it up tight.

12 Twist the wire or string around pieces of wood to hold the patch tightly against the inside of the panel until the epoxy adhesive cures. Heat lamps, placed 30 to 45 cm from the repair area, will speed the curing process. Since the epoxy is concealed between two layers of fibreglass, it

should be allowed to cure for at least four hours even with the heat lamps, and twelve hours if heat lamps aren't available.

13 After the epoxy holding the patch has completely cured, remove the wire or string.

14 Mix a quantity of epoxy filler and spread it over the damaged area with a putty knife or body filler applicator. Apply enough material to produce a new surface higher than the original surface. Be sure to use the putty knife or applicator to work all the bubbles out of the filler.

15 Use heat lamps to cure the epoxy solder for approximately one hour or let it cure overnight if heat lamps aren't available.

16 Use a grinder and body file to work the contour down to approximate the panel being repaired. Work carefully so you don't take off too much material. When you have it down to near the original panel, finish the contouring with 320 grit sandpaper and a sanding block, smoothing the filler and blending it into the original fibreglass surface.

17 Switch to 400 grit sandpaper and feather edge the paint down to the fibreglass.

18 Spray on several coats of primer, letting each coat dry before applying the next one, then wet sand the primer with 1000 grit wet or dry sandpaper.

19 When you've finished sanding, let the area dry completely, wipe it down with a tack cloth, then fog on a coat of paint from an aerosol 'touch up' can (available from most dealers and automotive parts stores).

20 Let the fog coat dry for ten minutes or so, then spray on a series of thin finish coats, letting each coat dry before applying the next one.

21 Let the paint dry for at least a week, then use a very fine rubbing compound to blend the new paint into the surrounding finish.

Pulling bent monocoque structures

When the word alignment comes up in conversation, at least where car people are concerned, everyone immediately thinks about getting the front wheels pointed, slanted and inclined the right amount. Which is fine, unless you happen to be working on a body, in which case you're going to be much more interested in how the doors hang than how the wheels track.

You can spend hour after hour pounding out a dent, filling, sanding, priming and painting – and the whole thing will be a waste of time if the door won't close or the bonnet sticks up 25 mm over the wing on one side. The panels not only have to have the right contour, but they have to fit as intended and match the other panels around them.

There are two kinds of alignment we'll be dealing with: Alignment of the basic structure – the monocoque or the chassis – and alignment of the various panels which are bolted or welded to the basic structure, such as the wings, doors and bonnet.

Getting the basic structure, the chassis everything else bolts or welds to, straight is an absolute necessity. If the substructure isn't straight, nothing else is going to fit. And that means taking the time to accurately measure and adjust the basic structure before making any attempt to align outer panels.

Whether you're dealing with a monocoque vehicle (most common these days) or a chassis and bolt on substructure, or even a hybrid where you have a monocoque centre section with bolted or welded on front and rear subframes (stubs), it's possible for the whole thing to be so completely out of alignment that nothing will fit right, and still look perfectly straight to the naked eye. The only way to find out if the structure is right is with a measuring tape.

Again, it doesn't matter if you're dealing with monocoque construction or a separate body and chassis, the secret is in picking 'benchmark' measuring spots and making comparisons from side to side. The factory body manuals often give the standard measurement for the distance from point A to point B, but they aren't really necessary to tell you if the structure is out of alignment. What is necessary are comparison figures, taken from opposite spots on the vehicle.

Any vehicle you're liable to be dealing with is basically symmetrical. That is, the left and right sides are mirror images of each other. The distance from the left rear of the bonnet to the right front of the bonnet is the same as the distance from the right rear to the left front (assuming the bonnet is straight). The distance from the top of the windscreen pillar to the lower rear edge of the door on the right side should be the same as on the left side. The distance from the right lower corner of the windscreen to the point where the radiator support bracket bolts to the left front wing should be the same as the distance from the left lower corner of the windscreen to the right side of the radiator support bracket. Taking the measurements and comparing them from side to side is called X checking, and it's the only certain way to determine if the basic structure is straight before you start bolting or welding outer panels into place. The most common areas to measure are:

- *The lower edge of the windscreen to the front edge of the chassis or monocoque of each side.*
- *The upper spring, shock absorber or strut mounting point to a spot on the opposite side of the scuttle.*
- *The top of the windscreen pillar on one side of the radiator support attaching point on the opposite side.*
- *The lower control arm balljoint on one side to the front of the chassis or monocoque on the opposite side.*
- *The top of the windscreen post to the bottom rear edge of the door.*
- *The lower door hinge to the top of the rear pillar.*
- *The front of the front door to the rear of the rear door.*
- *The top of the windscreen pillar on one side to the base of the rear pillar on the opposite side.*

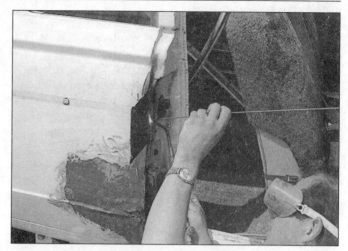

The damage to this door pillar was minimal, but it prevented the door from closing properly – to repair it, a plate was welded to the pillar, . . .

. . . the puller apparatus was attached to the plate . . .

- *The boot lid (or tailgate) hinge mounting point on one side to the centre of the boot lid (or tailgate) lock mechanism.*
- *The outer end of the rear axle (usually from one of the wheel mounting studs) to the end of the chassis or monocoque structure on the opposite side.*

Obviously, X-checks can be made in a variety of places. The more checks you make, the less chance there is of finding out after you've started replacing outer panels that the substructure is bent somewhere.

Keep in mind that the majority of measurements you make might show the structure to be perfectly straight – but all it takes is one area to be off for body panels to hang crooked. If a car is hit, let's say, in the right front wing, it's entirely possible that the right front windscreen post is pushed back out of alignment. The roof on that side will probably be too high, the door post will be too far back, the windscreen and bonnet won't fit and the door won't close. And the distortion of the lower part of the windscreen post might only be 6 mm or so – easily overlooked by the naked eye.

Generally the most structural damage to a car will be done in either a roll-over accident or a side (T-bone) collision. In a roll-over accident, it's typical for the structure, including the windscreen and rear top pillars and even the door pillars, to be pushed away from the direction of the roll-over. If the top alone is pushed out of shape, it can usually be straightened by the jacks inside the vehicle. However, if there's general collapse of the structure, it's often more effective to simply locate a new top in a breaker's yard, cut off the old top and graft the new one into place.

Where structural damage has extended down into the door pillars, or, in the case of a side collision, where major structural damage has been done, the extent of the damage must be carefully evaluated before starting work on the vehicle (see **Determining the extent of the damage** in Chapter 3 for more information). Bent door pillars can usually be pulled straight on a body alignment machine or pushed out with hydraulic jacks. In the case of monocoque vehicles, bent floor structures can generally be pulled out if the damage isn't too severe or, as an option, an undamaged section can be cut from another car and welded into the damaged vehicle. However, major structural damage to either a monocoque floor pan or a separate chassis structure should be evaluated in light of the financial advisability of even attempting to repair the vehicle. Often the cost, both in time and money, of the straightening procedures where this sort of damage has been done is more than the actual value of the vehicle.

. . . and the pillar was carefully and deliberately pulled back into alignment

The door alignment was carefully checked each step of the way to make sure the pillar wasn't moved too far

Notes

Body component replacement

7

Introduction

Bolt on components

Welded panels

Bonded panels

Body component alignment

Introduction

The amount of damage involved, and the time it'll take to fix it, is the most important factor to consider when deciding whether to replace a component, a panel or a section of a panel, or to try to straighten it. Also to be taken into consideration is the amount of time you're willing to invest in a repair job. A professional body repairer must count his/her time as money, and balance the cost in time to repair a panel against the cost of a replacement panel or component. The do-it-yourselfer may not consider the time element as important as a professional body repairer does, and can afford to spend more hours repairing or straightening a panel than a professional. And, at the same time, remember that a replacement panel or an entirely new component will almost always come out looking better than

a repaired panel, no matter how carefully the repair job is done.

Practically every body part on a car is available in replacement form from the manufacturer, from aftermarket suppliers or from car breakers. Even the substructures are often available, especially from car breakers, although they're usually repaired rather than replaced. Replacement is generally confined to sheet metal parts such as the top, quarter panels and sill panels and components like the wings, doors (covered separately in Chapter 10), bonnet and boot lid or tailgate. **Note:** *Take some time to read through the Introduction to replaceable panels Section in Chapter 1 and the first two Sections in Chapter 3 for additional information.*

Chapter 7

Bolt on components

Bonnet

The bonnet is normally bolted to hinges at each rear corner, although some vehicles have the hinges at the front. If the same bonnet is going to be reinstalled, be sure to paint or scribe around the bolt heads and around the edges of the hinge plates. This will ensure that the bonnet can be repositioned in the same location, minimising adjustments.

Also, before loosening the hinge bolts, place an old blanket or a large piece of cardboard between the rear edge of the bonnet and the scuttle panel to prevent damage if the bonnet swings to the rear during removal.

With a couple of assistants helping to hold the bonnet, remove the bolts and lift it away from the vehicle.

During installation, place the bonnet in position and move the hinges and bolts to their original locations, using the marks you made as a guide. Refer to the **Body component alignment** Section in this Chapter for the bonnet adjustment procedure.

Boot lid

Removal, installation and adjustment of the boot lid are essentially the same as the procedures for the bonnet. Note, however, that many boot designs have the hinges inside support members, with only the bolts accessible. In those cases, remove the bolts and slide the boot lid away from the hinges.

Boot lids usually have an adjustable opening feature which causes the lid to pop open on its own when the lock or latch is released. The design of this mechanism varies from manufacturer to manufacturer, but usually involves torsion bars positioned between the hinges in some fashion. The ends of the bars fit into holes of some kind, usually allowing for tension adjustment by moving the bar end to a different

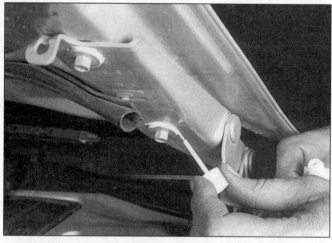

Mark the hinge-to-bonnet bolt washer positions before removing them so they can be reinstalled in the same place to preserve bonnet alignment

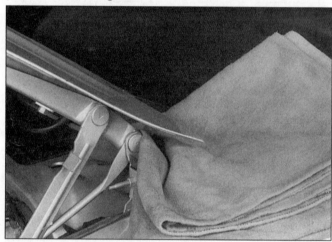

Protect the windscreen and surrounding scuttle area from damage with rags or cardboard in case the bonnet slides back during removal

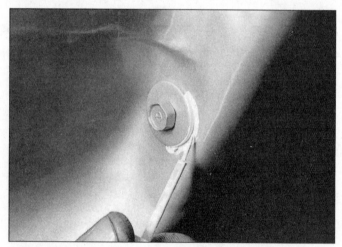

Before removing or adjusting the boot lid, paint or scribe around the bolt head washers to indicate the original positions and the extent of movement during adjustments

hole. Note that some designs incorporate much more tension than others, which can lead to a potential safety hazard during adjustment. Consult a repair manual for specific information concerning your model vehicle.

Hatch

The rear hatch or tailgate can be removed and adjusted following the bonnet information above. For access to the hinges, you may have to remove interior moulding pieces and/or peel back the headlining. Do this carefully to avoid tearing the material slightly – refer to the appropriate Haynes Service and Repair Manual. Like the bonnet, the rear hatch or tailgate is quite heavy and awkward to handle, so have at least one assistant available to help during removal and installation.

Front wings

These components are relatively easy to replace, since they normally are bolted to the monocoque structure along the top edge, rear edge, front end and both ends of the wheel opening arch. Be sure to disconnect all wires leading to lights mounted in the wing or remove the light assemblies before unbolting anything. Apply masking tape to the front edge of the door adjacent to the wing – this will prevent damage to the paint on the door as the wing is detached. The inner wheelarch liner or splash shield must be removed first (plastic fasteners are often used, so plan on buying new ones for installation of the shield). Prop the bonnet open so it doesn't close unexpectedly.

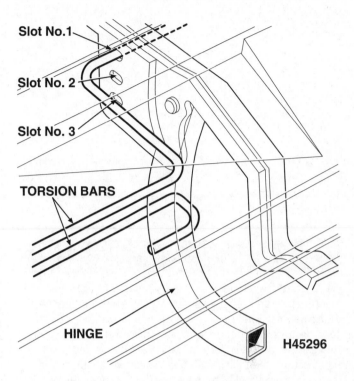

Typical boot lid torsion bar mounting details

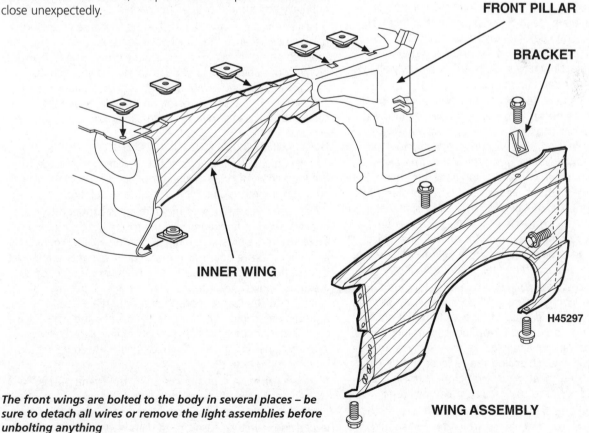

The front wings are bolted to the body in several places – be sure to detach all wires or remove the light assemblies before unbolting anything

Welded panels

While there are differences from manufacturer to manufacturer in how the various outer panels are attached to the substructure, generally large panels, which would be easily distorted by heat, are spot welded to the substructure. An example of this is the top, which is spot welded to the substructure, then filled with body solder, or arc brazed in place. Smaller panels, and panels with structure stiffening bends, curves or styling creases, are not so easily distorted by heat. They are often welded to the substructure, with the weld circling the entire panel.

If the damage to the vehicle is such that either part of a panel or a complete panel must be replaced, the first task, which should be done before the damaged panel is removed, is to make sure the area surrounding the panel, and the supporting structure underneath, is properly aligned (see Chapter 6 for more information).

After checking and correcting the structure alignment, it's time to remove the damaged panel. Just how it's removed depends on how it's attached and what tools you have available. Panels that are spot welded to the structure can be removed most easily by drilling out the welds. This can usually be accomplished with a drill bit, although special hole saws and spot weld cutters are available (see Chapter 4 for more information). A panel held on by a lot of spot welds, or one fastened in place by fusion welding, can usually be removed with a cutting torch, if you're careful. The critical factors are to limit panel distortion from heat to an absolute minimum and to avoid starting fires in the upholstery.

If you have access to one, there's no better tool for panel removal than an air chisel. The air chisel will quickly and accurately cut out a welded panel, or a section of a panel, with no heat distortion of the surrounding sheet metal. This is especially important when replacing items such as quarter panels, where the job of blending the replacement panel into the undamaged sheet metal can be made much easier by the clean and accurate cuts made with an air chisel.

When working on a panel that's been fusion welded to surrounding panels, or to the main structure, you should try to make the cuts about one inch from the weld into the damaged section of the panel. This could be very helpful if a torch is used to remove the damaged panel, since the weld area will help to control heat distortion in the panels on the other side of the weld. Even if you're using an air chisel to remove the damaged panel, try to maintain the one inch lip around the weld area to provide enough material for attaching the replacement panel. Remember when securing a replacement panel from a breakers yard, where you may have to cut it off another car, to cut closer to the weld, or perhaps even on the other side of it, to give you trim room and a lip for attaching the panel to your car. In both cases, the trimming must be careful and precise to get a good fit and easy attachment of the new panel.

Partial replacement of a panel, either because of collision damage or because the panel has rusted out, is probably the most common form of major car body repair. The sill panels, lower door panels and lower quarter panels are sections most often replaced. While the entire door or quarter panel can be replaced, it's more common to replace only the section of the panel that has been damaged.

Rear quarter panel replacement

For example, let's look at a car that's sustained damage to the lower part of the rear quarter panel, between the wheel arch and the rear bumper, as a result of a collision.

First, check to make sure the damage is confined to the quarter panel. If it extends into the roof pillar or boot section, a more extensive repair procedure will be required. Also check to see how much of the quarter panel is affected. Is it confined to the rear section of the quarter panel or does it extend above and/or forward of the wheel arch? If it's confined to the rear section, then only partial panel replacement is involved. If it extends beyond the wheel arch, then the entire panel should probably be replaced, along with the inner wing liner. A typical repair procedure should be done as follows . . .

1 If the car has a separate chassis, is the frame pushed in behind the axle or have the spring hangers been bent out of shape? If it's a monocoque design, make sure the underlying structure hasn't been damaged.

2 Using a grease pencil or chalk, mark off the area to be replaced. Whenever possible, follow the contour of the panel, but also try to make all cuts in straight lines. This will make matching the replacement panel to the vehicle much easier. Pick reference points, such as bumper mounts, mouldings and door openings, and measure from the reference points to the cut line. Jot down the measurements. If you're getting a replacement panel from a breakers yard, take them with you when you go to cut out the replacement panel.

3 With the replacement panel in your workshop or garage, transfer the cut lines from the damaged panel to the replacement, using the reference marks to ensure accuracy.

4 Use an air chisel to cut the replacement panel along the marked lines – keep the cuts as straight and accurate as possible. Note that at this point you still haven't cut the damaged section of sheet metal off the car (the section that's going to be replaced).

5 Position the cut replacement panel over the damaged section, lining it up carefully to make sure it matches the original contour of the body. You may want to drill a few 3.0 mm holes through both the replacement panel and the damaged panel underneath it and fasten the replacement panel temporarily in place with pop rivets.

6 With the replacement panel secured over the damaged panel, use a scribe to transfer the outline of the replacement panel to the original sheet metal.

7 Remove the replacement panel. You now have an exact fit cut line for removal of the damaged panel. Note that in this type of repair you don't want any sheet metal overlap, like you would if you were replacing the entire quarter panel.

8 Very carefully use an air chisel to cut the damaged panel along the inside edge of the scribed line. Inevitably the air chisel will cause some panel buckling along the cut edge. Use a hammer and dolly (very lightly) to straighten any bent areas – do the same along the edge of the replacement panel.

9 Use a wire brush in an electric drill to clean the edges of the body opening and the replacement panel – if rust was the reason for the repair, apply a rust arresting chemical to the exposed metal. **Note:** *Rust arresting chemicals are made by several manufacturers. They react with rust and transform it into a substance called 'black rust', which is chemically stable and won't continue to eat away at the metal.* After the panel is installed, apply rustproofing compound to the inner areas of the quarter panel as well.

10 Position the new panel on the body and use clamps or rivets to temporarily hold it in place.

11 Refer to Chapter 12 and tack weld the panel to the existing sheet metal, then weld the entire joint. Use a MIG welder and follow the instructions for butt welding large panels.

12 Grind down the welds, then finish the repair with plastic filler.

The body and the replacement panel must be clean before anything is welded in place – apply a rust arresting chemical to the exposed metal of the body (arrowed) and the back side of the new panel

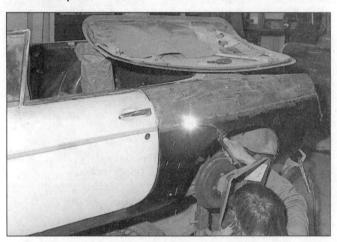

The welded in panel will restore the body to like new condition and greatly reduce the amount of filling and sanding required to finish the repair

If the weld bead is correctly formed, very little grinding will be needed to get the repair ready for the application of filler

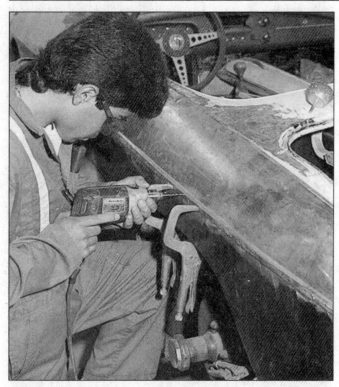

If rivets or screws are used, leave a flange on the body for the new panel to attach to and drill a row of holes to accept the fasteners

Installing with pop rivets or screws

An alternative to welding the new panel section in place, one that's especially good for do-it-yourselfers, is to install the replacement panel with pop rivets (or screws) . . .

1 After tracing the shape of the replacement panel onto the damaged panel with a scribe, make the cut about 12 mm to the inside of the line. This will result in a flange, which the replacement panel can be attached to.

2 Position the replacement panel and hold it in place with clamps.

3 Drill a series of holes through both panels, along the edges, then install the rivets or screws. If screws are used, try to find fasteners made of stainless steel.

4 Once the panel is securely attached, use a body hammer to force the rivet or screw heads and the replacement panel edge slightly below the original panel contour. If screws are used, you can grind the heads down to avoid having to use too much filler later.

5 Complete the repair with plastic filler. This doesn't result in a repair of the same quality as a weld, but it's much quicker, and for the beginner lacking well developed welding skills, will be much easier and more effective.

Sill panel replacement

Sill panel replacement is very similar to quarter panel replacement and is relatively simple, other than having to work close to the ground. It's much easier if you can get the

vehicle up on axle stands or ramps, where you'll have more working room and can see what you're doing better. Sill panels are usually spot welded in place – drilling out the welds, removing the panel and either riveting, MIG welding or brazing the new panel in place is all that's required. Keep in mind that in almost all cases, it's much easier to replace a damaged or rusted out sill panel than it is to repair it.

Door skin replacement

The most common partial panel or 'skin' replacement is the door panel. Doors are almost always damaged in any collision other than direct front or rear end hits, and they're also highly susceptible to rust damage due to plugging of the water drain holes. Use caution when repairing a door that's been extensively damaged by rust. Quite often a rusted door will also have rust damaged inner parts, which means it's more appropriate to replace the entire component with one from a breakers yard.

Depending on the extent of the damage and the design of the door, you may want to replace either the entire skin or a part of it. Quite often, replacing the section below the moulding (if one is used) may be all that's required. If there's no moulding to hide the rivets or weld seam, it's a good idea to replace the entire door panel, since working the middle of a low crown panel, especially where welding is required, is quite difficult. If part of the original panel is going to be cut out, the cut should be made either at the waistline (just below the window) or under the moulding (if one is used). The panel should be cut with an air chisel, leaving enough material for the replacement panel to overlap.

You'll note that the edge of the door skin is held to the door frame by a crimped hem flange. Use a grinder to remove the rounded over edge of the panel to separate it from the door frame. Both the outer panel and what's left of the flange will simply fall off, leaving the frame ready for the

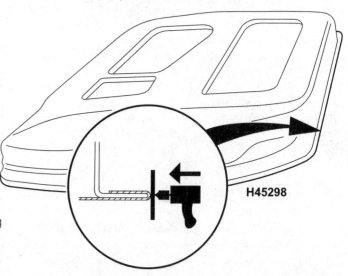

H45298

To remove a door skin, simply grind off the edge of the flange all the way around, and drill out any spot welds on the upper edge, near the window

new panel. Most replacement panels come with the flange already bent, ready to slip over the frame. All that's necessary is crimping and, in some cases, a few spot or plug welds to secure the panel to the door frame.

When attaching a replacement panel with a lap joint, use sheet metal screws to hold the panel in place while short sections around the perimeter are welded, then remove the screws and fill the holes with plastic filler.

If the panel is going to be butt welded to the old panel, refer to Chapter 12 and use a MIG welder to fasten the panel in place. If possible, do the welding from the inside of the door so you won't have to deal with grinding the weld down to the door contour before applying plastic filler.

Bonnet and boot lid skin replacement

Bonnet and boot lid panels are crimped to the reinforcing framework the same way door panels are secured to the inner door structure, so replacement is similar – you're just working with a larger piece of metal. Before attempting to replace a bonnet or boot lid skin, check with a breakers yard – a complete replacement component may be cheaper to install.

Roof skin replacement

The roof is usually the easiest major panel to replace on a car. Of course, you'll have to first make sure the substructure is properly aligned and, if not, get it back into the proper shape. Once the substructure has been pushed out (if necessary) and aligned with the doors, the damaged roof panel (skin) can be removed. Use an air chisel to make the cut about 25 mm from the drip rails, windscreen and rear window edges and lift off the panel. The remaining strip, which is usually spot welded to the underlying structure, can then be 'peeled' off or the spot welds, which were not readily visible when the entire panel was in place, can be drilled out and the flange removed. Use sheet metal screws to hold the new top panel in place, spot or plug weld it to the substructure, then use plastic filler to complete the repair.

Bonded panels

Increasingly, on later models, some panels (usually front wings or rear quarter panels) are being bonded into place during their assembly. Replacement of a damaged bonded panel is reasonably straightforward. Using an air chisel, cut the panel away leaving a strip of the original panel about 25 mm wide where it is bonded to the substructure, then cut through the bonding material and remove the remains of the damaged panel. It is possible to cut through the bonding material using a sharp knife or scalpel, but it's hard work! Use a heated knife (like the ones used by windscreen fitters) to make the job much easier. Prior to fitting the new panel, remove all traces of the original bonding material.

When it's time to fit the new panel, the material used to bond is often a 'Two-pack' paste. Here, the two substances (usually an adhesive and an activator) must be mixed together then applied to the substructure. Take care though, because once mixed, there is a limited time before the bond 'sets' – check the instructions supplied with the bonding material. Position the new panel in place, then hold or clamp it in place until the bond 'sets'. Often, bonded panels are also secured with a few bolts or screws for extra security.

Body component alignment

Front end components

Most vehicles have either a frame, bolt-on sub frame, or sheet metal structural section in front, which the outer cowl, bonnet, wings, inner wings, radiator/grille support, suspension components and, in some cases, engine support crossmember are bolted or welded to. Because of this design feature, it's common to replace rather than repair major front end components. Once the alignment of the front structure has been checked and, if necessary, corrected, only minor adjustments of the components attached to it are needed.

Manufacturers allow for them by using adjustable mounting points for the wings and bonnet. In some cases shims are used to adjust the component location. In others, the mounting holes are elongated to allow the piece to be moved in relation to the structure and the surrounding sheet metal.

The main reason for this, whether you're replacing a component with a piece from a breaker's yard or installing a new component direct from the manufacturer, is they very seldom fit exactly right. Tolerances in components can 'stack up', leading to a bonnet that's straight and true in blueprint terms, but one that won't match up with the wing or the scuttle. At the factory, when the car is coming down the assembly line, this is usually taken care of by one or more specialists who use nothing more sophisticated that their eyes, some leverage and a length of wood to fit the panel. You won't have the constantly moving assembly line to contend with, so you can take a bit more time when adjusting wing height and spread, latch and hinge location, etc. However, you'll still find that a large block of wood will come in handy for 'tweaking' panels for a perfect fit.

Front end component adjustment should focus on getting the bonnet opening to match the shape of the bonnet. In almost all cases, the wings and radiator support are bolted in place, then the bonnet is mounted and everything is shifted around until the bonnet fits. Although the bonnet can be moved fore and aft, as well as up and down, during the initial alignment (getting the hole the right shape) you must move the wings and radiator support – then move the bonnet as required for the final fit.

Chapter 7

Moving a wing is simply a matter of loosening all the bolts, then prying the wing in the required direction. In some cases, especially when moving it forward or backward, you may have to use a hydraulic jack – this should be a last resort, when nothing else will make the bonnet fit right. Before you make major changes in alignment though, go back and repeat all the X-check measurements (Chapter 6) to make sure the monocoque structure or chassis is straight.

Quite often when major front end sheet metal repair has been done on a car, the bonnet opening will end up being too narrow at the front. The best way to cure this problem (again, assuming you've made the necessary X-checks and the structure alignment is correct), is to unbolt the wings (don't overlook the bolts at the radiator support bracket), use a hydraulic jack or a large hammer and block of wood to spread the wings apart and add shims, an equal number on each side, to the bolts between the wings and radiator support.

Once you have the panel alignment as close to correct as practical, it's time to use the bonnet adjustments to get things perfect.

Start with the bonnet hinges, if only because they'll give you more range of movement – more placement options – than any other adjusting point. By moving the hinge mounting plates or the bonnet itself, after loosening the bolts, or by adding or subtracting washers/shims under the bolt heads, you can move either side of the bonnet up or down, fore or aft, or move it left or right in the bonnet opening. Remember to just barely loosen the bolts when making the adjustments and snug them down when checking for fit. The hinge springs can very easily change the bonnet position when you try to close it, and move it again when you open it, making the adjustments an over and over again repetition that'll get you nowhere.

Most bonnets have rubber bumpers mounted on the radiator support to control the height at the front, keep the bonnet under tension when it's closed and reduce flutter and vibration in the sheet metal. Before making any other adjustments at the front of the bonnet, use the bumpers to set the proper height in relation to the wings on each side (usually, the bumpers can be turned to raise or lower them after loosening a lock nut on the threaded post). Just remember, the bonnet must rest securely on the bumpers when it's in the closed position. Use the latch adjustment to ensure that the bonnet is held securely against the bumpers.

Occasionally, especially when you've bought a new bonnet from either the original manufacturer or an aftermarket company, you'll find that it's 'tweaked' slightly. That is, even with all the adjustments correct, one corner may be too high while the other corner aligns perfectly with the wing. To fix it, use a small block or a large rubber hammer and give the sheet metal a little nudge in the direction you want it to go. Lay the block (or hammer) between the bonnet edge and the top of the wing, blocking it up, then gently lean on the bonnet to bend it ever so slightly. The idea is to 'warp' the bonnet a little to bring it into alignment, not actually bend it

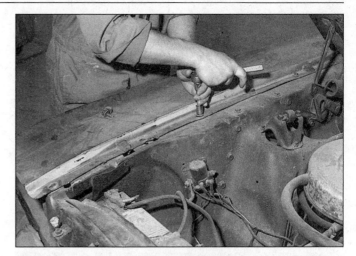

Wings can be adjusted by removing the mounting bolts (don't forget the bolts at the radiator support bracket) . . .

. . . and persuading them in or out, forward or backward, with a jack or a large hammer and a block of wood

Loosen the hinge-to-bonnet bolts to move the bonnet forward or backward or from side to side

(in the sense of putting a kink in the metal). Work slowly and carefully until you have it right.

The final bonnet adjustments are made with the latch mechanism, half of which is mounted on the bonnet and the other half on the radiator support. Just as with the bonnet hinges, the bonnet latch can usually be moved from side to side and up and down (to hold the bonnet closed snugly against the rubber bumpers).

The easiest way to adjust the position of the bonnet latch is to loosen the bolts slightly, just enough so the latch mechanism will move when pressure is put on it, then close the bonnet. The latch mechanism should centre when the bonnet is closed. Carefully open the bonnet and tighten the bolts. Finally, adjust the bonnet latch up or down as necessary so the bonnet is held snugly against the bumpers. Also, check to make sure the bonnet safety catch is working.

Rear end components

Getting the boot lid or hatch adjusted properly after collision repair is much more difficult than adjusting the bonnet, simply because there are less places adjustments can be made. While the front wings and radiator support/grille are bolted in place and are, to a certain extent, adjustable, the rear quarter panels and the sheet metal below the rear window and the back of the boot lid are welded in place and in general can't be moved. This means that if the boot lid can't be adjusted by moving the hinges and latch mechanism and X-checks have shown that the structure is straight, then the only alternative is to change the contour of the boot lid.

The first thing that has to be checked, just like the bonnet, is if the hole is the right shape for the lid. If the hole is too narrow at one end or the other, or too wide, then there's something wrong with the structure and further checking,

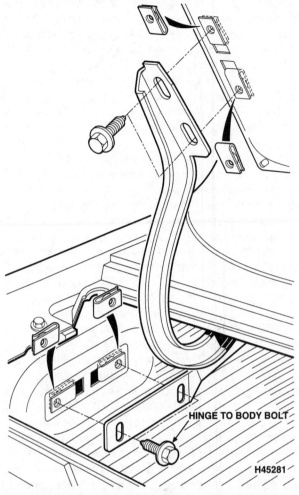

HINGE TO BODY BOLT

H45281

Loosen the hinge-to-body bolts to move the bonnet up and down

The front of the bonnet, adjacent to the wings on each side, is normally adjusted by loosening the locknuts on the bonnet bumpers and turning them slightly to raise or lower it

This type of bonnet latch can be adjusted to hold the bonnet snugly against the bumpers after the lock nut has been slackened

and possible structure pulling, is required. When dealing with the boot lid or hatch, you have to assume the shape of the lid is correct (unless its been damaged and incorrectly repaired), and the shape of the car must be adapted to fit the lid in terms of overall size.

One major difference between the bonnet and boot lids is in sealing – the bonnet, for all intents and purposes, doesn't seal. That is, it's not expected to keep water out. The boot, on the other hand, is expected to stay dry. Rubber weather stripping is used around the boot edge to accomplish this. Refer to Chapter 5 to check the weatherstrip seal.

With the boot lid centred and the latch adjusted properly, if it's misaligned it must be corrected using a block of wood, just like the bonnet. The most common adjustment needed on a boot lid will be for greater contact against the weather stripping on one side or the other, or possibly on both sides. The easiest way to make this adjustment is to place a wood block (or rubber hammer) between the lower edge of the boot lid and the latch, then push down very gently on the side that needs greater contact with the weather stripping. If both sides must be lowered, get a friend to help and do both sides at the same time rather than taking a chance on warping the boot lid by doing one side at a time.

Most of the time, misalignment of the boot lid will mean it isn't making full contact with the weather stripping. Occasionally, however, especially where extensive bodywork has been done, the weather stripping will be too high, either keeping the boot lid from closing or raising the edge above the wing. If this is the case, tapping with a rubber hammer will usually lower the flange enough to align the lid.

The boot lid can be slightly out of alignment in several areas. Moving the wood block or rubber hammer around and judiciously applying pressure can bring it back into

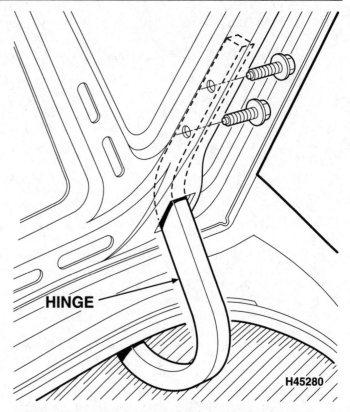

HINGE

H45280

A typical hinge that fits into a structural member doesn't allow for very much adjustment of the boot lid

alignment. Just remember, be careful when you're 'tweaking' sheet metal – a little patience can prevent needless damage and repairs.

Preparation for painting

Old paint preparation

The best paint in the world, applied with the highest degree of expertise, won't look any better than a coat of house paint applied with a brush if it starts falling off or is full of peeled, blistered or bubbled spots. And that's exactly what will happen to your new paint job if the old paint isn't properly conditioned before you start spraying the new stuff on.

Probably close to ninety percent of the problems which occur with a new paint job can be directly traced to improper preparation of the old finish. If you don't get every trace of contaminants off the finish, the new paint won't stick. If you don't properly sand out and primer nicks and scratches in the old finish, they will show up clearly when the new paint is applied. If you forget those hard to reach areas like under the door handles and in the scuttle louvers, the paint will probably peel off after a couple of days, and you'll end up doing half the paint job over again – or living with a car that has a case of the uglies.

The first thing to do is clean the car – thoroughly! And not just with soap and water. To get the surface really clean, you need a cleaner designed specially for pre-paint surface preparation. They're usually referred to as pre-cleaning solvents or wax/silicone removers. Silicone, used in many polishes and cleaners, is the number one enemy of new paint, followed closely by wax and oil, so make sure you get a cleaner that's effective for removing silicone.

Most wax/silicone removers are applied with a clean rag, then immediately wiped off with another rag. Some include instructions to use a non scratching abrasive pad, such as a Scotch-Brite, for application. In either case, follow the instructions on the container – and use lots of rags! It doesn't make a lot of sense to dissolve the silicone, wax and oil, then try to clean it off with a dirty rag which will just leave behind a film of those very contaminants you're trying to remove. Your best bet is to buy cheesecloth washing rags from a car accessory shop, use them and discard them as they become contaminated.

Because sanding won't really remove silicone or oil, it's very important that you clean the entire car with wax/silicone remover. This is especially true of those hard to reach spots like around the windshield wiper drive posts, key lock cylinder holes, radio aerial, etc. And don't forget inside the doors and boot lid. The best way to make sure you don't miss anything is to do only a small area at a time, making sure you have it thoroughly clean, then move on to another area.

With all the contaminants removed from the old paint, it's time to start sanding. This isn't the finish sanding that you'll be doing before applying the paint, but the roughing and cleaning of the top layer of paint to produce a workable surface. Because of this, you'll be using a relatively coarse grade of sandpaper, using it dry, and looking for a dull and even somewhat scratched surface.

Use 320 grit open face sandpaper to sand the old paint. While we have repeatedly said in this manual that sanding should be done only with a sanding block to produce a level finish, this is a case where you should use the sandpaper with your hands – one hand to sand and the other to follow along behind to feel the sanded surface.

Fold the sandpaper in thirds (this will give your palm something to grip and keep the paper from slipping) and start sanding a small area in straight, back and forth lines. As you finish a small area, run your other hand over it, feeling for small imperfections or 'glossy' unsanded areas. Nicks in the paint and deep scratches will show up here, but don't worry about them at this time. Just make a note of where they are so you can come back to them when you've finished rough sanding the entire surface of the car.

It's important that every square centimetre of the car's old surface be sanded with the 320 grit sandpaper until it has a rough, dull appearance. If it still looks glossy, even when wiped with a clean cloth to get rid of the sanding residue, it hasn't been sanded enough. That top, glossy layer of paint has to be removed or chances are the new paint simply won't stick to the old finish. Be especially critical around the edges of panels, such as the back edge of the bonnet and the edges of the door panels where they wrap around into the inner door panels, since unsanded areas here have a sharp contour that paint can easily peel off of. Speaking of inner door panels (and inside the hood and trunk lid), these areas generally don't need as extensive sanding as the outer panels, since they probably haven't been repeatedly coated with waxes, polishes, etc. But they must be thoroughly cleaned with wax/silicone remover and, where practical, they should receive a surface sanding.

With the entire surface rough sanded, it's time to go back and take care of those nicks and deep scratches you noticed during sanding. If you leave them, no amount of primer coating and sanding before painting will eliminate them, and they'll be painfully obvious when you spray on the new paint. They have to be taken out at this point and the only way to do it is by sanding them down until they feather edge into the old paint. Then primer over the bare metal and sand the primer until it blends into the paint.

Here is another of those areas where sanding must be done with a sanding block, rather than your hand. If you use your hand to sand away a nick or a scratch, you'll leave a depression in the paint the shape of your fingers (or possibly

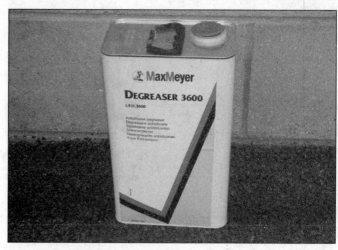

Wax/silicone remover solvent is probably the most important item needed for preparing the body for primer and new paint – if it isn't used for cleaning, the new primer/paint won't adhere properly and the finished paint job will be unsatisfactory

your whole hand). Even though the depression will probably be invisible at this stage, or even at the primering stage, it'll show up sharply in the new paint.

Start with the same 320 grit sandpaper you used for rough sanding the finish and block sand the nick or scratch down until you reach the bottom of the imperfection. This doesn't necessarily mean all the way down to bare metal, although in many cases, especially in door dings, this will be the case. Sand out between 25 mm and 40 mm around the nick or scratch to featheredge the base into the top layer of existing paint. Make sure there's no 'edge' left when you finish sanding or it'll show up later.

When you think you've got the area properly feather edged, wipe it clean with wax/silicone remover, then use an aerosol can of lacquer type primer to cover the area. Allow the primer to dry thoroughly, then apply another coat and a third after that. Don't apply the primer so heavy that it runs, but don't just fog it on either. You want to end up with a relatively thick coat of primer over the sanded area.

When the primer is completely dry, take a sheet of 400 grit wet or dry sandpaper and sand it smooth without using water. You don't need to get the glass smooth surface you'll want later in the full coat primer sanding, but you do need a smooth enough surface to reveal any ridge lines between the nick and the old paint. If you've properly feather edged the old paint, you shouldn't be able to tell where the sanded area ends and the old paint begins.

If you're going to go directly into the painting process, wipe down the entire car with wax/silicone remover again (being careful in the primered areas not to wipe the primer off), then do a dry wipe down with a tack cloth to remove any sanding residue. Read the Section on Use of primers in this Chapter before proceeding. In many cases where new paint is being applied over sanded old paint, a sealer (bar coat) or high-build primer should be used next.

Sanding techniques

The secret to a successful paint job is the sanding that's done before you even unpack the spray gun. If the surface you spray the paint on isn't smooth and clean, the finished job won't be right – and might be wrong to the point where you'll have to take it off and start over from scratch. Putting on a first class paint job can easily take two or three days, only an hour or so of which is actually spraying paint on the car. The rest is preparation and sanding mostly sanding, sanding and more sanding.

And let's get one thing straight right from the start. There's no way to get the surface of a car sanded properly for painting by dry sanding. To get a surface that's smooth enough to produce the high quality paint job you're after, you have to wet sand, which means that you're going to need a water supply, an area where the water can drain away (and to keep your neighbours from forming a lynching party, one that doesn't drain sanding residue into their gardens), wet or dry sandpaper and clothes that you don't mind getting wet – because you will get wet. It's possible, barely, to wet sand a car with a bucket of water rather than a hose, but the results are generally less than satisfactory, and we highly recommend that you use a hose with a constantly running supply of water to do the wet sanding.

In general, there are two stages to finish sanding a car. Sanding the old finish (assuming the car hasn't been stripped to bare metal), and sanding the primer coat. We've already looked at rough sanding the old paint and finishing bare metal for sanding is covered in the Section on **Use of primers**, so let's get started with the finish sanding you'll need to do before applying primer.

Initial sanding

You don't need a lot of water for wet sanding, but you do need a steady supply, and it's best if the water is coming from a source that won't scratch or ding the surface you're sanding. Most hoses have a brass fitting on the end and when you're trying to keep your balance on a stepladder so you can reach the roof, sand with one hand and hold the hose with the other, it's almost guaranteed the brass end is going to put some dings in the paint. One answer is to cut the end off the hose, but this sort of spoils the hose for connecting up to the sprinkler or other hoses. A more practical way of preventing hose damage is to wrap the end of the hose with a rag, tying or taping it in place, then turn the water on very low so the rag won't blow off. Again, you don't need a lot of water – what will pass through the rag should be plenty.

In finish sanding, the pattern you sand in is extremely important. The thing you don't want to do is sand in circles, which is a very natural tendency, but one that should be avoided since it'll leave circular sanding marks if you sand that way. Sand in a straight line and, where possible, make the lines run the length of the panel you're working on, rather than across it.

Although wet sanding can be done with the paper held in the hand, since you aren't really cutting into the paint, it's better to use a sanding block. If you're sanding long, flat panels, use a hard rubber block. If you're sanding curved (high crown) areas, use a piece of sponge for the sanding block. For tight areas, go ahead and use your hand, with the paper folded in thirds to give your hand something to grip.

The hardest part of this initial wet sanding will be getting the 'feel' of how the paper is working. You'll be using a relatively coarse grit sandpaper (for wet sanding), say 220 or 280 grit, and you're going to have to learn to feel the difference between paper that's cutting and paper that's just sliding over the finish. If the paper clogs with paint debris, it will either slide over the old finish or gouge into it. In either case, it won't be doing the job right. The paper must be kept clean while you're sanding (that's what the running water is for) so it doesn't either slide or grab, but will have just that trace of 'bite' that tells you it's sanding properly.

Even though you feather edged all repaired areas and nicks and scratches in the rough sanding phase (**Old paint preparation**), you may want to work them down even more when wet sanding. Remember, the smoother the undercoat is, the smoother the final paint job will be. Wet sanding a feather edged area until the old paint layers and primer layer are feathered out for 18 to 25 mm will give you a really smooth surface to work with later.

Primer sanding

When primer is sprayed on a panel, if it has been mixed right and sprayed right, it'll dry with a slightly rough texture. The rough texture must be sanded out, without cutting all the way through the primer, before the finish coat can be applied.

Spraying primer is covered in **Use of primers**, so let's assume that you've got the entire car covered and you're ready to sand.

To start with, it would be best if you gave the primer a couple of days to 'cure' before sanding it. While most primers can be sanded an hour or less after spraying, it's better if you give it plenty of time to harden and shrink before sanding (this takes at least two days).

Whether you're sanding relatively fresh primer, or have waited a couple of days, the idea is to smooth the primer coat, not cut into or through it. If you do cut through the primer when wet sanding it's not a disaster – you'll just have to spray on some more primer and wait for it to dry, but it can be time consuming and frustrating if you want to get on with the job of painting a car.

To sand the primer you'll want a good supply of 1000 grit wet or dry sandpaper. This is a fine standard sandpaper, and it's what you'll need to get the finish really smooth. Tear a sheet of paper in half, fold it in thirds, and use your hand and lots of water to take the 'nap' off the primer coat. This is a case where the less sanding you do, the better off you are, since the whole idea is to get the surface polish smooth, not sand out imperfections in the surface (which should have already been taken care of). After sanding each section, run your hand over the surface while it's still wet to check for smoothness. Any unsanded areas will show up quite clearly.

When you've got the primer smooth, use compressed air to blow all dust off the surface, then start taping and masking (see **Masking techniques**). When you've got the entire car masked and ready for the first colour coat, wipe the primer down with wax/silicone remover (yes, wipe it down again – there's no way you can get a surface too clean before painting). Wipe the solvent off with clean towels and you're ready to start painting.

Use of paint strippers

If the paint is badly deteriorated, you should consider removing it completely to prevent incompatibility problems with the new paint. Large amounts of paint can be removed relatively easily with chemical paint strippers (they're very effective because they won't warp or otherwise affect the metal of the body).

Before using a chemical paint stripper, be aware that several precautions must be taken . . .

- *Work only in a well ventilated area!*
- *Always wear eye protection and rubber gloves when using chemical paint strippers. If you get any in your eyes or on your skin, injuries will occur.*

Before applying the paint remover to the car body, mask off any areas that you don't intend to strip (apply a double layer of masking material when using paint strippers). Be especially careful to cover any crevices that could allow the material to seep into areas that you don't want it to contact. Remove all trim pieces.

Use a cheap bristle paint brush to apply the paint stripper to the body, one panel at a time. Flow the stripper on in one direction only – don't try to brush it out. Don't be stingy with the stripper or you'll end up repeating the procedure. The chemical will lift the paint very effectively and it'll be easy to scrape off with a putty knife. If acrylic lacquer is involved, it will get very sticky and be harder to remove with a scraper. You may need to use coarse steel wool on it.

At any rate, allow the stripper to 'work' for at least 15 minutes, or until the paint is completely softened, before trying to scrape it off. When it's all off, wash the exposed metal, then sand it and remove any remaining paint residue with 60 grit sandpaper.

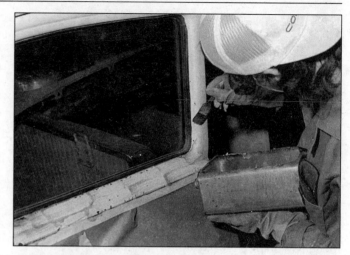

Apply the chemical paint stripper with a paint brush, let it work for several minutes . . .

. . . (until the paint blisters and separates from the sheet metal), then scrape it off with a putty knife and coarse steel wool

Preparing bare metal for painting

Bare metal surfaces should be chemically clean to ensure good primer adhesion. Cleaning the metal is a three step process that includes **cleaning** to remove oil, grease, wax and other contaminants, application of a **metal conditioner** to remove rust and corrosion and the use of a **conversion coat** to ensure the best possible primer adhesion. This process is usually ignored completely or done incorrectly, which will lead to poor primer/paint adhesion and eventually corrosion.

Cleaning

Use paint thinner or reducer to clean the metal. Apply it to the surface and remove it while the metal is still wet with a second clean cloth. Work on 1 metre square areas and use plenty of cleaner.

Conversion coating

There are several different types of conditioner/converters available from Automotive accessory shops / paint shops. Most off them involve painting on a rust converter/preventer. Once applied the treatment converters rust into a neutral chemical compound known as 'black rust', which can then be sanded and painted over as normal. It's a good opportunity to treat the whole of the panel with the converter/preventer, to ensure your paint job will last, even on panel where no rust was visible. Make sure you following the instructions supplied by the treatment manufacturer.

Use of primers

Primers are the most common undercoats used when refinishing car bodies. They're used to build up and level feathered areas or rough surfaces and to provide a smooth surface for paint. Primers have several unique characteristics . . .

- **Adhesion** – they provide a strong bond between the sheet metal or old paint and the new paint
- **Rust resistance** – they resist the formation of rust where they adhere to the sheet metal
- **'Build'** – they're able to fill sanding and grinding marks in old paint, sheet metal and fillers
- **Sanding ease** – they can be sanded smooth and levelled quickly and easily
- **'Hold out'** – they prevent the paint from soaking in, which results in a dull finish
- **Drying speed** – a good high-build primer should be ready to sand in as little as 30 minutes

The two main types of primers are: Primer lacquer (also known as 1K or 1-pack, or just Primer) and Etch primer.

Primer Lacquer

This type of primer is normally available as 'high-build' primer. High-build primer has three main functions:

- *To provide a relatively thick coating which will fill any small imperfections (eg. minor scratches and sanding marks) in the finish underneath.*
- *To provide an element of stone chip resistance; if a stone penetrates the top-coat, the high-build primer has an element of elasticity to absorb the impact, preventing the chip from penetrating through to the bare substrate underneath.*
- *To provide a coating which can be sanded to give a smooth, sound base on to which colour coat can be sprayed.*

High-build primers are usually 2-pack products which are mixed from 3 elements (primer, activator and thinner). The term 'high-build' is used by most paint manufacturers to refer to the primer used to prepare a surface for application of colour coat. High-build primer can be mixed with thinners in various ratios to provide coatings of various thicknesses. 'High-build' primer is not necessarily applied to give a thick 'high-build' layer, and can be sprayed to give a thin layer purely to provide a key fo colour coat.

Etch primer

The purpose of etch primers is to replicate the cataphoretic dip priming process used by vehicle manufacturers to protect panels against corrosion. Etch primers contain an acid which etches bare metal, ensuring that there is a very strong bond between the primer and the panel surface. Etch primers are normally used on bare metal, but most types are equally effective on other materials such as plastic and fibreglass (check the manufacturer's recommendations as to suitability for non-metallic surfaces). Etch primers can also be used on galvanised metal or on top of existing primer to cover any minor damage in the protective galvanising coating. Etch primers are usually two-component products, which contain an acid activator. The acid etches the bare metal, allowing the primer to adhere strongly to the panel, and providing excellent corrosion resistance. Some paint manufacturers also produce etch primer 'ready-to-spray' in an aerosol can for repairs to small areas. Generally, etch primers do not require sanding, and 1K primer (high-build or otherwise) is usually spayed over the top before preparing the panel to receive the colour coat. Etch primers are the only primers suitable for use directly on galvanised panels.

Other common undercoat products that may be confused with primers are sealers or primer-sealers (some sealers prime as well as seal and are known as 'primer-sealers', while others only seal). Primer-sealers do the same job as primers, but they also seal better over a sanded old paint coat to provide uniform colour 'hold out' when the new paint is applied. Sealers don't have the same characteristics as primers – they're applied over a primer or sanded paint coat to improve adhesion between the old paint and the new paint, provide a uniform colour background and 'hold out' for the new paint and to form a solvent barrier to help prevent sand scratch swelling and 'show through'.

Sealers are usually lacquer based, so they're easy to apply and dry very fast. Primer-sealers are generally enamel based. They can be used to prime bare metal and as a sealer under any enamel paint job.

The type of sealer to use depends on the paint to be applied. Check with an automotive paint shop to be sure you match up the primer-sealer or sealer correctly with the paint you intend to use. Depending on the condition of the old paint, the type of new paint being used and the repairs that were done, sometimes a sealer must be used and sometimes a sealer should be used.

The decision to use a particular type of primer, high-build primer, primer-sealer and/or sealer depends on whether or not the car's surface is smooth or rough, bare metal or painted, if painted, the type of paint already on it, and the type of paint you intend to apply. Paint manufacturers offer a variety of products that should be used in specific combinations for the best results, so check with your local automotive paint shop before buying primer and paint – they'll recommend items that are compatible.

The first and most important step when applying primer is to get the body's surface ready first. Use compressed air to remove all dust and dirt from joints and recessed areas, then wipe the entire car down with wax/silicone remover. If the old paint has been completely removed, exposing bare metal, refer to the **Preparing bare metal for painting** Section in this Chapter before proceeding.

Next, tape and mask off all trim and glass just as you would for painting, then mix up the primer (where necessary). Always remember to check that the primer and paints you plan to use are compatible – don't be afraid to ask advice from your local automotive paint shop.

No matter what kind of paint is going to be used, use the recommended multi purpose primer with the appropriate thinner (where applicable – ask for advice at your local automotive paint store). Mix them according to the directions, then stir thoroughly. For primer, adjust the spray gun so the spray pattern is about 200 mm wide, 300 mm from the gun head (see Chapter 9 for spray gun adjustment).

If the pattern is too wide, there will be a thin spot in the middle; if it's too narrow, the pattern will appear as a tight band. The fan (pattern) adjustment is the top knob above the handle on the spray gun. The second knob is for material (primer or paint) adjustment.

Make several practice passes on a piece of cardboard with the compressor regulator set at 60 psi (4.1 bar). Notice that when the paint gun trigger is first depressed, there's a moment when only air comes out, quickly followed by the paint. Practice making a smooth pass, keeping the gun at a constant distance from the surface until the pass is completed. Start the pass on one side, swing horizontally to the other limit, raise or lower the gun nearly a fan width and go back. Keep the gun nearly a fan width lower and make a

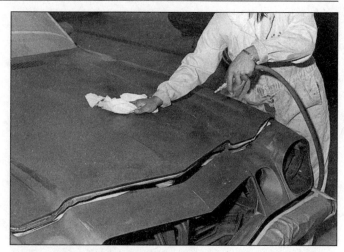

After sanding, and before applying any primer, use compressed air and a clean cloth to remove all dust and debris from the entire body – don't overlook cracks and joints between body panels

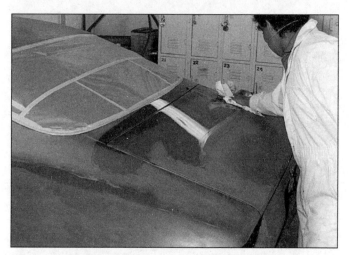

Then wipe the entire body with wax/silicone remover one more time – work on a small area and dry it off, then move to the next section of the car

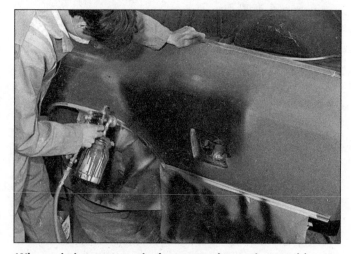

When priming spot repairs (as opposed to entire panels), overlap the primer coat onto the existing paint

Be sure to keep the air hose away from the car when spraying on the primer (or paint) – drape it over your shoulder when spraying the top of your vehicle . . .

. . . and hold it in your free hand when spraying lower sections

second pass. The gun should be kept parallel to the surface, so one end of the fan isn't closer than the other. See Chapter 9 for more information on painting techniques.

If you're spot priming isolated repairs, overlap the primer onto the existing paint about 25 or 50 mm all the way around the sanded surface. If the entire vehicle is being primed, start with the doors, bonnet and boot lid/tailgate openings. Spray the primer on evenly, in smooth strokes. When they're done, allow them to dry for 10 to 15 minutes, then close everything up and start on the outside metal.

Start spraying on the top, which is the hardest area to reach, and remember these hints . . .

- *Throw the air hose over one shoulder and hold it away from the car with your other hand*
- *Wrap a piece of rag around the gun/cup connection point to keep paint from dribbling out when painting with the gun in a nozzle down position*
- *If the primer is going on correctly, it will appear smooth and wet for just a short time; if it looks grainy, the primer is too thick or you're holding the gun too far away from the surface*
- *If the primer runs, it's too thin or you're holding the gun too close to the surface*
- *If the primer alternates wet dry wet or wet runny wet, your passes are inconsistent*

Primer is the basic foundation of a fine paint job, so don't skimp. It takes about 4 litres of unthinned primer for the average car, so keep going around it until you're sure you have it covered well.

After the primer has dried for 20 or 30 minutes, the tape can be removed. Although it's possible to go right ahead and sand the car (dry) and follow with the paint, it's a good idea to allow the primer to cure for several days, or even a couple of weeks if possible. The primer will shrink as it dries, so allow time for it to cure completely before painting.

After the primer has cured and shrunk, use wax/silicone remover again, completely washing the car, even in the tiniest cracks. This is vital – any foreign substance will invariably ruin an otherwise perfect paint job. For instance, just the marks left by your fingers will leave dark splotches under the final colour. When washing the car with the solvent, always use clean, lint free rags. Don't use workshop rags, as they're often cleaned with low-grade solvents that contain contaminants which will prevent good paint adhesion. If wax/silicone remover isn't available, in a pinch you can use thinner, applied with a very wet rag and immediately wiped off with a dry rag. Don't wait even a minute if you use thinner, as it'll quickly soften the primer's surface.

Masking techniques

One of the easiest ways to tell the difference between an amateur and professional paint job is to look at how much paint there is on the trim, glass, frame, etc. In other words, how good a job was done on the masking before the painting job was started.

The problem with masking is that it starts off easy and quickly becomes a very boring, time consuming and sometimes even uncomfortable job. You're generally working with a lot of small pieces that have to be masked very accurately if the finished paint job is going to look right, as well as large glass areas that have to be masked with paper as well as tape. Before you're half way through, you may start wondering why you didn't just let a professional do the job. Hang in there, though. Getting the car masked right is essential to getting a good paint job – and the extra work will be worth it in the end.

Chapter 8

The key to a good masking job begins before you even get close to the car – with the tape you buy. And in this case we don't mean masking tape from your local hardware store. Masking tape dries out in a hurry, and the tape that will work fine on the doors in your house and the cabinets in your kitchen will be a disaster on your car. Go to a professional paint supply shop and purchase fresh masking tape. When you pick up the roll of tape and squeeze it you should be able to feel the freshness. The roll of tape should feel soft. If it doesn't, find another store. Masking tape is available in two general types. One type is for use with air drying paints and the other type is for use with paints that must be baked on in an oven.

The next thing you'll need to buy is masking paper. Most people, when masking the windshield, side windows, grille, etc., get out yesterday's newspaper for masking. And while this might work fine, chances are it won't. Newspaper tears easily, letting paint seep through, which will later have to be removed. If the paint is thinned too much, even intentionally as with a fog coat, it can blot right through newspaper and, worst of all, newspaper masking seldom goes on flat, leaving pockets which collect dust that will later end up embedded in the new paint job. A roll of heavy-duty masking paper doesn't cost much and it can make your job a lot easier.

Finally, before starting work, spend some time figuring out what pieces of trim you can pull off, unbolt, unclip or otherwise get rid of (see Chapter 11). Pulling a bumper off is a major job – until you start masking it. Then you'll realize that spending ten minutes taking off bolts might have been a lot easier than spending thirty minutes trying to get the tape and paper to protect all that chrome or flat black plastic. Getting trim pieces off can likewise be a real pain, but those trim pieces, especially the badges telling the world you're driving a GTI Turbo Ghia, can take you all day to mask off correctly.

But, if you can't get the trim off, and it simply has to be masked, take your time and do it right. Apply the tape evenly, without stretching it, use a razor blade or scalpel type craft knife to trim the tape where necessary to make sure it doesn't cover an area that needs to be painted, and don't start the masking job until just before you're ready to start painting. The tape will dry out in a hurry once you have it on the car, and the dryer it gets the harder it'll be to get off once you've finished painting.

If you're painting only a portion of a vehicle, the adjacent panels will have to be masked off. Here, it's a good idea to use a double layer of paper and tape to prevent the paint that accumulates there from seeping through onto the panel under it.

If you're doing spot repainting of small areas, reverse masking techniques should be used to help blend the paint in and make the transition less noticeable. This is done by taping a piece of paper over the repaired area, then lifting it up and taping it in place so it presents a curved surface to the spray gun. You can repeat the masking application at the sides and bottom of the repair area to form a mask all the way around it.

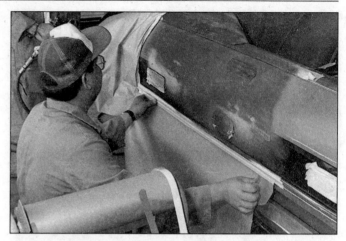

Buy professional quality masking tape and paper from an automotive paint supplier – don't use hardware store tape and don't buy tape that's been sitting around a long time

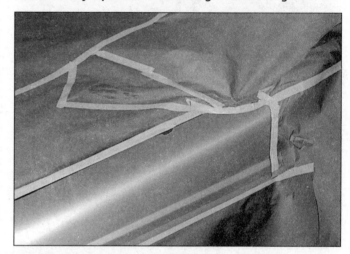

Use double layers of tape and paper when masking off the body panels next to a repaired panel – the paint will invariably build up on the tape and paper and could soak through it, causing damage to the paint underneath

Many trim pieces can be removed faster and easier than masking them off

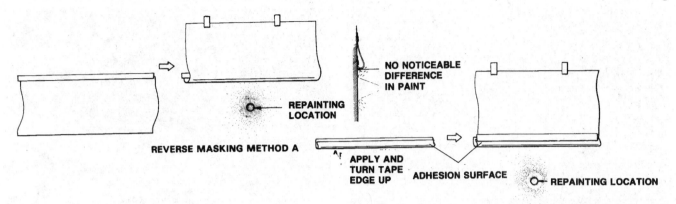

REVERSE MASKING METHOD A

NO NOTICEABLE DIFFERENCE IN PAINT

REPAINTING LOCATION

APPLY AND TURN TAPE EDGE UP

ADHESION SURFACE

REPAINTING LOCATION

REVERSE MASKING METHOD B

Be sure to cover the tyres/wheels so they don't get primer or paint on them. Paper and tape can be used to protect them, but the cheapest, easiest, and most effective covers you can use are large plastic dustbin bags – hold them in place with tape if necessary.

Keep the following tips in mind as you work – they'll make the paint job look more professional . . .

- *Run the masking tape in long strips down the piece of trim to be masked – avoid short pieces that will give the paint a seam to leak through*
- *When taping chrome trim, it's better to leave a little gap between the edge of the tape and the edge of the trim than to have the tape overlap the surface to be painted (it's easier to clean excess paint off the chrome than to touch up a missed spot on the body)*
- *A ball point pen can be useful for wrapping tape over the back edges of trim pieces – it will ensure the trim is completely covered, but there's still room for the paint to get in under the edge of the trim*
- *Whether you're using masking paper or newspaper, try to get it as flat as possible when covering large areas such as the windshield or rear window – folds and pockets in the paper will catch dust, which will later blow out onto the fresh paint*
- *A key area for masking that always shows up on an 'amateur' paint job is the under side of the car – overspray on the exhaust pipe is a sure sign the car wasn't masked properly*
- *If you're masking off an area of the body that's going to be painted a different colour, you'll often have to deal with tight curves – 3 mm wide masking tape is best for this sort of work (just make sure the tape is very fresh or it will either tear or lift in the curves)*
- *When masking the grille opening, it's a good idea to open the bonnet and extend the masking paper well inside the engine compartment to avoid overspray onto the radiator, etc.*
- *If you remove headlight, taillight and side marker light assemblies, rather than masking around them, be sure to cover the inside of the openings to prevent paint*

Run the tape in lengthwise strips down the piece of trim to be masked – avoid short pieces that give the paint a seam to leak through

Professional paint workshops have tyre covers, but large plastic dustbin bags work very well (just make sure there are no gaps for paint to spray through – it's awfully hard to clean off rubber)

Whether you're using masking paper or newspaper, try to get it as flat as possible when covering large areas such as the windscreen and rear window – folds and pockets in the paper can catch dust, which can later blow out onto the fresh paint

Open the bonnet and extend the masking paper down over the top of the radiator before masking off the grille opening

overspray from getting into the boot and engine compartment

• When you've finished painting, let the paint dry to the point where you can touch it with your fingers without leaving any marks, then begin removing the tape

• If you start pulling the tape up too soon, you risk getting the sticky edge of the tape into the fresh paint and leaving marks

• If you wait too long after painting (like a day or so) to pull up the tape, you'll find it has dried out until it tears instead of pulling up in strips, making the clean-up job a lot harder than it should be

Put paper over the inside of all openings to keep paint out of the interior, boot and engine compartment

Painting

Painting equipment

There's no way you can do a decent job of painting a car unless you thoroughly understand the operation of the paint spraying equipment you'll be using.

Spray guns

The paint spray gun is a device that uses air pressure to atomize a sprayable material, in this case, paint.

There are three basic types of spray gun in common use; *suction feed, gravity feed,* and *pressure feed.* The suction feed gun draws paint up from a reservoir attached to the underside of the gun body. The gravity feed gun works in exactly the same way, but features a top-mounted paint reservoir from which paint enters the gun body due to gravity. The pressure feed gun uses a remote fluid reservoir, which can be useful if a large quantity of fluid is to be sprayed (this requirement will be rare for normal automotive work). The choice between suction and gravity feed guns is very much down to the personal preference of the sprayer.

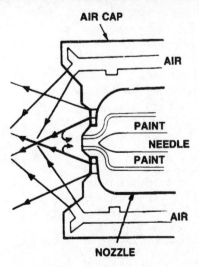

External mix spray gun air cap details – the air and paint passages must be kept clean!

GRAVITY FEED TYPE

SUCTION FEED TYPE

PRESSURE FEED TYPE

Spray guns commonly used for automotive painting come in three basic types – gravity feed, suction feed and pressure feed (a do-it-yourselfer will probably end up using a suction feed gun)

It's important to note that the spray gun set-up for a specific type of paint will be different for suction and gravity feed guns. The appropriate set-up data will be provided on the paint manufacturer's technical data/application sheet.

For fine work, such as spraying narrow stripes or custom paintwork, small spray guns are available. These guns are usually known as *detailing guns*, and are lighter and easier to manoeuvre than a full-size gun.

For automotive work, suction feed, gravity feed, and pressure feed guns are external mix guns. Here, the sir and paint are mixed and atomised just outside the cap. A suction feed gun uses the force of a stream of compressed air to cause a vacuum, which causes the paint to push out of the container. The fluid tip extends slightly beyond the air cap on this design. If the fluid tip is flush with the air cap, chances are the gun is a pressure feed type where the paint is forced to the gun by air pressure in the container attached to the spray gun.

The air cap is located at the extreme tip of the paint gun, with a knurled face so it can be gripped and removed by hand. Such a cap may have one to four orifices for air which is directed into the paint stream to atomize the mixture. As a rule, the average bodyshop gun will have two orifices, but the more orifices available the better. Heavy materials will atomize better with multiple orifice caps.

A small removable nozzle is held in the gun body by the air cap. This is the fluid tip which meters and controls the flow of paint into the air stream. The fluid tip is a seat for the fluid needle valve, which controls the flow of material from the cup. These tips are available in a wide range of nozzle sizes. The larger the nozzle size, the larger the amount of paint that can be sprayed. The needle and fluid tip come in matched pairs, ranging up to 2.2 mm, but for average use something in the 0.9 to 1.1 mm range is best.

Because of the way a suction feed gun is made, it tends to apply an uneven layer on anything but vertical surfaces. This is because paint in a tipped container will flow over the vent in the cup cover. The only partial solution is to unplug the vent periodically and keep it toward the rear of the cup. The same air flow that atomizes and sprays the paint creates a siphon. If very large areas are being painted, where the fluid adjustment is wide open for maximum pattern, the atomization pressure can get as high as 35 to 40 pounds (2.0 to 2.8 bar), which means the pressure required to operate the siphon is greater than that required to atomise the paint. The pressure feed gun eliminates most of the disadvantages of the suction feed gun, but it requires more skill because it applies a greater volume of paint in less time.

The main trigger on a spray gun is not simply an on/off switch, it has two distinct stages of operation. Initial pressure on the trigger operates the *air valve* to allow compressed air to flow from the *air holes* in the *air cap* at the front of the gun. Pulling the trigger beyond the first stage progressively

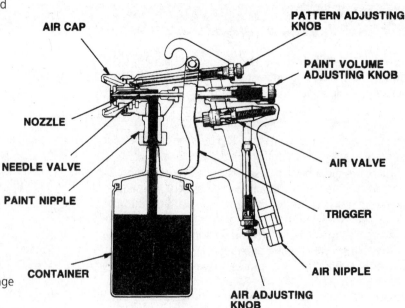

AIR CAP

PATTERN ADJUSTING KNOB

PAINT VOLUME ADJUSTING KNOB

NOZZLE

NEEDLE VALVE

PAINT NIPPLE

AIR VALVE

TRIGGER

AIR NIPPLE

CONTAINER

AIR ADJUSTING KNOB

Suction feed spray gun components

operates the *fluid needle*, which allows paint to flow from the *fluid tip*. Note that the trigger should always be pulled fully back against its stop when spraying, to ensure a consistent spray pattern.

The fluid needle can be adjusted using the *fluid control knob*. The fluid control knob controls the maximum movement of the fluid needle, and can be used for fine control of the quantity of paint sprayed.

An *air needle* is fitted, which can be adjusted using the *air (fan) control knob*. The air needle controls the quantity of air allowed into the air passages which leads to the air cap. Note that the air (fan) control knob does not control the air pressure, it is used purely for fine-tuning of the airflow when adjusting the spray pattern.

The fluid and air (fan) control knobs are normally located at the rear of the spray gun, above the handle. On most spray guns, the lower adjustment knob is the fluid control knob, and the upper adjustment knob is the air (fan) adjustment knob.

Some spray guns are fitted with a fine air pressure control which allows fine adjustment of the air pressure reaching the gun. It's common practise to fit an air pressure gauge either between the air supply line and the spray gun, or in the air supply line close to the gun; this allows the air pressure to be easily checked during spraying.

Setting up the gun for spraying involves balancing the air (fan) and paint controls to suit the type of paint being sprayed, and the pressure at which it is being sprayed.

It is absolutely imperative to keep all spray painting equipment as clean as possible – that means cleaning the gun after each and every use. If the gun isn't cleaned, the paint will dry in those difficult to clean nozzles. When cleaning a suction feed gun, loosen the cup and hold the gun handle over it with the siphon tube inside the container. Unscrew the air cap several turns, then cover the cap with a rag and pull the trigger. Air pressure will be diverted through the fluid passages and will force any paint in the gun back into the cup.

Empty the cup and clean it thoroughly with thinners (often called 'gunwash'), then pour a small amount of thinners into it. Spray the thinners through the gun to flush the fluid passages. It's a good idea to keep a small can of thinners ready for gun cleaning. Either wipe the gun housing with a rag and thinners or use a bristle brush (the preferred method).

The air cap should be removed and cleaned by soaking it in clean thinners. Dry the cap with compressed air. If the small holes are plugged, soak the cap longer, then open the holes with a toothpick. DO NOT use a metal object as it may enlarge the orifice.

Never soak the entire spray gun in solvent, as this allows sludge and dirt to collect in the air passages or removes lubricants necessary for smooth gun operation. The lubricant points include the fluid needle valve packing, air valve packing and trigger bearing screw. The fluid needle valve can

be lightly coated with petroleum jelly. Never use a caustic alkaline solution to clean a spray gun, as it will corrode the aluminium and die cast parts. It takes only minutes to clean a gun shortly after use, but sometimes the cleaning requires hours if the gun has been left uncleaned for a long period of time.

Servicing a spray gun

Note: *The following strip-down and cleaning sequence shows the procedure for the DeVilbiss conventional (non-HVLP) JGA spray gun, but the procedure for most other common spray gun types will be similar. Refer to the spray gun manufacturer's information for specific details.*

General

Spray gun overhaul should be carried out in accordance with the manufacturer's recommendations. Major overhaul is unlikely to be required unless there's been a noticeable deterioration in the performance of the gun.

Dismantling

Note: *For cleaning and minor servicing, proceed as described in steps 1 to 4 inclusive. For major overhaul, follow steps 1 to 10.*

1 Air cap removal

Unscrew the air cap from the front of the spray gun **(see illustration 9.1)**.

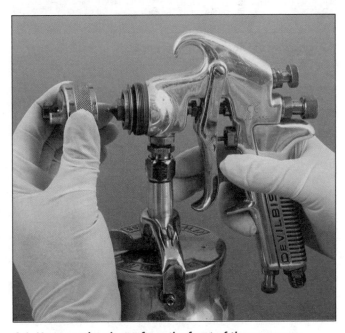

9.1 Unscrew the air cap from the front of the spray gun

2 Fluid needle removal

Unscrew the fluid adjustment knob, and withdraw the adjustment knob and spring, then carefully withdraw the fluid needle. Unscrew the bushing from the gun body using a spanner **(see illustrations 9.2, 9.3 and 9.4)**.

3 Fluid tip removal

Slacken the fluid tip using a spanner or socket, then continue unscrewing the fluid tip by hand. Gently prise off the baffle and seal to inspect for damage **(see illustrations 9.5, 9.6, 9.7 and 9.8)**.

4 Paint reservoir and diaphragm removal

Release the securing clip and remove the paint reservoir from the reservoir cover/paint pick-up tube (or unscrew the reservoir as applicable) **(see illustration 9.9)**.

Pull the paint filter from the end of the pick-up tube, then withdraw the diaphragm from the reservoir cover, and slide it down over the paint pick-up tube **(see illustrations 9.10 and 9.11)**.

5 Air (fan) control removal

Slacken the air (fan) control knob bushing, using a spanner,

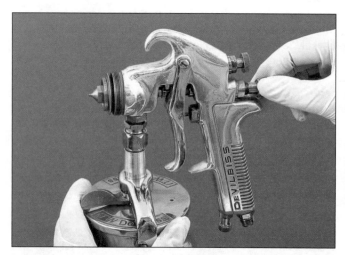

9.2 Unscrew the fluid adjustment knob . . .

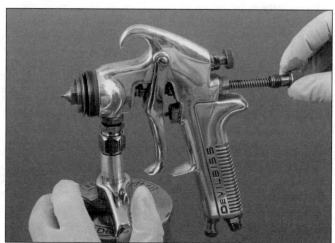

9.3 . . . and withdraw the adjustment knob and spring . . .

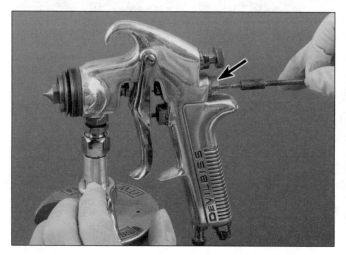

9.4 . . . then carefully withdraw the fluid needle. Bushing arrowed

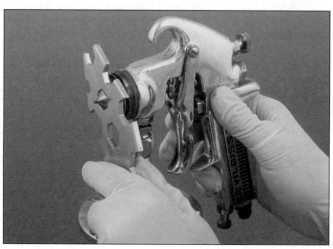

9.5 Slacken the fluid tip using a spanner or socket . . .

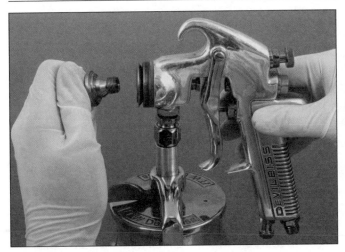

9.6 . . . then continue unscrewing the fluid tip by hand

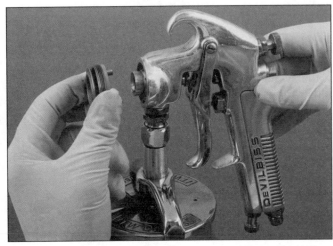

9.7 Gently prise off the baffle . . .

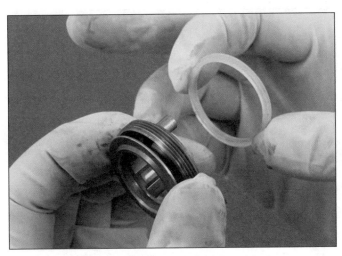

9.8 . . . and seal to inspect for damage

9.9 Remove the paint reservoir . . .

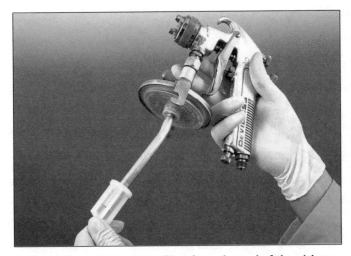

9.10 . . . then pull the paint filter from the end of the pick-up tube . . .

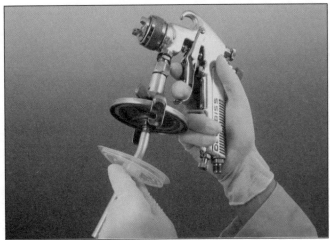

9.11 . . . and withdraw the diaphragm

then continue to unscrew the bushing by hand, and withdraw the bushing and air needle assembly **(see illustrations 9.12, 9.13 and 9.14)**.

6 Fine air pressure control removal (not applicable to HVLP spray guns)

Where applicable, slacken the fine air pressure control knob bushing, using a spanner, then continue to unscrew the bushing by hand, and withdraw the bushing and air pressure valve assembly **(see illustrations 9.15 and 9.16)**.

7 Trigger removal

Using two screwdrivers, counterhold the trigger pivot, and unscrew the pivot retaining screw. Remove the pivot,

retaining screw, and the trigger **(see illustrations 9.17 and 9.18)**.

8 Paint reservoir cover/paint pick-up tube removal

Using an open-ended spanner, unscrew the paint reservoir cover retaining nut, then continue to unscrew the nut by hand, and remove the reservoir cover/paint pick-up tube **(see illustrations 9.19 and 9.20)**.

9 Air valve removal

Slacken the air valve using a spanner, then continue to unscrew the air valve by hand. Withdraw the air valve assembly, complete with the spring, from the gun body. Remove the plastic seal ring from the air valve assembly, then

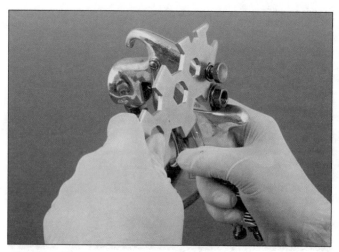

9.12 Slacken the air (fan) control knob using a spanner . . .

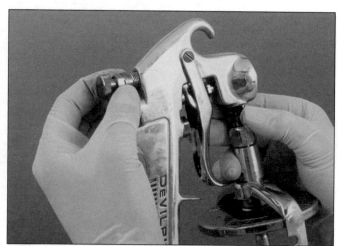

9.13 . . . then continue to unscrew the bushing by hand . . .

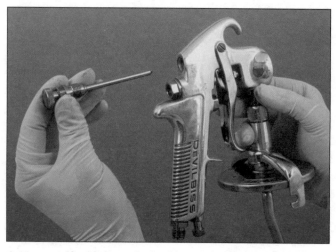

9.14 . . . and withdraw the bushing and air needle assembly

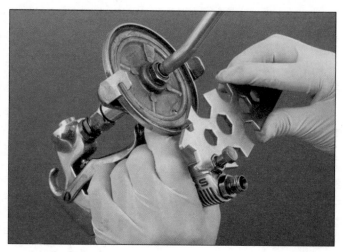

9.15 Slacken the fine air pressure control knob bushing using a spanner . . .

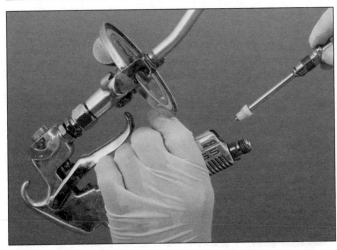

9.16 ... then withdraw the bushing and air valve assembly

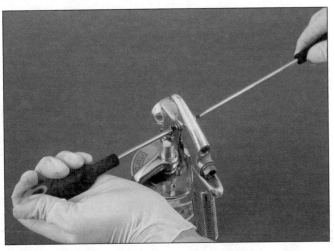

9.17 Counterhold the trigger pivot and unscrew the pivot retaining screw . . .

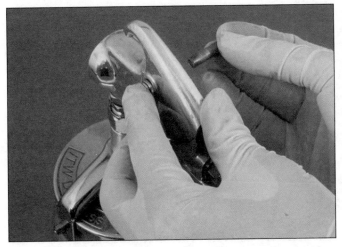

9.18 ... then remove the pivot, retaining screw and trigger

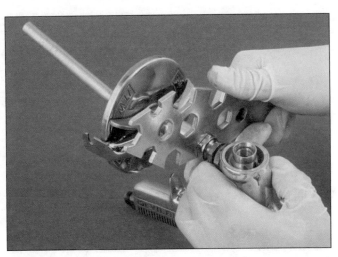

9.19 Unscrew the paint reservoir cover retaining nut . . .

9.20 ... then remove the reservoir cover/paint pick-up tube

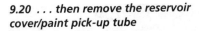

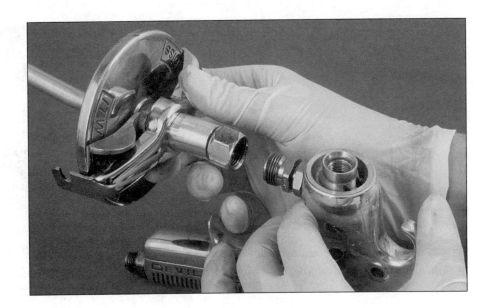

withdraw the control rod/spring assembly from the valve **(see illustrations 9.21, 9.22, 9.23 and 9.24)**.

10 Fluid needle packing piece removal

Using an open-ended spanner, slacking the fluid needle packing piece retaining nut, then unscrew the nut by hand. Carefully lever the packing piece from the gun body, using a small blunt instrument, taking care not to damage the surfaces of the gun body **(see illustrations 9.25 and 9.26)**.

Reassembly

Note: *When lubricating spray gun components, always use the manufacturer's recommended gun lubricating oil where possible.* ***Do not*** *use silicone-based oil.*

1 General

With the gun fully dismantled, clean the paint and air holes in the gun body using a suitable brush. Also clean the paint pick-up tube **(see illustrations 9.27 and 9.28)**.

2 Air valve

Check the condition of the valve components, and renew any components which show signs of wear or damage. Check that the valve stem is not bent. Renew the plastic seal ring at the rear of the valve as a matter of course **(see illustration 9.29)**.

On JGA and GFG guns, the wire circlip can be removed from the front of the valve to allow inspection of the front seal. Renew the seal if there are any signs of wear or contamination.

Reassemble the air valve components, renewing the sealing ring(s) where necessary, then lubricate the assembly just below the rear seal **(see illustration 9.30)**. Screw the assembly into the gun body by hand, then carefully tighten the valve using a spanner.

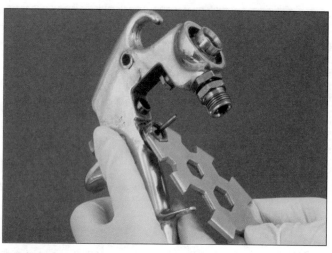

9.21 Slacken the air valve using a spanner . . .

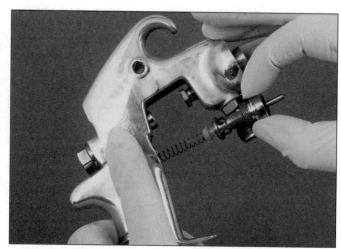

9.22 . . . then withdraw the air valve assembly, complete with spring, from the gun body

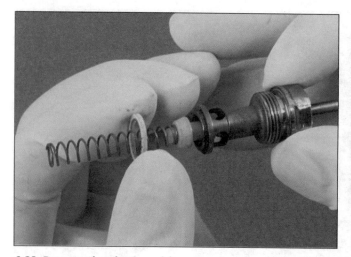

9.23 Remove the plastic seal from the air valve assembly . . .

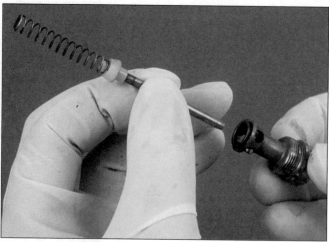

9.24 . . . then withdraw the control rod/spring assembly from the valve

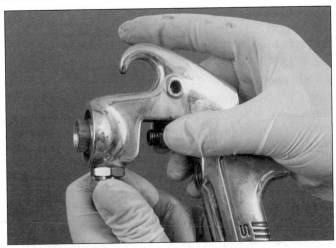

9.25 Unscrew the fluid needle packing piece retaining nut . . .

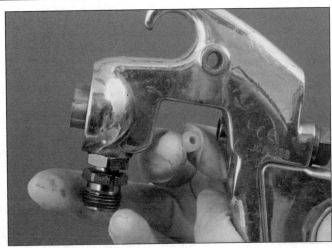

9.26 . . . then carefully lever the packing piece from the gun body

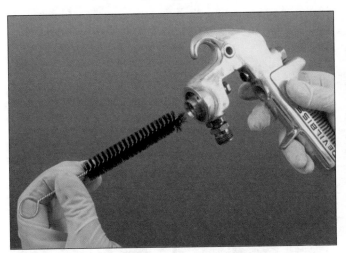

9.27 Clean the paint and air holes in the gun body . . .

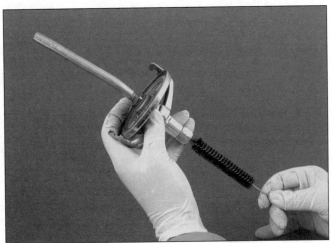

9.28 . . . and the paint pick-up tube, using a brush

9.29 Renew the plastic seal ring at the rear of the air valve as a matter of course

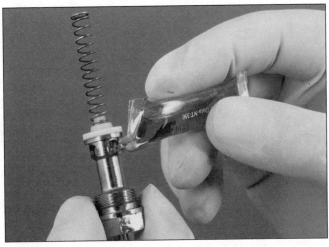

9.30 Lubricate the air valve assembly just below the rear seal

3 Fluid needle packing piece

Carefully fit a new fluid needle packing piece to the gun body (with the wide end facing towards the front of the gun) **(see illustration 9.31)**. Refit the packing piece retaining nut, and tighten **finger-tight only**.

> **hint** *Do not fully tighten the nut until the fluid needle is in position.*

4 Fluid tip

Soak the fluid tip in gun cleaner, then if necessary clean the hole in the fluid tip using a wooden stick or a brush – **do not** use wire or a metal rod. After inspection and cleaning, blow through the fluid tip using an air line.

Check the condition of the baffle and seal ring. Check the seal ring for cracks, holes and splits, and renew if worn or damaged.

Check the condition of the fluid needle (see step 7) before refitting the fluid tip.

Where necessary, fit a new seal to the rear of the baffle, then refit the baffle to the gun body **(see illustration 9.33)**. Refit the fluid tip, and tighten gently using a spanner or socket.

5 Fine air pressure control

Note: *Not applicable to HVLP spray guns.*

Check the condition of the rubber O-ring on the control assembly, and renew if necessary **(see illustration 9.34)**. To renew the O-ring it will be necessary to remove the circlip securing the control rod to the bushing. On JGA guns, renew the O-ring as a matter of course. Lubricate the O-ring with a little petroleum jelly before screwing the assembly back into the gun body. Tighten the bushing using a spanner.

6 Air (fan) control

Check the condition of the rubber O-ring on the control assembly, and renew if necessary. To renew the O-ring it will be necessary to remove the circlip securing the air needle to the bushing. Lubricate the O-ring before screwing the assembly back into the gun body **(see illustration 9.35)**. Tighten the bushing using a spanner.

7 Fluid needle

Check the fluid needle for wear and contamination (see Haynes Hint below). Needles which have been in use for some time are prone to suffering from wear rings, which will show up as narrow shiny bands around the needle **(see illustration 9.36)**.

Clean off any paint contamination, but do not use abrasive products, as they are likely to damage the needle **(see illustration 9.37)**. If noticeable wear is found on the needle, the needle and fluid tip should both be renewed.

Inspect the seal on the needle adjustment control bushing, and renew if necessary. Screw the bushing into the gun body, and tighten gently with a spanner.

Carefully slide the fluid needle into the gun.

Lubricate the bushing, then refit the adjustment knob, ensuring that the spring is in place **(see illustration 9.38)**.

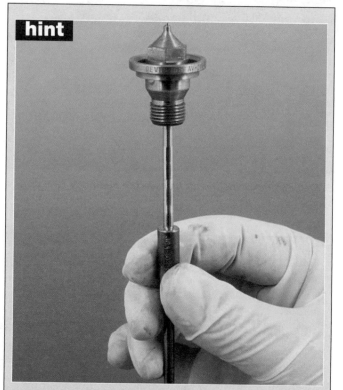

hint

Hold the fluid needle vertically, with the tapered end facing upwards, and slip the fluid tip over the end of the needle. Gently shake the needle. There should be very little movement between the fluid tip and the needle; if the fluid tip is loose on the needle, the needle and/or tip are worn, and both components should be renewed

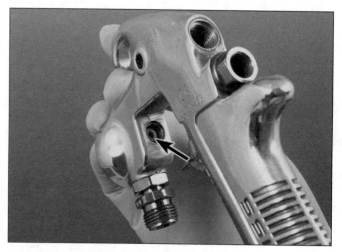

9.31 Fit a new fluid needle packing piece (arrowed), with the wide end facing towards the front of the gun

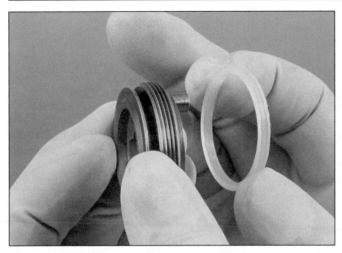

9.33 Fit a new seal to the rear of the baffle

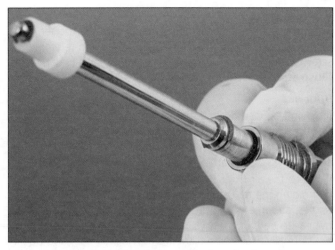

9.34 Check the condition of the O-ring on the fine air pressure control assembly

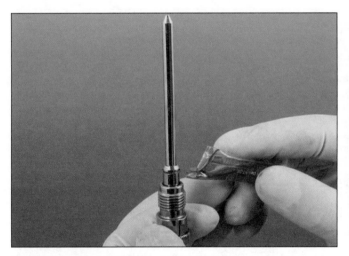

9.35 Lubricate the air (fan) control O-ring

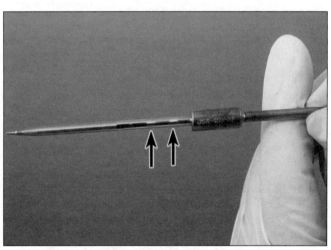

9.36 Check the fluid needle for wear rings (arrowed)

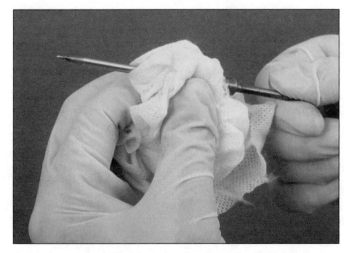

9.37 Clean any paint contamination from the fluid needle

9.38 Lubricate the fluid needle bushing

8 Trigger

Slide the trigger into position, then lubricate the trigger pivot, and refit and tighten the trigger pivot and retaining screw using two screwdrivers, as during removal **(see illustration 9.39)**.

9 Air cap

On some guns, if desired, the air cap itself can be separated from the retaining ring by using long-nosed pliers to remove the clip inside the retaining ring. Soak the air cap in gun cleaner, and clean with a bristle brush.

Check the air holes in the air cap for damage or blockage by holding the air cap up to the light (tilt the air cap at right-angles, as some of the drillings may be at an angle, and may appear to be blocked if viewed with the cap head-on). There are normally four holes in the front of the air cap, and one in each of the air horns. The air holes can be cleaned using a wooden stick or a brush – **do not** use wire or a metal rod. After inspection and cleaning, blow through the air holes using an air line. Also check that the air cap horns are not bent **(see illustrations 9.40 and 9.41)**.

Screw the air cap into position, and tighten securely by hand.

10 Paint reservoir cover/paint pick-up tube

Offer the paint reservoir cover/paint pick-up tube into position, with the pick-up tube angled towards the front of the gun, then tighten the retaining nut securely using a spanner.

11 Paint reservoir and diaphragm

Check the diaphragm for splits, and check that the air hole in the diaphragm is clear. If any damage or wear is evident, renew the diaphragm. If a major gun overhaul is being carried out, renew the diaphragm as a matter of course.

Slide the diaphragm over the paint pick-up tube and position it on the paint reservoir, ensuring that the holes in the diaphragm and reservoir cover are aligned.

Fit a new filter to the end of the paint pick-up tube.

12 Finally

Lubricate the fluid needle by applying one of two drops of spray gun lubricant, just ahead of the packing piece retaining nut.

Pull the trigger and tighten the needle packing piece retaining nut **by hand**. Pull and release the trigger whilst backing off the packing piece retaining nut until the trigger and needle move smoothly.

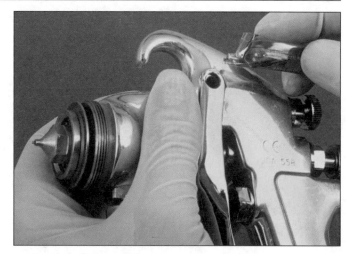

9.39 Lubricate the trigger pivot

9.40 Check the air holes (arrowed) in the air cap for damage and blockage

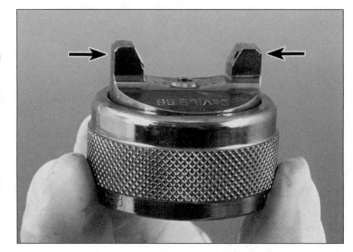

9.41 Check that the air cap horns (arrowed) are not bent

Air compressors

Air compressors are normally classified as single or two stage. The single stage unit has a single cylinder and will produce about 100 psi (6.9 bar). A two stage unit has twin cylinders of unequal size with an intercooler between the cylinders and will pump well over 100 psi (6.9 bar). In the two stage design, air is compressed first in the large cylinder, then it's compressed further by the small cylinder before being fed into the high pressure storage tank.

The size of compressor needed will depend entirely upon what the job calls for. A do-it-yourselfer working at home can usually do very well with a single stage compressor that will hold at least 60 psi (4.1 bar) while the gun is being operated. A paint gun requires on average 8.5 cubic feet (240 litres) per minute of air.

Seldom included with a new compressor is a regulator, which is used to maintain a close check on the air supply to paint guns. The regulator also prevents oil, water and dirt from entering the air lines. The regulator has numerous filter elements to trap foreign materials and a drain in the sump to release oil and moisture. Gauges on the regulator show exactly how much pressure is available and how much is being used.

Respirators

Another very important piece of equipment needed when applying paint with a spray outfit is a respirator, which filters out fumes, dust and dirt that would otherwise enter your lungs. You can't overstate the importance of a respirator, so buy a good one and use it correctly. Never mix or spray primer or paint, especially in an enclosed area, without one! If you're going to spray two-pack (2K) paint, you <u>must</u> use an air fed mask. Here fresh air is fed to the inside of the mask by a separate hose from the regulator.

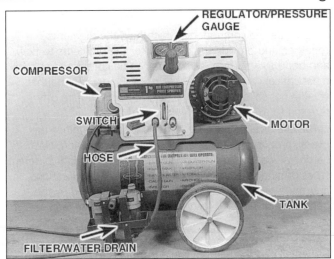

Typical air compressor components

A good respirator is absolutely essential when spraying paint (note that some paints – acrylic 2-pack etc. – often require SPECIAL RESPIRATORS/AIR FED MASKS – be sure to read the paint can label carefully and follow all instructions)

Paint types

Paint constituents

Paints are designed to give protection to the surfaces to which they are applied, and to give an attractive decorative finish. The fundamental principle behind all paints is that they are manufactured, handled, stored, and applied as liquids, which then harden to form a protective solid film of the desired finish.

Paints are made up of three main groups of components; pigments, binders and solvents. Additional additives are normally used to give the paint specific characteristics.

Pigments

Pigments give a paint its colour and opacity, and are responsible for the bulk of the paint. Pigments consist of very fine particles of solid material which are not soluble in the binder. There are two different types of pigments which

are used together to give a paint its colour and 'body'. 'Finish' pigments give the paint its colour, and may be used to give the finish special effects (eg, aluminium and mica pigments give metallic and pearlescent effects respectively). 'Extender' pigments affect the paint's 'body' and durability, including factors such as the adhesion properties, and the ease with which the paint can be sanded and compounded when it has cured. Additional special pigments may be used to give the paint certain properties such as protecting the substrate from corrosion.

Most modern paints are 'high solid' paints, which contain increased amounts of pigment to give greater coverage. High solid paints tend to achieve a good quality finish with very few coats when compared with conventional paints.

Chapter 9

Binders

Binders are the components which hold the pigments together, and provide the medium for the pigments to flow and bond to a surface, so binders can be considered as the most critical components of the paint. Binders are neither volatile nor solid when the paint has dried, and are often referred to as 'resins'.

The chemical composition of the binder determines the overall properties of the paint, such as the adhesion, elasticity, hardness, weather resistance, and method of drying. Different types of binders are available to suit different applications, and the type of binder used in a paint is indicated by the general paint type; eg, acrylic, polyester, cellulose, etc.

Solvents

Solvents keep the paint in liquid form during manufacture and storage, and they control the viscosity of the paint. The solvents evaporate as part of the drying process after the paint has been applied. No solvents remain in the final coating paint film which bonds to the panels.

If paint is required to be less viscous (or more liquid), it can be thinned using a solvent-based thinner. The main paint solvent and thinner do not necessarily have to have the same chemical composition, but both the solvent and the thinner must have a chemical composition which is compatible with the binder.

There are two distinct groups of solvents which are used in automotive paints, and these give rise to two groups of paints:

Solvent-based paints

Contain solvents and thinners consisting of Volatile Organic Compounds (VOCs), such as acetone, petroleum products, and butyl acetate. Solvent-based paints are usually stored in metal containers.

Water-based paints

These are paints in which water forms the main constituent of the solvent and thinner (the paint still contains some solvent). Water-based paints are normally stored in plastic containers to prevent corrosion problems.

Note that water-based paints are fully compatible with solvent-based paints, and a solvent-based paint can be sprayed over the top of a water-based paint (and *vice versa*) with no adverse effects.

Water-based paints were developed to alleviate environment concerns regarding cellulose and acrylic (2-K) paints, which are solvent based. It's this evaporating solvent that's deemed to be harmful to the environment. The curing principle is similar to cellulose paints, but instead of the solvent evaporating, the water does. Consequently, instead of using heat to speed up the curing process, water-based paints are cured by increasing the air flow over the painted surface – blowing the paint dry!

Because they are much less toxic than 2-K paints, water-based paints are a good proposition for the DIY-er. The only drawback is cost – water-based paints are much more expensive.

Additives

Various different additives may be used depending on the type and application of the paint. Additives can be used to prevent oxidation, thicken the paint, give the paint a matt appearance, change the way in which the paint flows, and to control various other attributes.

Types of paint

The types of paint used for automotive refinishing work can be broadly divided into two groups. The first group consists of paints which dry through solvent evaporation or by oxidation of the binder (sometimes called 'lacquers' – not to be confused with clear-coat lacquer finishes). The second group consists of paints which dry due to a chemical reaction between two or more elements (often called 'enamels'). Both groups of paint contain solvents, and initially, the solvent contained by the 'lacquers' evaporates in the same way as the 'enamels', but then a chemical reaction takes place to finish the drying process. The chemical reaction can be triggered in a number of ways, but oxidation, heat, or the presence of a catalyst or activator are the most common. 1-pack acrylic, cellulose and synthetic paints fall into the 'lacquers' group, whilst 2-pack acrylic and 2-pack polyurethane paints fall into the 'enamels' group.

Note that solvent evaporation occurs during the drying of all types of paint, but does not necessarily affect the drying process.

Cellulose paints

Cellulose paints fall into the 1-pack category, and were once the industry standard. Cellulose paints have now been almost entirely superseded for professional use by modern 2-pack alternatives, although cellulose paint is still widely available for DIY and classic/restoration use.

1-pack paints ('1K', or '1C' paints)

1-pack paints dry by solvent evaporation. Drying by solvent evaporation is the simplest form of drying. The paint dries because the solvent keeps the paint in liquid form, and as the solvent evaporates, the binder in the paint solidifies. Heat accelerates the drying because it speeds up the evaporation of the solvent. Cellulose and 1-pack synthetic paints are good examples of paints which dry through solvent evaporation.

The chemical properties of cured 1-pack paint are the same as those of the liquid paint, and so concentrated solvent will dissolve the cured paint.

Some 1-pack paints dry by oxidation of the binder, in addition to solvent evaporation; as the solvent evaporates, the oxygen in the air reacts with the binder, causing it to solidify.

1-pack synthetic paints tend to be confined to the commercial vehicle spraying industry.

2-pack paints ('2K', or '2C' paints)

2-pack paints derive their name from the fact that two elements must be mixed in order for the paint to cure. 2-pack colour coats and 2-pack clear coats must be mixed with an activator ('hardener' or 'catalyst') liquid before it can be

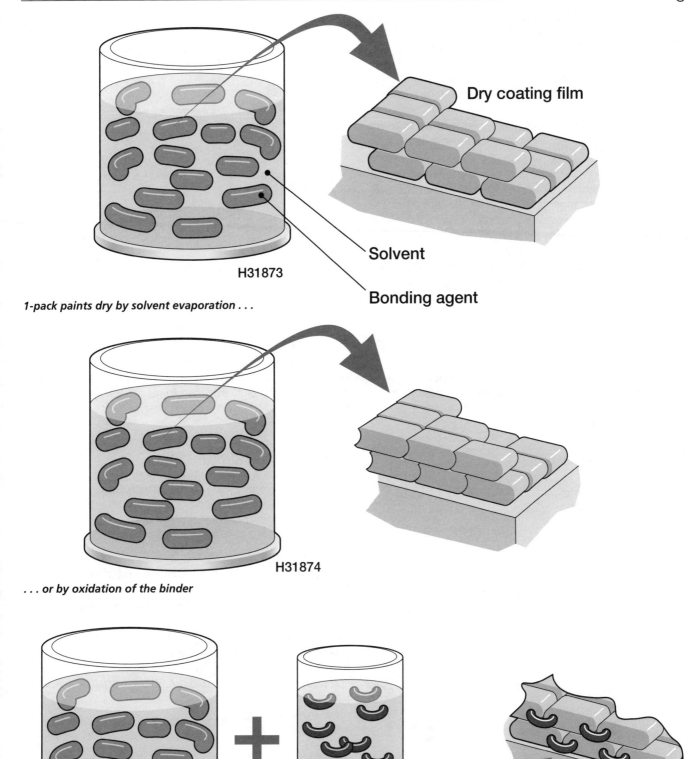

H31873

1-pack paints dry by solvent evaporation . . .

Dry coating film

Solvent

Bonding agent

H31874

. . . or by oxidation of the binder

H31875

2-pack paints dry due to a chemical reaction between two elements

sprayed. Once the colour coat and activator, or clear-coat and activator are mixed, a chemical reaction takes place, and the two liquids eventually form a solid layer through chemical bonding ('polymerisation'). The chemical reaction (curing) can be speeded up by raising the temperature, which is why a low-bake oven or infra-red lamps are usually used during curing.

The chemical properties of the final solid layer are different from those of the two elements, and so the type of solvent used does not affect the properties of the cured paint.

Note that in addition to the base coat or clear-coat and the activator, a third element in the form of thinner is usually added to the mixing formula. The thinner allows the paint to be thinned to give the required viscosity for spraying.

2-pack paints form a very hard finish which is highly resistant to chemical and impact attack. However, 2-pack paints contain Isocyanides which are extremely toxic, and it's essential that an air fed mask is used, and ideally, a proper extraction system with the correct filters etc. Consequently, it's not recommended for DIY use.

Colour coats ('base coats')

Colour coats may contain various different types of pigments. The pigments used determine the colour and the overall effect of the paint finish. The pigments used in colour coats can be divided into three basic groups:

- *Colour coat pigments.*
- *Metallic pigments.*
- *Pearl-effect pigments.*

Base coat pigments

Colour coat pigments are organic or mineral substances which are opaque and colour-fast.

Metallic pigments

Metallic pigments are very fine particles of aluminium. The particles act as tiny mirrors, and give the finish an opaque and metallic quality. The appearance of the finish depends on the number, size and shape of the metallic pigments.

By combining colour coat and metallic pigments, metallic colours can be produced, such as metallic red and blue. If metallic pigments are used alone, silver or metallic grey colours are produced.

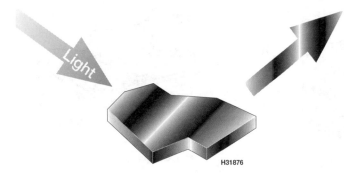
H31876

Metallic pigments reflect light

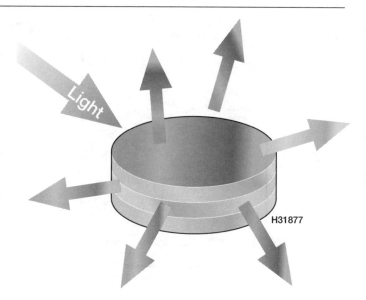
H31877

Pearlescent pigments reflect and refract light

Pearl-effect pigments

Pearl-effect pigments are made from synthetic materials, which are coated with oxides of titanium or iron. The oxide coatings and the pigments themselves are transparent, and the thickness of the oxide coating determines the degree of pearl-effect.

When light passes through the pigments, it's reflected and refracted to give variations in colour.

To ensure that a pearlescent paint layer is fully opaque, the pearl-effect pigments must be mixed with colour coat pigments, otherwise the primer colour will alter the appearance of the pearl-effect paint layer.

Lacquers ('clear-coats')

A lacquer is a transparent clear-coat which is sprayed over the top of a colour coat (solid colour, metallic or pearlescent) to give a high gloss finish. A lacquer is always used with metallic and pearlescent colour coats, and may or may not be used with solid colour coats.

Lacquer coats are sprayed directly onto the colour coat before the colour coat has fully cured. No sanding or compounding need be carried out on the colour coat before the lacquer is applied.

Lacquers are usually 2-pack products.

Tinters

Tinters are the base colours which are mixed together according to the paint manufacturer's specifications to produce a specific colour. Refer to Chapter 12 for more information on matching paint colours and mixing paint.

Once the appropriate tinters have been mixed together, thinner and, in the case of 2-pack paints, activator must be added before the paint can be sprayed.

Many paint additives are also available – be sure to use materials made by a single manufacturer to ensure compatibility

Next to the paint itself, the most important material you'll need is paint thinners

Activators ('hardeners' or 'catalysts')

Activators are used with 2-pack paints. When the activator and the paint are mixed together, a chemical reaction takes place, and the paint begins to cure.

The recommended mixing ratio for the paint and the activator will be given on the paint manufacturer's technical data/application sheet. Refer to Chapter 12 for more information on mixing paint.

Adhesion promoters

When spaying some types of plastic, if the original primer has been damaged, and new primer is to be sprayed onto bare plastic, it may be necessary to use an adhesion promoter in order to ensure that the new primer adheres to the plastic.

Isolators

An isolator can be used to act as a barrier between two incompatible types of paint. For example, if 2-pack paint is sprayed on top of cellulose paint, the solvent in the 2-pack paint may affect the cellulose paint, causing it to soften.

In practice, situations where isolators are required are rare in the body shop, and a suitable primer is usually used to perform the function of an isolator.

Anti-stone chip paint

Anti-stone chip paint is often applied to vulnerable body panels such as the lower edges of wing panels and doors, and front valances. Anti-stone chip paint may provide a smooth finish, or it may dry with a textured finish, with an effect similar to 'orange peel'.

Anti-stone chip paint provides a thick, rubberised layer, which is resistant to penetration by flying stones and road debris. Colour coat can usually be sprayed over anti-stone chip paint to match the surrounding finish.

Painting techniques

Spraying the paint

There are three things you **must** do before you start painting a car. The first is **clean the painting equipment**, the second is **clean the paint**, and the third is **wipe down the car and remove all dust**.

Cleaning the painting equipment, is one of those 'professional' secrets that makes the difference between a good paint job and an excellent finish. No matter how well you cleaned your spray gun after the last time you used it, there's going to be some dirt or dust in it. Getting it out before you start spraying can make a big difference in the final results.

Use compressed air and wax/silicone remover to remove all dust from the car and prepare the surface for the paint – you simply can't get things too clean!

Be sure to blow out all cracks, seams . . .

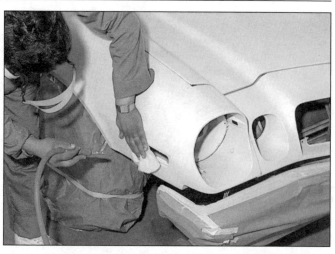

. . . and recessed areas – if you don't, the blast from the spray gun will dislodge dust and other debris, which will end up mixing with the paint

Getting the paint clean is even more important, because no matter how well the paint is mixed, there's bound to be some lumps in it and they can clog up a paint gun in a hurry.

Most paints will have to be thinned before they can be sprayed through the gun and some acrylics need hardeners, activators and other additives. Mix them in first, then use a paint strainer (not a wire strainer, but a professional, one use **paint strainer**), to pour the thinned paint from the can into the spray gun cup.

 Caution: Never pour unstrained paint (or unthinned paint) into a spray gun!

Tighten the locking handle on the spray gun cup securely, but remember that no matter how tight you get it, leaks will happen! Because of the design of the spray gun, the cup is unsealed, and it will leak, if not around the junction between the gun and cup, then out the air hole. And if you don't take precautions, such as wrapping an absorbent cloth around the top of the cup, the leak will drip paint all over the middle of that big panel you just finished spraying without a single run.

Before you start spraying paint at your car, **test the gun!** Set the regulator on the compressor to deliver the recommended air pressure to the spray gun (read the instructions that came with the paint). Turn both the top (pattern) and bottom (paint volume) knobs in all the way, then turn the pattern knob out all the way and the paint knob out until just the first thread is showing. Set up a flat piece of metal against a wall, hold the gun 150 mm from it, pull the trigger all the way back and then release it. There's no need to move the spray gun. All you want to do is get a sample of the pattern or 'fan'.

The pattern you get should be even from top to bottom, with no blank spaces and no overly wet areas. If it isn't, make **small** adjustments to the gun. If they don't result in an even pattern, the gun probably needs a thorough cleaning.

Okay, you've got an even pattern, picking up just the right amount of paint. Now you've got to get your mind, and your hands, to move the spray gun in just the right way to put the paint on the metal in an even layer, without either missed spots or areas so heavily covered with paint they begin to run or sag.

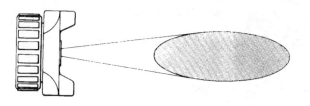

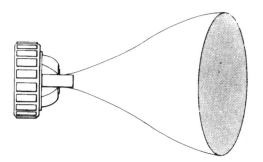

Use the spray gun air cap to adjust the spray pattern orientation

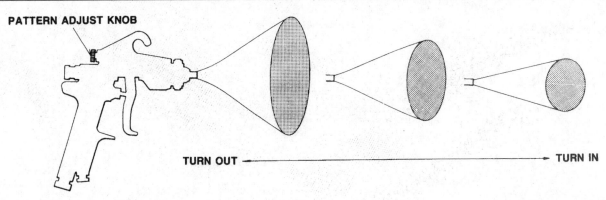

PATTERN ADJUST KNOB

TURN OUT ⟶ TURN IN

The spray pattern width can be changed by turning the pattern adjust knob on the gun – turn it very slowly and see how each adjustment affects the pattern

PATTERN	CAUSE	SOLUTION
FLUTTERING	1. Air entering paint passage from needle valve packing. 2. Air entering between paint nozzle and taper sheet of gun. 3. Air entering from paint container installation nut or paint pipe joint. 4. Insufficient paint in container. 5. Paint passage clogged. 6. Paint viscosity too thick. 7. Container lid hole clogged.	1. Tighten needle valve packing nut. Lubricate or replace packing. 2. Clean taper sheet. Tighten paint nozzle. 3. Tighten joint. 4. Refill with paint. 5. Clean gun. 6. Thin paint. 7. Clean hole.
CRESCENT MOON PATTERN	1. Side holes clogged. 2. Air cap damaged. 3. Paint nozzle clogged. 4. Paint nozzle damaged. Rotate the cap 180°. If the deviation changes, the problem lies with the air cap. CLOGGED	1. Clean side holes. 2. Replace air cap. 3. Clean paint nozzle. 4. Replace paint nozzle.
DEVIATED PATTERN	1. Paint nozzle clogged. 2. Paint nozzle damaged. 3. Paint nozzle not installed correctly.	1. Clean paint nozzle. 2. Replace paint nozzle. 3. Reinstall paint nozzle.
WIDE CENTER PATTERN	1. Caliber of paint nozzle enlarged due to wear. 2. Center hole enlarged. 3. Air pressure too low. 4. Paint viscosity too thick.	1. Replace paint nozzle. 2. Replace air cap and paint nozzle. 3. Raise air pressure. 4. Thin paint.

Spray gun pattern troubleshooting chart

Chapter 9

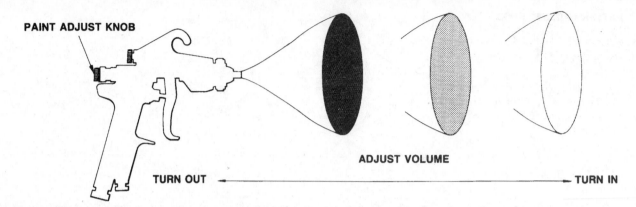

PAINT ADJUST KNOB

ADJUST VOLUME

TURN OUT ← ──────────────────────── → **TURN IN**

The volume of paint exiting the air cap can be adjusted by turning the paint adjust knob on the gun

Hold the spray gun so it's pointing along the panel, but not pointed directly at it, then squeeze the trigger and turn the gun until it's at a right angle to the panel

Just like baseball or golf, the secret is in the swing. Every time you spray paint at the panel, you're going to start with the gun pointed along (not towards) the panel to be painted. **After** you've pulled the trigger and the paint starts to flow, twist your wrist until the gun is pointed **at** the panel, 200 to 300 mm (8 to 12 inches) away. As your wrist brings the gun around to point directly at the panel, your hand should begin to move down the panel, holding the gun at the 200 to 300 mm (eight to twelve inch) distance. Don't move too fast, which would 'fog' the paint on rather than leaving a full coat, and don't move too slow, which would leave runs in the paint. At the end of the panel, don't let go of the trigger – keep it down while twisting your wrist until, once again, the spray gun is pointing down the length of the panel instead of directly at it.

The first time you paint a car, you're going to find the biggest problem you'll have is getting a consistent coat of paint laid on. That's a big part of the reason for the wrist

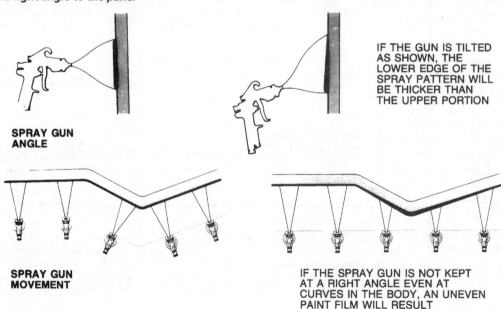

SPRAY GUN ANGLE

IF THE GUN IS TILTED AS SHOWN, THE LOWER EDGE OF THE SPRAY PATTERN WILL BE THICKER THAN THE UPPER PORTION

SPRAY GUN MOVEMENT

IF THE SPRAY GUN IS NOT KEPT AT A RIGHT ANGLE EVEN AT CURVES IN THE BODY, AN UNEVEN PAINT FILM WILL RESULT

The gun must be held at a right angle (in both the vertical and horizontal planes) and moved parallel with the panel to avoid the application of an uneven paint film

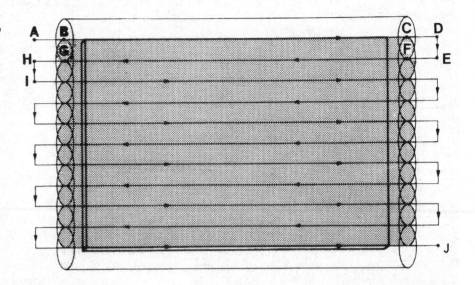

Since the paint thickness is thinner at the outer edge of the pattern, the strokes must be overlapped about 1/3 to 2/3 of the pattern width as shown here

1 The gun is held at point A as the spraying begins
2 Paint application begins at point B and ends at point C
3 The gun is moved down about 1/2 the width of the spray pattern (D to E)
4 From C to F, only air is being discharged from the gun
5 Paint discharge begins again at F and continues to G
6 The gun is moved down again about 1/2 the width of the spray pattern (H to I)
7 The procedure is continued uninterrupted until the entire panel is covered (point J)

motion at the beginning and end of every stroke. It produces an 'overlap' area, where the next stroke can begin without a heavy, uneven build-up of paint. If the paint doesn't overlap evenly, the streaks are going to be very visible when the paint dries.

Here's where you're going to run into the first of the major differences between the different types of paint.

If you're painting with a 2-pack paint, you'll have to take into account the fact that it dries very slowly, and can't be applied all at once. If you try to put a full, heavy coat of 2-pack on a surface, it's guaranteed that it'll run. Instead, the first time around you need to apply what is called a tack coat. That is, a very light, almost fogged on coat of paint. It'll take only a few moments for the tack coat to dry to the sticky to the touch stage, which is just what you want to put the second coat over. The second, heavier coat should be allowed to dry for at least fifteen minutes, then spray on the final coat.

Remember, 2-pack paints dries very slowly. In general, if you don't have a drying oven in your garage, the paint is going to have to dry for two, and maybe even three, days before it's ready to be worked on. If you find some runs that you missed when you were painting, you're going to have to give the paint at least two weeks to cure before they can be sanded out.

Cellulose has one major advantage over 2-pack when painting – by the time you finish putting a coat of paint over the car, the area where you started has completely dried and it can receive a second coat. In addition, with cellulose there's much less danger of runs or sags in the paint, so you can put the paint on a little heavier right from the start. However, several coats are needed, since you'll be cutting into the top coat when sanding and there's always a chance you might sand completely through the paint if you put it on all in one layer. The ideal way to lay on cellulose would be to

spray on several coats, give it two days to dry, colour sand with 600 grit wet or dry sandpaper, then spray on several more coats.

Finishing up

A couple of days after you finish painting, the paint will feel dry to the touch. And it is – on the outside. Underneath, though, the paint's still soft, still wet, and it will be for at least a month. Because of this, don't set anything heavy on the paint unless you want the outline of whatever it was to become a permanent part of the paint job. To allow the paint underneath to dry, don't try to wax the car for at least four months (six would be better), and be very careful when you wash the car. Paint which hasn't had a chance to dry underneath can be scratched very easily, and it can develop permanent water spots if you wash it with anything except cool water and fail to dry it thoroughly with a chamois immediately after washing.

Many paints require colour sanding after painting to bring out the full shine in the paint. Even if colour sanding isn't done, most paints must be rubbed or buffed out to finish the job.

Paints which dry very quickly generally don't flow together. Therefore, there will be a surface unevenness – almost a sandy feel to the finished paint. It's this unevenness that colour sanding and rubbing out is intended to get rid of.

There's no big secret to colour sanding other than using the right materials and knowing when to stop. The right materials are 600 grit wet or dry sandpaper and lots of water. Never use a coarser grade of paper to colour sand. If you let the paper run dry, or fail to wash away the sanding residue from under the paper, chances are you'll scratch the surface, leading to the need for more painting. Keep the water running (this is the time to use a hose – not a bucket of water), make sure you don't scratch the paint with the end of the hose, and sand **only until the surface feels glass smooth**. Check the feel of the surface often, since it doesn't take much to remove the rough top layer.

When you finish the colour sanding, let the car dry completely, and when you look at it you'll swear you've got to go back to step one, take all the paint off, and start all over again. The finish will be dull, probably even streaked looking, and might even have a grey looking uneven film over it. Don't panic – that's the way it's supposed to look.

Now you've got to make the paint shine. For this you're going to need machine polishing compound, hand rubbing compound, a fine rubbing compound and an electric polisher. Renting an electric polisher is the best bet – although you can do the job with a polishing disc on an electric drill. DO NOT try to use a high speed machine like a body grinder with a polishing wheel on it or you'll go right through the paint.

That's the biggest problem the first time painter is going to have when rubbing out a paint job – going completely through the paint. Rubbing out requires a very light touch. Go slow, and use water if necessary to thin the rubbing compound. At this point, you're probably figuring that the

safe way to do this would be to forget the electric polisher and just do the rubbing out by hand. Well, you could, but it's going to take a **long** time, and you probably won't get as good results as you would with the electric polisher. The rubbing compounds designed for use with an electric polisher are much finer than the hand rubbing compounds, and give a finer finish. But if you try to use the machine compounds by hand, you'll still be polishing when your car stops being transportation and becomes a classic. You'll have enough hand polishing work when doing the spots the electric polisher won't reach.

Once you've gone over the whole car with the rubbing compound, you'll find all the steaks and the film are gone, and the paint shines. But there's one more thing you should do as a final touch. Go over the entire surface with a very soft cloth and liberal amounts of **very fine** rubbing compound. It'll change the shine to a glow.

With the car parked in shade, using cool or cold water and no soap or cleaners, wash the paint thoroughly, then dry it immediately with a chamois. As soon as you have it completely dry, apply a good coat of wax (see Chapter 2), then step back, grin, and pat yourself on the back – you did it!

Troubleshooting

To avoid problems, ensure that the paint is mixed in accordance with the manufacturer's recommendations, and ensure that the paint manufacturer's recommended spray gun set-up data is observed.

This Chapter does not aim to provide comprehensive information on all the possible faults which may be encountered during refinishing work, but aims to deal with

the most common faults which are likely to be visible in the final finish, particularly those likely to be encountered by inexperienced sprayers.

The recommendations appearing in this table apply primarily to modern 2-pack paints, but much of the information applies equally to cellulose-based paints, etc.

Acid and alkali spotting

Appearance
Spotty discoloration of the surface (different pigments react differently when exposed to acids or alkalis).

Cause
Chemical change of pigments due to atmospheric contamination, in the presence of moisture.
Battery acid spills.
Brake/hydraulic fluid spills.
Acid rain (near industrial areas).

Prevention
Avoid contaminated atmosphere around finish. If finished surface is contaminated, flush the surface immediately with cool water and detergent.

Remedy
Wash with detergent and water, followed by diluted vinegar.
Sand and refinish.
If contamination has reached the substrate or sub-coating, sand spot down to metal before refinishing.

Bleaching or peroxide bleaching

Appearance
Discolouring of paint surface corresponding to areas of body filler in substrate.

Cause
Excess quantities of hardener (peroxide) used in filler.

Prevention
Take care to calculate and measure hardener quantities accurately.
Observe recommended working temperature of filler.
When using filler in cold ambient temperature, raise ambient temperature.
Do not use extra hardener to compensate.

Remedy
Totally remove affected paint and underlying filler, and start repair process again.

Bleeding

Appearance
Discoloration of the surface of the refinish colour (halo, or complete colour change).

Cause
Solvent from refinishing material dissolves original finish, releasing dye which comes to the surface.
Usually reds and maroons.
Painting white over red colour.

Prevention
Apply 2-pack high-build primer over any areas which it suspected may bleed, before spraying new colour.

Remedy
Either:
• Remove all colour coats, and re-coat.
Or:
• Allow surface to cure, then re-coat.

Blistering

Appearance
Small swollen areas, similar to water blister on human skin.
Lack of gloss in small blisters.
Broken-edged craters if blisters have burst.

Cause
Corrosion under surface.
Paint applied over oil or grease.
Moisture in spray gun lines.
Trapped solvents in paint layer.
Prolonged or repeated exposure to high humidity.
Moisture absorbed in body filler.
Inadequate cleaning of panel surface.

Prevention
Thoroughly clean metal and treat against corrosion.
Frequently check spray gun air line for water.
Ensure paint thinner used is suitable for ambient temperature.
Allow sufficient drying/flash-off times between coatings.

Remedy
Sand and refinish blistered areas.

Chapter 9

Blooming and Blushing (acrylics and lacquer)

Appearance	Cause	Prevention	Remedy
Milky looking finish. Haze or mist on surface.	Incorrect thinner used in high humidity (associated with cellulose paints). Condensation on original finish. Incorrect thinners used in low ambient temperature (associated with cellulose paints). Paint sprayed at correct temperature, then left in lower ambient temperature – paint then absorbs moisture as it cures (associated with flat panel surfaces). Excess activator in paint (usually due to low ambient temperature).	Ensure ambient temperature is not too cold. Keep paint and surface to be sprayed at ambient temperature. Use good quality 'anti-bloom' thinner (cellulose paints). Ensure correct quantity of activator is used.	Either: • Add thinner/activator and re-spray. Or: • Sand and refinish. • Polish paint surface (cellulose paints).

Chalking

Appearance	Cause	Prevention	Remedy
Lack of gloss. Powdery surface.	Natural weathering of paint film. Use of strong traffic film removers. Use of poor quality thinner (cellulose paints). Natural breakdown of main tinter (usually due to age or prolonged strong sunlight).	Mix colour coats thoroughly. Use good quality thinner (cellulose paints).	Sand to remove soft surface material, then clean and refinish (cellulose paints). Use paint restorer/polishing compound. Sand and refinish in severe cases.

Checking, crazing and cracking

Appearance	Cause	Prevention	Remedy
Crowsfoot separation (checking). Appearance similar to shattered glass (crazing). Irregular separation (cracking).	Insufficient drying/flash-off times between coatings. Repeated extreme temperature variations. Excessively heavy coats. Paint constituents not thoroughly mixed. Mixing of incompatible paint constituents. Re-coating a previously checked finish. Thinner attacking the surface of a cured acrylic lacquer (crazing). Solvents or petrol penetrating paint film (especially thermo-plastic acrylics).	Allow sufficient drying/flash-off times between coatings. Avoid extreme temperature changes (hot climates). Spray even coats, avoiding excess, particularly with lacquers. Mix all paint constituents thoroughly. Use appropriate, good quality thinner and activator. Don't re-coat over a checked finish.	Remove damaged paint layer(s) and refinish.

Dirt in finish

Appearance

Foreign particles embedded in paint film.

Cause

Poor cleaning, drying and tacking-off of surface to be sprayed.

Faulty spray gun air cleaner filter.

Dirty working area.

Faulty or dirty spray booth air inlet filters.

Dirty spray gun.

Prevention

Blow out all cracks and body joints using air line.

Use panel wipe and tack cloth on surface before spraying.

Ensure all equipment is clean.

Ensure spray area is clean.

Renew spray booth air inlet filters.

Strain any foreign matter from paint.

Keep all containers closed when not in use to prevent contamination.

Remedy

Rub finish with polishing compound.

If dirt is deep in finish, sand and compound.

Metallic finishes may show mottling after sanding and compounding, and will require additional colour coats.

Fisheyes and poor wetting ('sissing' or silicone marks)

Appearance

Separation of the wet paint film.

Previous finish can be seen in spots.

Craters (smooth).

Dishes (sometimes clustered, or individual).

Cause

Poor cleaning of surface.

Spraying over finishes which contain silicone.

Silicone polishes.

Use of space heaters (paraffin and diesel).

Recently-valeted vehicle.

Finger prints (not wearing latex gloves).

Dried soap.

Washer jet fluid.

Prevention

Use panel wipe to remove all waxes, oils and silicone from surface

Remedy

Remove paint whilst still wet (wash immediately)

Allow paint to cure, then sand and refinish.

Use 'anti-sissing' additive.

Lifting or reacting

Appearance

Lifting and swelling of the wet paint film.

Peeling when the surface is dry.

Crocodile skin.

Cause

Insufficient drying/flash-off times between coatings.

Sandwiching base coat between two layers of acrylic or lacquer.

Spraying onto poorly cleaned surface

Prevention

Clean surfaces thoroughly.

Allow sufficient drying/flash-off times between coatings.

Remedy

Isolate whole surrounding area, then remove paint, and refinish.

Mottling or striping

Appearance	Cause	Prevention	Remedy
Streaks in base coat – with metallic finishes.	Excessive wetting of some areas. Inconsistent film thickness. Poor spraying technique. Poor spray pattern. Incorrect spray gun set-up.	Avoid excessive wetting or heavy film build-up in localised areas. Ensure correct thinner is used. Do not use excessive thinner. Ensure correct spraying technique. Ensure correct spray gun set-up.	If colour is freshly applied, apply a drop coat. Avoid excessive thinner. In extreme cases, if colour has dried, flat down and apply additional colour coat.

Orange peel

Appearance	Cause	Prevention	Remedy
Finish resembles skin of an orange. Finish resembles small ball-pein hammer dents in paint.	Insufficient thinning of paint. Incorrect thinner used. Poor flow from spray gun. Incorrect spray gun pressure. Surface drying too fast.	Check set-up of spray gun. Use correct thinner and activator. Check paint manufacturer's recommended viscosity and spraying/drying temperature.	Either: • Base coat: rub surface with mild polishing compound. • Lacquer: sand or use flatting compound. Or: • Sand and refinish.

Peeling or de-laminating

Appearance	Cause	Prevention	Remedy
Separation of paint film from surface underneath (from primers up to lacquers).	Poor surface preparation. Incompatibility between paint types. Contamination of underlying surface. Etch primer not used on galvanised metal surfaces. Inadequate keying of surface. Surface too hot or too cold when sprayed. Incorrect primer process. Paint film applied too thickly. Final base coat applied far too lightly (lacquer adheres to final base coat and peels). Too much time allowed between base coat and lacquer.	Thoroughly clean and prepare surface. Use appropriate primer. Ensure materials used are compatible with each other and with original finish.	Remove all peeling paint, prepare surface correctly and refinish.

Pitting or cratering

Appearance	Cause	Prevention	Remedy
Small craters. Appearance similar to dry spray or overspray.	Refer to *Blistering* (except that blisters have broken).	Refer to *Blistering*.	Refer to *Blistering*.

Water spotting

Appearance

Dulling of gloss in spots.
Mass of spots which appear as a large distortion of the paint film.

Cause

Spots of water drying on a finish which is not thoroughly dry.
Washing finish in bright sunlight.

Prevention

Don't allow water or rain to contact a newly painted surface.
Don't allow water to dry on a new finish.
Avoid strong sunlight when washing finish.

Remedy

Flat and use polishing compound.
Extreme cases: Sand and refinish.

Wrinkling

Appearance

Puckering of paint surface.
Prune skin effect.
Loss of gloss as paint dries (minute wrinkling not visible to the naked eye).

Cause

Excessive thinners in base coat.
Excessive paint film thickness.
Solvents trapped in surface layer during drying (particularly synthetic finish).
Fresh paint film exposed to heat too soon (particularly synthetic finish).

Prevention

Use recommended type and quantity of thinner and activator.
Check spray gun set-up.
Allow sufficient flash-off time before forced drying.

Remedy

Sand to break open top surface, then allow paint to dry (synthetic paints).
When paint has dried, sand and refinish (sealing with a primer may be needed to cover damaged area).

Runs

Appearance

Running of wet paint film in rivulets.
Mass slippage of entire paint film.
Wavy lines on vertical surfaces.

Cause

Excess thinner and activator with insufficient air pressure when spraying.
Spraying onto cold surface.

Prevention

Check paint viscosity.
Check set-up of spray gun.
Don't spray onto cold surface.

Remedy

Severe cases: Remove paint and refinish.
Minor runs: Flat surface and use polishing compound.

Sags

Appearance

Partial slipping of paint in curtains, caused by a paint film which is too heavy to support itself.

Cause

Insufficient drying/flash-off times between coatings.
Spray gun air pressure too low.
Spray gun held too close to panel.
Incorrect spray gun set-up.

Prevention

Use recommended type and quantity of thinner and activator (eg, fast or slow activator as appropriate).
Allow sufficient drying/flash-off times between coatings.
Check spray gun set-up.
Keep spray gun at correct distance from panel.

Remedy

Sand and refinish.

Corrosion under finish

Appearance

Peeling or blistering.
Raised surface spots.

Cause

Poor preparation of metal.
Broken paint film allowing moisture to creep under surrounding finish.
Water in spray gun air lines (during initial priming).

Prevention

Ensure metal is correctly prepared and primed (using etch primer).
Locate any sources of moisture and rectify.
When refitting trim, take care not to break the paint film, or to allow dissimilar metals to come into contact (this can cause electrolysis which may cause corrosion and/or a loss of adhesion with the paint film).

Remedy

Remove any sources of moisture.
Sand down to bare metal, treat, prime and refinish as necessary.

Doors and glass

Door replacement and adjustment

Glass repair, replacement and adjustment

Door replacement and adjustment

Door replacement

Because they are so susceptible to damage, doors are a common item to be repaired or replaced during body repair. Faced with damage to a door – either from collision or rust – a vehicle owner has essentially three options. If the damage is minor, the original door can be repaired using one of the methods shown elsewhere in this book. If damage or rust is limited to the outer sheet metal, a new door 'skin' can be welded into place on the door frame. Finally, a completely new or used door assembly can be installed to replace a badly damaged door.

If it's decided to repair the door rather than replace it, refer to Chapter 5 or 6 for the proper procedures to follow. Replacing an exterior door skin takes some skill with a cutting torch and welder, so it may be best left to a professional, although additional information can be found in Chapters 6, 7 and 12.

The best bet for the do-it-yourselfer may be to just simply find a replacement and bolt it on. Dealerships and body shops will be able to order new components and most car breaking yards have a large inventory of complete doors awaiting your inspection.

Doors and wings can normally be found in car breakers' yards. Choose a replacement carefully however (check for damage and rusted areas)

When choosing a used door, check it very carefully for damage and/or rust. Determine which parts (like interior trim panel, armrest, mirror, etc.) can be transferred from the original door to the replacement if necessary. Be sure to roll up the window to inspect the glass and verify that the window regulator works properly (manual windows).

Door hinges vary from manufacturer to manufacturer and dictate just exactly how a door is removed and installed. Some models will have a simple bolt on hinge where removal of the bolts allows the door to be lifted away. Other manufacturers use a hinge which is welded in place, incorporating a pivot pin which is driven out for door removal. Most door hinges also have some kind of device to hold the door in an open position. If the hinge, or any part of it, has a spring loaded component, be very careful during removal that the pieces don't fly apart and cause injury.

Before actually removing a door, make sure that all wires and cables leading into it (for power windows, remote mirrors, etc.) have been disconnected. You'll have to remove the trim panel and feed them back through the door jamb. Also keep in mind that car doors can be very heavy and awkward to handle. Support the door during removal and have a strong helper available to lift it away.

Door adjustment

Due to an accident, or merely with age, automotive doors will require adjustment to ensure they latch securely and seal properly against the weatherseal/stripping.

To determine if a door requires adjustment, look carefully at the seams all around the door edges – where the door meets the wings, roof line and lower body panel. The gap all around the door should be uniform. If the space between the door and these panels is narrow in some places and wider in others, the door needs adjustment.

Like removal above, adjustment will be dictated by the type of hinges on the car. With bolt on hinges, the bolts are loosened slightly, the door is repositioned and the bolts are tightened. If welded hinges are involved, adjustment is difficult and in many cases impossible – for these hinges, consult a body repair workshop or Service and Repair Manual for adjustment procedures which may require applying heat or using special tools to bend the hinges.

Before actually loosening any bolts for adjustment, there are a few preliminary steps. First, use a marker or scribe to trace around the bolt heads and the hinge assembly. This will give you a point of reference and allow you to see how much, and in what direction, movement is occurring. Also, plan your moves very carefully – know which direction you want the door to go before loosening the bolts.

With a helper holding the door, loosen the bolts a little at a time until the door can be moved. Adjust the door and tighten the bolts securely. Don't slam the door shut. Instead, slowly swing it to an almost closed position and check the fit of the latch and striker which is bolted to the opposite door jamb. If necessary, the striker can also be adjusted in order to be in alignment with the latch.

When buying a door from a breaker's yard, choose one on the basis of overall condition, rather than trying to match a certain paint color or trim type

Doors are heavy – axlestands with rags as pads are used here for support. In addition, an assistant to help lift the door away is mandatory for this job

When removing a door to be reinstalled later, or adjusting a door for better fit, scribe or trace around the door hinges and bolt heads before loosening or removing anything (to use as a point of reference)

Small chips in the windscreen don't necessarily mean it must be replaced. There are now many repair kits on the market which, when used properly, make the damage disappear. Follow the directions on the package carefully, or seek help from a windscreen replacement specialist who does this work

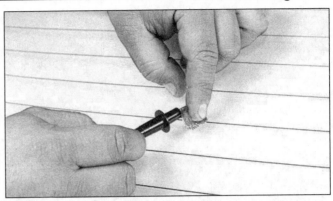

When measuring the voltage at the rear window demisting grid, wrap a piece of aluminum foil around the positive probe of the voltmeter and press the foil against the wire with your finger

Glass repair, replacement and adjustment

Automotive glass will fall into the categories of either laminated safety plate, used for windscreens, or solid tempered plate glass which is used for side and rear windows. Windscreens commonly come with a tinted band across the top and some have radio aerials as well. Many rear windows (and some front windscreens) are equipped with strands of elements which make up an electric window demisting system.

For purposes of removal and installation, automotive glass can be classified as either fixed or opening. Fixed glass is typically the windscreen, rear window and quarter windows. Opening glass would be the door windows and perhaps the rear hatch found on some models.

Glass repair

Minor chips or 'bullseyes' in a windscreen, which once meant replacement, can now be successfully repaired with new kits on the market. These kits use a special clear liquid which fills the damaged area and, when properly done, will leave little evidence of damage and not impair vision through the glass. These kits are commonly available at car accessory shops and some windscreen repairers have started using the procedure as well.

Scratches in window glass can also be repaired in most cases. After using a grease pencil on the inside of the glass to mark problem areas, a creamy paste made from cerium oxide is used to buff out the scratches. A low speed polisher or drill motor with a wool felt polishing pad should be used with light pressure to remove the imperfections.

Another common glass repair job involves fixing the electric grid which runs on the inside of rear windows equipped with this option. Breaks in this grid are common and special repair kits are available at car accessory shops

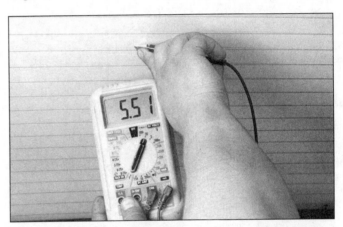

To determine if a wire has broken, check the voltage at the centre of each wire. If the voltage is 5 to 6 volts, the wire is unbroken; if the voltage is 10 to 12 volts, the wire is broken between the centre of the wire and the earth side; if the voltage is 0 volts, the wire is broken between the centre of the wire and the power side

To find the break, place the voltmeter negative lead against the demister earth terminal, place the voltmeter positive lead with the foil strip against the the heat wire at the positive terminal end and slide it toward the negative terminal end – the point at which the voltmeter deflects from several volts to zero volts is the point at which the wire is broken

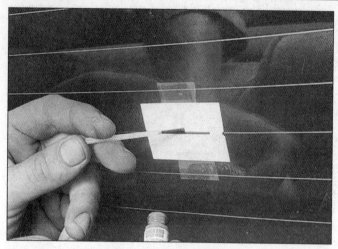

To use a demister repair kit, apply masking to the inside of the window at the damaged area, then brush on the special conductive coating

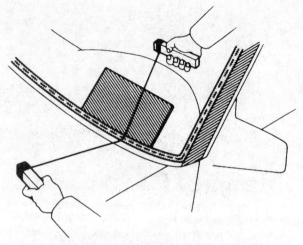

Most late-model windscreens and fixed glass windows have the glass bonded in place. A common removal technique requires a piano wire stretched between two handles. Using a sawing motion, cut all the way around the glass to break the bond

and dealer parts departments. The repair can be done at home and involves filling the grid break with a special silver plastic. The accompanying illustrations will help you locate and repair a break in the grid.

Fixed glass replacement

The most common method of attaching fixed glass is with a special urethane bonding agent which seals the entire perimeter of the glass and remains flexible enough to withstand the constant vibrations of driving. Chrome or painted mouldings sometimes cover the urethane and also help to secure the glass in place.

The exact procedure for replacing a windscreen or fixed window will vary from vehicle to vehicle, but there are many similarities. The first step is to remove all interior and exterior moulding pieces to expose the edge of the glass.

Next, the bond between glass and body must be broken. The most common method of doing this is to feed a length of piano wire just under the glass at the bottom centre of the window and wrap each end of the wire around wooden handles. With one person on the outside of the car and one on the inside, the wire is worked back and forth, all the way around the glass.

This will cut through the urethane, allowing the window to be removed. After a thorough cleaning of the window cavity, the new glass is bonded in place and the window moulding pieces are put back into position.

Although this process may sound fairly easy, in reality there are many pitfalls for the do-it-yourselfer attempting fixed glass replacement. If you decide to attempt this procedure, consult a windscreen replacement company for the special urethane sealers, primers and other materials which may be required.

Some fixed windows – used mostly in pickups and older models – have the glass secured by a rubber weatherseal which goes completely around the window. The weatherseal fits over a flange in the body opening and the glass then sits inside a groove in the inner circumference of the rubber. The glass is removed by gently prising it out of the groove. For installation, a long piece of cord is placed in the groove and when the cord is pulled out, the lip of the weatherseal pops outside the glass, sealing the glass in the groove.

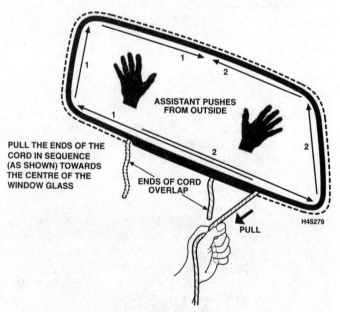

Where a rubber weatherstrip secures the fixed glass to a channel in the body opening, a nylon cord is used to set the glass in place. After installation, the cord is pulled out of the weatherstripping, forcing the lip over the glass

Opening glass replacement

The replacement of door glass is somewhat easier than fixed window glass, but depending upon make and model, is not without its challenges.

Generally speaking, the door glass is either bolted or riveted to a mechanism inside the door called a window regulator. This regulator has a series of arms and gears/cables

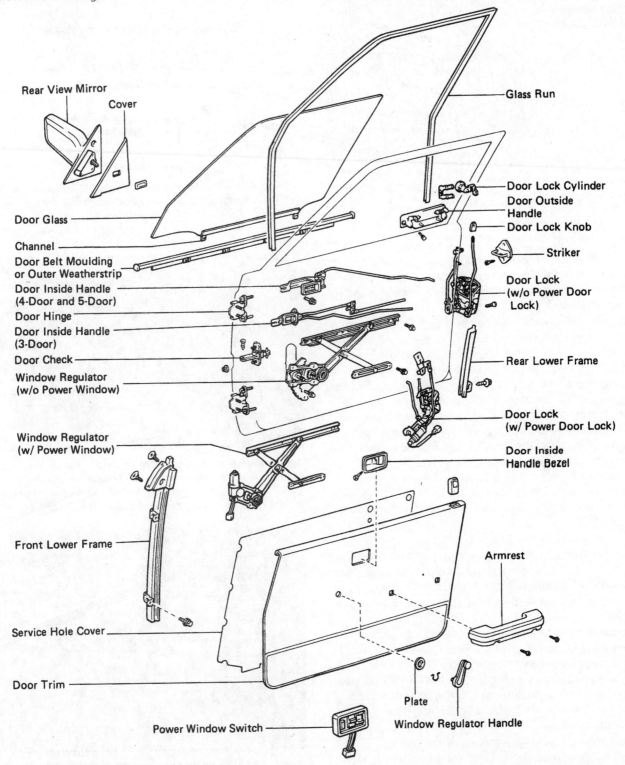

Rear View Mirror
Cover
Glass Run
Door Glass
Channel
Door Belt Moulding or Outer Weatherstrip
Door Inside Handle (4-Door and 5-Door)
Door Hinge
Door Inside Handle (3-Door)
Door Check
Window Regulator (w/o Power Window)
Window Regulator (w/ Power Window)
Front Lower Frame
Service Hole Cover
Door Trim
Power Window Switch
Door Lock Cylinder
Door Outside Handle
Door Lock Knob
Striker
Door Lock (w/o Power Door Lock)
Rear Lower Frame
Door Lock (w/ Power Door Lock)
Door Inside Handle Bezel
Armrest
Plate
Window Regulator Handle

These are the typical components making up a door assembly. Since most parts are hidden from view, study the illustration carefully to learn how each part works

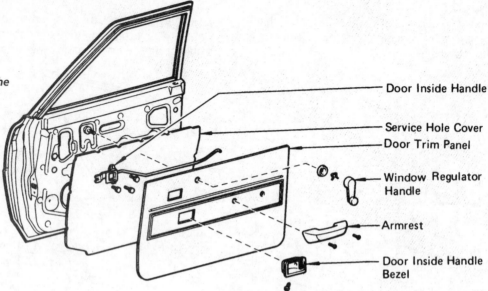

Interior door panels can be tricky to remove. There are usually screws at the armrest with simple push in fasteners around the edge of the panel

- Door Inside Handle
- Service Hole Cover
- Door Trim Panel
- Window Regulator Handle
- Armrest
- Door Inside Handle Bezel

which move the window up or down, with a small electric motor powering the mechanism on models so equipped. To remove the glass, it's unfastened from the regulator and lifted out of place.

To gain access to the regulator and the window attachments, the first step is to remove the interior door trim panel. Once the panel has been pried away and the waterproof membrane has been peeled off, the window to regulator fasteners should be accessible through one of the large holes provided in the inner panel. You may need to raise or lower the window to remove the nuts, or drill out the rivets, but then lower the window before attempting to pull the glass out of the door frame. On some models it may be necessary to remove the door glass stoppers or glass guides in order to pull the window free. For a detailed description of the replacement procedure specific to your vehicle, consult the appropriate Service and Repair Manual.

Glass adjustment

Door window glass can be adjusted to eliminate poorly closing windows that produce wind noise, water penetration and rattles. The window should move smoothly up and down in its tracks and seal evenly in the weatherseal across the top and sides.

To adjust the glass position, remove the interior door trim panel, exposing the bolts which secure the window regulator to the metal inner panel. You will note the regulator mounting bolts are located in slots rather than round holes. Use a pen or scribe to draw around the bolt heads for reference, then loosen the bolts slightly and move the regulator as necessary to adjust the glass.

This may be a lengthy process of making small adjustments, tightening the bolts and then checking the window for fit. Once the window is adjusted properly, tighten all the bolts and replace the door trim panel.

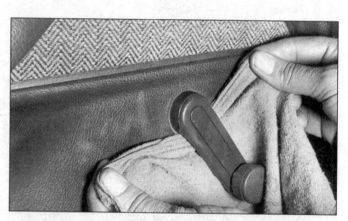

Most window crank handles are secured to the shaft with a horseshoe shaped clip. The clip can be seen by pushing the panel back as much as possible and can be removed by working a cloth back and forth, forcing the clip out of its groove

A screwdriver or pry bar can be used to release the clips from the door. Wrap the blade with tape to prevent damage and work slowly when prying the fasteners out of position

Trim and accessories 11

Introduction

This Chapter covers basic removal and installation procedures for exterior body mouldings, emblems and accessories like mirrors, bumpers and light lenses.

Many times, the components discussed in this Chapter are removed from the vehicle prior to performing body repairs and/or painting. Doing so eliminates the need for careful masking to prevent damage and paint overspray. Removing these items also simplifies the actual painting process, since the paint can be sprayed in nice complete sweeps and not around exterior parts which can easily lead to uneven application.

Not to be overlooked when replacing many of the items discussed in this Chapter is the replacement of the gasket which seals the accessory to the body. Exterior pieces such as door handles, mirrors, taillight lenses and door key lock cylinders often have a gasket or seal to prevent water leaks. With age, this gasket will deteriorate and allow water to enter the body, ultimately contributing to rust damage.

The most difficult part of removing exterior trim and accessories is determining how they are fastened to the body. Manufacturers have used numerous methods of attaching these pieces, from a rear taillight lens attached with wing nuts, accessible only after first removing a trim panel in the luggage compartment, to side moulding attached with special industrial strength double-faced tape.

Trim and accessory removal and installation

Bumpers

Early model bumpers – before the advent of 'energy absorbing' designs – were bolted to the vehicle chassis to help protect the body in the event of an accident. These chrome plated, heavy steel components are often removed prior to painting to simplify the task of getting paint to the body areas behind the bumper, which are often visible but nearly impossible to reach with the spray gun.

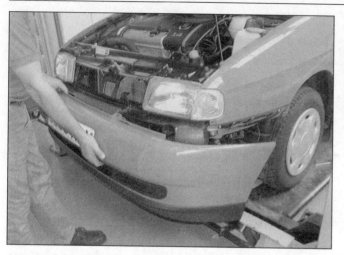

Late model wrap-around bumpers are retained by a mixture of clips and screws

Some mirror designs on classic cars will have screws or bolts visible from the outside, simplifying removal and installation

During a restoration or as a final touch to a new paint job, many vehicle owners will install new, shiny replacement chrome bumpers or have the original ones re-chromed.

Bumper removal is usually quite straightforward, with the bumper attached to the vehicle chassis or chassis brackets with bolts and nuts. Special chrome plated carriage bolts are usually used (the square section of the shank fits into a square opening in the bumper). Before removing the nuts, accessible from under the vehicle, it may be a good idea to first soak the bolt threads with some liquid rust penetrating fluid. These nuts have a habit of 'welding' themselves to the bolt threads due to rust and the elements to which they are exposed.

Late model bumpers are different in design and are made of a composite plastic cover bolted to isolators. These isolators act as shock absorbers to cushion the effects of a low speed crash. The isolators, once compressed in an accident, will usually have to be replaced to restore the bumper to its original position. As replacement of these type of bumpers is different on each model, refer to the appropriate Service and Repair Manual for a detailed procedure description specific to your vehicle.

Mirrors

Externally mounted mirrors can generally be divided into two categories – those which are chrome plated and those which are painted to match the colour of the vehicle (although many are also painted with dull or flat black trim paint). During a paint job, chrome plated mirrors are either covered and masked off, so they can be painted around, or removed prior to painting. Colour coordinated mirrors can be painted right along with the vehicle, as long as the paint type is compatible with the mirror housing, which is usually a plastic.

The mounting of external mirrors is also normally done in one of two ways. Either the mounting screws are accessible from the outside, attaching the base of the mirror to the

A typical late model exterior rear view mirror

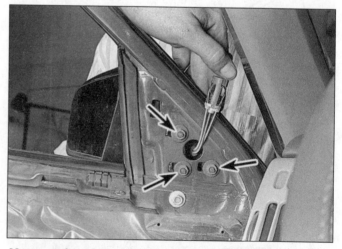

Most exterior mirrors on late model vehicles have the attaching hardware accessible only from the inside of the door (arrowed) – here bolts extend through the door and into the mirror (the adjuster mechanism is in the middle)

body, or the mirror will have threaded studs, which pass through holes in the door, and accept nuts on the inside. With the latter type, the interior door panel is often removed to gain access to the nuts.

If the mirrors are adjustable from inside the vehicle, either electrically or by a manual operated cable, the removal process will be complicated to some degree by the necessary disconnection of the various wires and cables. Work carefully when disconnecting them and mark each wire and cable with pieces of numbered tape to help guide the installation later on. Refer to the appropriate Service and Repair Manual.

Door handles

Exterior door handles come in a variety of types and styles, but generally operate in the same manner by moving a rod inside the door to release the latch mechanism.

The handle can be removed from the door after first removing the interior door trim panel and disconnecting the operating rod from the handle. The rod is usually held in place by a special clip which can be pried off the rod with a screwdriver. The handle itself will be attached to the door by screws threaded through the inside of the door and into the handle, or by captive nuts, such as discussed above for mirrors. During installation, remember to place the appropriate gasket or seal between the handle and the door to prevent water leakage into the door cavity.

If you remove the door handle for a paint job, don't make the mistake of removing the handles without first allowing access to the interior through another door or an open window with the interior handles still connected to the latch mechanism – otherwise you may find yourself in the embarrassing situation of being locked out of your own car.

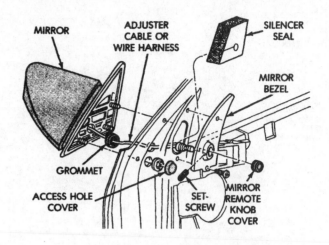

If the mirror is adjustable from inside the car, a cable or electrical wiring will also have to be disconnected to remove it

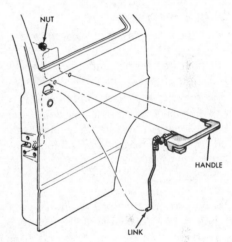

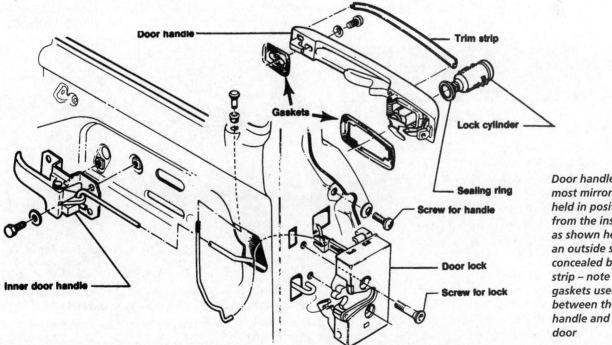

Door handles, like most mirrors, are held in position from the inside or, as shown here, by an outside screw concealed by a trim strip – note the gaskets used here between the handle and the door

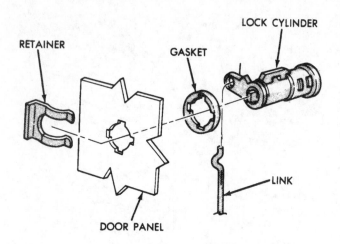

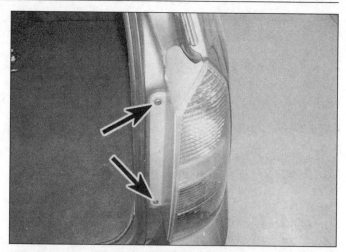

A standard door key lock cylinder will have a gasket and be held tightly by a special retainer clip like the one shown here – the clip can be slid out with a pair of pliers

Some exterior light lenses have screws (arrowed) which are accessible from the outside

Door key lock cylinders

When turned by the key from the outside, the lock cylinder operates the locking mechanism in the door jamb, effectively preventing the door from being opened any other way. The lock cylinder operates the lock either directly, or via a rod.

The lock cylinder is usually attached at the inside of the door by a special retainer which simply wedges around the cylinder housing. Access to the retainer, as well as the operating rod and locking mechanism, is through the inside of the door after removing the trim panel.

Like the door handle and mirror, the key lock cylinder may have a gasket or seal which must be in good condition to prevent water leakage into the door. Some styles will also have a drain hole to drain water which has entered through the key passage; this drain hole must be facing down during installation.

Other light designs incorporate threaded studs with attaching nuts on the inside of the body. Often the bulbs and attaching nuts for the lens are behind inner luggage compartment panels or carpeted sections

Exterior light removal and installation

Exterior light lenses

Exterior light lenses are common replacement items when bodywork is required due to an accident or as a part of a vehicle restoration. These lenses include the taillight lenses and side marker lenses.

The lenses are attached to the body either by screws through the lens, accessible from the outside of the vehicle, or by nuts on the inside of the body panel or in the trunk or cargo area.

It's very important to prevent water leaks at the taillight area when removing and installing taillight lenses. If a gasket or seal is used, make sure it's in good condition. If no gasket is incorporated in the design, sealer (body caulking compound or the equivalent) should be used.

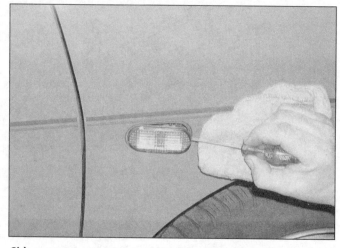

Side repeaters are removed by sliding them forwards or backwards . . .

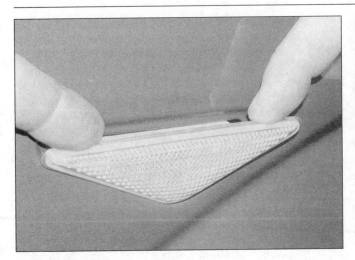

. . . or downwards

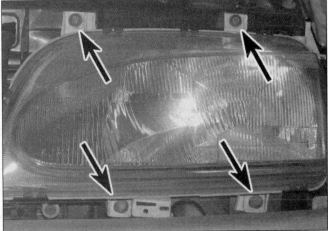

Here the headlamp (Ford Galaxy) is secured to the front panel by four screws (arrowed)

Headlights

Headlights may be either a sealed beam design (up until the mid-'70s) or, in the case of most late models, halogen type. Sealed beams are an all in one headlight and lens assembly, while halogen headlights have a removable bulb. The headlight assembly, whether sealed beam or halogen, is either mounted inside an adjusting bucket or ring, which is in turn secured to the body with spring loaded adjustment screws, or the headlamp body is fixed directly to the vehicle body, with internal adjusters that moved the reflector elements within the headlamp body. In either case, the adjustment screws should not be disturbed during headlight removal and installation. On some models, it's necessary to remove the bumper prior to removing the headlamps – refer to the appropriate Service and Repair Manual.

To remove a conventional sealed beam headlight, begin by removing any trim rings or mouldings which may be around the headlight assembly. With these removed, the headlight can be pulled out of the adjusting ring behind it and the wire harness connector at the rear of the light can be unplugged.

Halogen bulbs are usually removed from the back side of the headlight assembly, so they're accessible from under the bonnet. After unplugging the wire harness and releasing a retainer/clip, the bulb can be pulled out of the headlight reflector.

> ⚠ *Warning: Halogen gas filled bulbs are under pressure and may shatter if the surface is scratched or the bulb is dropped. Wear eye protection and handle the bulbs carefully, grasping only the base whenever possible. Do not touch the surface of the bulb with your fingers because the oil from your skin could cause it to overheat and fail prematurely. If you do touch the bulb surface, clean it with surgical alcohol or methylated spirits..*

Headlight adjustment

Adjusting the headlight aim should be left to a professional with the proper aiming equipment. However, you can make temporary adjustments for a lighting system which is critically out of adjustment.

Each headlight has two adjusting screws: one on the top for controlling up and down movement and one on the side to control left and right movement of the light beam. There are several do-it-yourself ways to adjust the headlights. The simplest method requires a blank wall 8 metres (25 feet) in front of the vehicle and a level surface in front of the wall. Adjustment should be made with the fuel tank half full and no unusually heavy load in the luggage compartment.

1 Park the vehicle on the level surface 100 mm away from the wall.
2 Attach masking tape vertically to the wall in reference to the vehicle centerline and the centerlines of each headlight.
3 Now position a long piece of tape horizontally in reference to the centerline of all headlights.

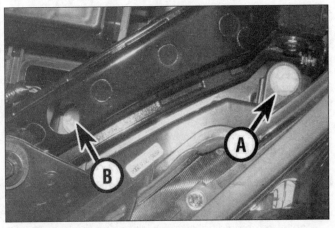

Visible here are the vertical (B) and horizontal (A) adjustment screws at the top of each headlight (Ford Focus)

4 Move the car straight back to a point 8 metres (25 feet) from the wall.

5 Starting with the dipped beam adjustment, turn the adjusting screws to get the brightest area of the light 50 mm below the horizontal line and 50 mm to the left of the headlight vertical line.

6 With the main beams on, the center of the light area should be vertically centered, with the exact center just below the horizontal tape line.

7 Since it may not be possible to position the headlight aim exactly for both main and dipped beams, if a compromise is required, keep in mind that the low beams are most frequently used and have the greatest effect on driver safety.

Emblem and moulding removal and installation

Emblems

Manufacturer's emblems are a common item removed prior to bodywork or painting. Although there are a number of attachment methods used, most exterior emblems, logos and nameplates are easily removed from the various body panels.

There are three common types of attachments used for emblems: threaded studs attached to the emblem and held in place with nuts, unthreaded studs which merely push into holes in the body and an adhesive backing or special cement. It's important that you recognize which method is used before attempting to remove the parts.

Before prising on the nameplate or emblem to remove it, make a thorough check on the rear of the panel for nuts or fasteners which are securing it. Occasionally, inner trim panels, carpet and other decorative items must be removed to inspect the area immediately behind the emblem. Only after checking carefully should you start to prise on the trim piece to loosen it from the body. Prise with a putty knife or screwdriver which has been wrapped with masking tape. This will help prevent damage to the paint and body. Even so, prise very carefully!

Body side mouldings

Body side mouldings, installed to help prevent minor door dents and improve appearance, come in a wide variety of styles and sizes. Like other trim pieces and accessories discussed in this Chapter, body side mouldings are attached by various methods.

When removing mouldings, your first check should be for obvious screws and/or rivets which may be securing the moulding pieces. They are often found inside a door jamb, at the end of a moulding strip, or perhaps on the inside edge of a wheelarch moulding. Next, check behind the body panel for nuts which are attached to threaded studs. It may be necessary to remove interior panels for access to them. If obvious fasteners are not visible, attempt to slide the moulding strip along the body, which in some cases will release the clips and allow the moulding to be removed. Sometimes a vinyl or rubber insert in the moulding can be slid or prised out of an outside railing which will then expose the fasteners to the body. A final method of attachment is with tape or an adhesive, requiring you to gently prise the moulding away from the body with a putty knife wrapped with masking tape.

If the above procedures and the accompanying illustrations fail to help when removing mouldings, consult a Service and Repair Manual for your specific vehicle or seek advice from a body repair workshop.

Colour coordinated body side mouldings are commonly added to a vehicle after body work and painting is complete. They help protect the body and add a final finishing touch to the job. These mouldings are available in kit form from dealer parts departments as well as from car accessory shops. The mouldings are easy to install by following the instructions supplied.

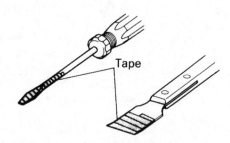

When it's necessary to prise emblems or moldings from a vehicle, use a putty knife or wide blade screwdriver with the end wrapped with masking tape or electrician's tape to help prevent damage to either the emblem or the body

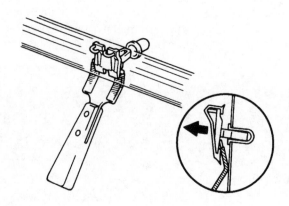

A special curved prising tool is available for removing molding and trim pieces

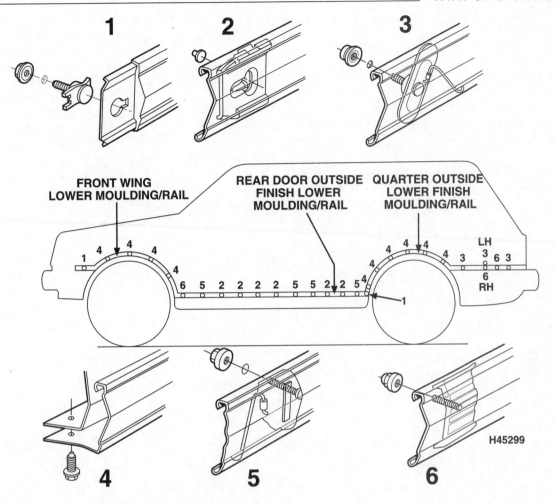

Typical locations of body side mouldings and fastening techniques

Notes

Welding 12

Introduction

There are two basic ways to join metal pieces together – mechanical fasteners (rivets, bolts, etc.) and fusion (welding). Welding is a method of joining metal where heat is applied to two pieces of metal, which 'fuses' them together.

Since body repair occasionally requires welding and flame cutting, anyone interested in doing bodywork should become familiar with the processes and the tools and equipment involved. Chapter 4 includes a brief description of equipment and the types of welding commonly associated with car bodywork.

Like any manual skill, welding requires a lot of practice to become proficient – just make sure you're using the proper techniques and compatible materials or all the practice in the world will be useless. Don't attempt to weld any pieces on a car body until you've become comfortable joining pieces of scrap metal of the same material and thickness. It's better to make mistakes on something that can be discarded easily. If you're really serious about learning to weld, consider enrolling in a welding course – most communities offer adult education or vocational classes designed for learning such

skills (they're usually scheduled in the evenings so they don't interfere with a person's normal work schedule).

Be sure to read the *Safety first!* Section in Chapter 1 before doing any welding or cutting with a torch.

Types of welding

Welding is divided into three main types: *Pressure welding, fusion welding and braze welding* . . .

1 Pressure Welding – In this type, the metal is heated to a softened state, pressure is applied and the pieces of metal are fused together. Of the various types of pressure welding, electric resistance welding (spot welding) is the most common method used in automobile manufacturing and, to a lesser degree, in repair operations.

2 Fusion Welding – In this type of welding, the pieces of metal are heated to the melting point, joined together (usually with a filler rod) and allowed to cool. Electric arc welding and gas welding are the two basic types of fusion welding.

3 Braze Welding – Commonly known as 'brazing'. In this process, metal filler rod with a melting point lower than the pieces of metal to be joined is melted at the joint of the pieces being welded (without melting the base metal). Braze welding is classified as either 'soft' or 'hard' brazing, depending on the temperature at which the brazing material melts. Soft brazing is done with brazing material that melts at temperatures below 450°C (840°F) and hard brazing is done with brazing material that melts at temperatures above 450°C (840°F).

When welding a car or truck body, keep in mind that strength and durability requirements differ, depending on the location of the part that's being welded. The factory decides the most appropriate assembly welding method by first noting the intended use, the physical characteristics and the location of the part as it's assembled. It's extremely important that appropriate welding methods, which don't reduce the original strength and durability of the body, be used when making repairs. This will be accomplished if the following points are observed:

• *Try to use either spot welding or MIG welding*

• *DO NOT braze any body components other than the ones brazed at the factory*

• *DO NOT use an oxy-acetylene torch for welding late model car bodies*

MIG welding

MIG is an acronym for 'Metallic Inert Gas' and is a welding process that utilizes a metallic electrode and a shielding gas that's emitted around the electrode. The gas prevents air from contacting the weld, which eliminates oxidation of the metal and the formation of slag. The term MIG originated when the gases used for shielding the weld were inert (helium and argon – which are still used when welding non ferrous metals). However, carbon dioxide, which isn't really inert, or argon, is used for welding most steels, which is the predominant metal in car bodies. It's very simple to change gas cylinders or regulators and switch from argon or helium to carbon dioxide gas when welding during body repairs.

> **(!)** *Caution: Be sure your work area is shielded from wind of any kind, since the gas must surround the arc at all times; if not, the weld will be brittle and spotty.*

This welding method uses a welding wire that's fed automatically, at a constant speed, as an electrode. A short arc is generated between the base metal (the body components) and the wire. The resulting heat from the arc melts the welding wire and joins the base metal pieces together.

MIG arc welding uses a short arc, which is a unique method of depositing molten drops of metal onto the base metal. The welding of thin sheet metal on automobiles can cause welding strain, blow holes and warped panels. To prevent these problems, the amount of heat near the weld must be limited. The short arc method uses very thin welding rods, low current and low voltage, so the amount of heat introduced into the panel is kept to a minimum and distortion is virtually eliminated.

To summarize, MIG welding characteristics that make it ideal for body repair procedures include . . .

• *Panel warpage and burn-through is minimal*
• *You don't have to be an expert welder to get good results*
• *The temperature around the molten metal is low, which permits a high speed, full penetration weld with good workability*
• *There's little slag generated, so slag removal operations are unnecessary*

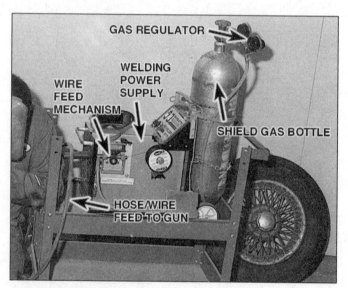

Typical MIG welder

MIG welder in operation

MIG welding equipment

A MIG welder consists of a gun, a wire feed mechanism, a shield gas supply and a welding current power supply. Although they're manufactured by many companies, MIG welder construction and use are common. Be sure to read the instruction booklet accompanying any MIG welder you may be using – if the information with the welder conflicts with anything in this manual, follow the instructions with the welder.

Factors that determine the results obtained with a MIG welder include input voltage (to the welder), welding current, arc voltage, welder tip to base metal distance, gun angle, weld direction, gas flow volume and welding speed. The input voltage isn't adjustable – it'll be either 110 or 220 volts, depending on the welder design.

Welding current affects penetration of the base metal, wire melting speed, arc stability and the amount of weld spatter produced. As the current is increased, penetration, bead height and bead width also increase. The best setting for welding current depends on the wire diameter and thickness of the panel being welded – specific current settings should be listed on the welder or included in the welder instruction booklet.

Arc voltage influences the length of the arc. When it's properly set, a continuous light hissing or cracking sound will be heard coming from the welder gun tip. If the voltage is too high, the arc will be too long and lots of weld spatter will result. Also, the bead will be wide and flat and won't penetrate the base metal very far. If it's too low, the arc may disappear or a sputtering sound may be heard. The bead will be narrow and dome shaped and penetration will be deep. **Note:** *Arc length is affected not only by the voltage, but also by the wire feed speed. The arc length will become constant when the wire melting and feed speeds are the same. If the feed speed is slow, the arc will be too long – if it's fast, the arc will be too short.*

The distance the gun tip is held from the weld is very important – the standard distance is 8 to 15 mm (5/16 to 19/32 inch) for most welders. If it's too great, the wire protruding from the gun becomes pre-heated and melts

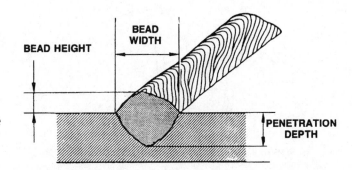

Welding current affects the penetration of the weld and the bead height and width – ideally, good penetration, with a relatively short bead is what you're looking for

faster. Also, the effect of the gas shield on the weld is diminished. If the tip distance is too short, the weld will be hidden by the gun and progress will be difficult to see.

If the gun is held so the tip is pointing in the direction of movement, it's called 'forward method'. Conversely, if it's pointing away from the direction of movement, it's called 'reverse method'. With the forward method, the bead is flat and penetration is shallow. With the reverse method, lots of metal is deposited in the weld and penetration is deep. The gun should be held at an angle of 10 to 30 degrees, regardless of the direction of the weld.

Precise gas flow is essential to a good weld. If it's too high or low, the shield effect will be diminished. The flow is based on the tip to base metal distance, welding current, welding speed and stillness of the surrounding air. Standard flow volume is 10.0 to 15.0 litres/min (0.35 to 0.53 CFM), but be sure to read the instructions accompanying the welder before making any adjustments.

Welding speed is determined by the panel thickness and machine voltage – factors that cannot be adjusted. If the speed is too high, penetration and bead width will decrease and the bead will be dome shaped. If it's too slow, holes may be burned through the panel. The welder should have a label with the recommended welding speed for panels of various thicknesses.

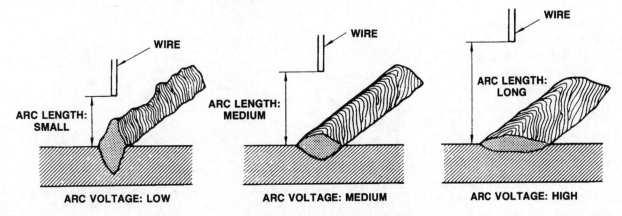

Arc voltage and length affect the shape of the bead and penetration of the weld

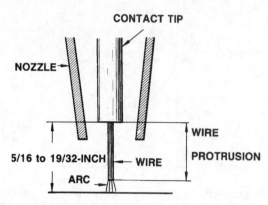

The tip-to-base metal distance is very important – it takes practice to learn how to maintain it (5/16 to 19/32 inch = 8.0 to 14.0 mm approx.)

MIG welder operation

To weld successfully with a MIG welder, the equipment must be handled properly. Following are some general pointers to keep in mind . . .

- *To start an arc, hold the tip of the gun near the panel, then activate the switch. The wire and shield gas will be fed through the gun. Bring the end of the wire in contact with the metal and create an arc. If the end of the wire forms a large ball, the arc will be difficult to strike, so hold the tip away from your face and quickly cut off the end of the wire with a side cutter.*
- *Remove weld spatter from the nozzle tip as soon as it forms. If it sticks to the end of the nozzle, the gas shield will be interrupted and a bad weld will result. If spatter builds up, it will also prevent the wire from moving freely. If the wire is jammed and the feed switch is activated, the wire will get twisted inside the welder. After removing built up spatter, make sure the wire feeds smoothly. Special spray compounds that prevent spatter from adhering are available from welding supply houses – spray it on the nozzle.*
- *To ensure a stable arc, replace the tip if it's worn. Also, make sure it's tight (the tips have flats to accept a spanner for tightening).*

MIG welding techniques

MIG welding is often used to fasten two panels together with a plug type weld. Proceed as follows . . .

1 Make a hole in the upper panel with a drill, hole saw or plug cutter. The thicker the material, the larger the hole should be.

2 Clamp the panels together with a vice-grip or C-clamps. The two panels must fit tightly together.

3 Hold the gun vertically (at a right angle to the panels) and weld through the hole in the top piece until the hole is completely filled with metal. Move the gun slowly around the edge of the hole to fill in the cavity; for small holes, aim at the center of the hole and keep the gun stationary. A flat,

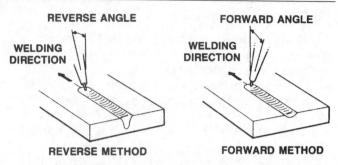

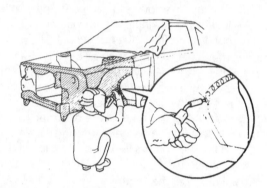

Gun tip inclination and the direction of the weld can be changed to match different welding conditions

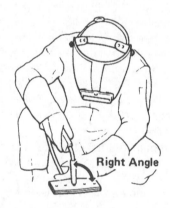

The MIG welder can be used to fasten panels, especially odd shaped ones, together with plug welds

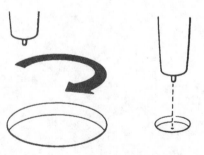

When forming a plug weld, hold the gun at a 90-degree angle to the panel . . .

. . . and move it slowly around the edge of the hole to fill the cavity with weld metal – if the holes are small (right), don't move the gun

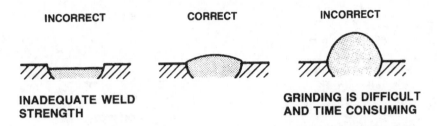

INCORRECT **CORRECT** **INCORRECT**

INADEQUATE WELD STRENGTH **GRINDING IS DIFFICULT AND TIME CONSUMING**

Try to form a bead that's slightly raised and gently sloping away from the center on the plug weld

gently sloping bead is strong and keeps grinding operations to a minimum.

Butt welding (where two panels are welded together in one continuous seam) can also be done with the MIG welder. It's used where panels are replaced in sections (for example, where the rear of a quarter panel is welded to the front section to form one continuous panel). For thick panels such as side members and frame rails, proceed as follows . . .

1 Tack weld the panels sections together. This will keep them positioned and prevent warpage. Space the weld points apart a distance equal to about 30 times the thickness of the panel (for example, if the panel is 2.0 mm (1/16 inch) thick, space the tack welds about 50 mm (2 inches) apart).

2 With the gun supported securely so it doesn't wobble, move it down the seam, using the 'forward method', at a constant speed. Keep the torch at a 10 to 15 degree angle and look frequently at the bead being formed.

3 Watch the panel and wire to see how they're melting and make sure the wire doesn't wander away from the joint. When stopping and starting, generate the arc a short distance ahead of the end of the weld, then move the wire back into the bead. The bead width and height should be uniform.

4 If the bead isn't forming correctly, the tip to base metal distance may not be right. Try holding the tip at several distances away from it until the desired results are obtained.

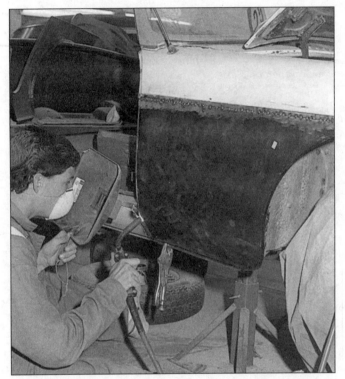

MIG welding can be used to fasten large, thin panels together with butt welds

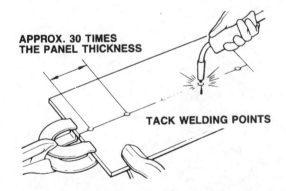

APPROX. 30 TIMES THE PANEL THICKNESS

TACK WELDING POINTS

To prevent shifting and warping, "tack weld" large panels at regular intervals before welding the entire joint

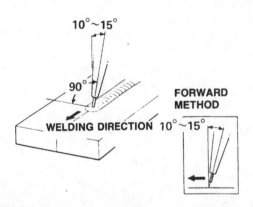

10°~15°

90°

WELDING DIRECTION 10°~15°

FORWARD METHOD

When butt welding relatively thick panels or pieces, use the "forward method" weld direction and hold the gun at a 10 to 15 degree angle – move the gun at a constant speed and watch the bead as it forms

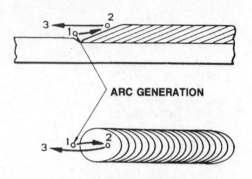

ARC GENERATION

OVERLAPPING BEADS

Generate the arc at a point slightly ahead of the weld (1), then move the wire back into the bead (2) and continue moving the gun forward to create a continuous bead (3)

5 Moving the gun too fast or too slow is also bad, even if the wire feed speed is constant. If the gun speed is slow, you'll blow holes in the base metal. if it's too fast, shallow penetration and poor weld strength will result.

6 To avoid panel warpage, start the weld in the center of the panel and change the location of the welding operation frequently. Move to the coolest portion of the joint and lay down a short bead each time.

The above method can't be used on thin sheet metal panels. Butt welding of thin panels requires a special technique. If a continuous bead is run on panels less than 0.8 mm (0.030 inch) thick, holes will be burned through the material. To avoid burn through, welding should be done intermittently or in cycles so heat build up is kept to a minimum. Use the 'reverse method' weld direction so the bead will be easier to see and wait for the bead to cool before beginning the next weld cycle.

Typical MIG welding problems, and solutions for each of them, are outlined in the accompanying chart.

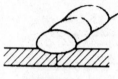

INCORRECT

Insufficient penetration. Weld strength is poor and the panel could separate when it is finished with a grinder

CORRECT

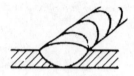

Good penetration and easy to grind

INCORRECT

There is good penetration but finish grinding will be both difficult and time consuming

This is what the finished bead should look like (centre)

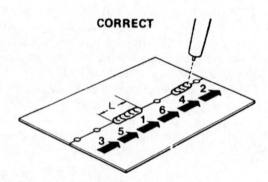

CORRECT

On large panels, warpage is a real problem, so form the bead in short sections – move to the coolest part of the panel when changing locations

INCORRECT

CONTINUOUS

CORRECT

INTERMITTENT

DO NOT attempt to weld one long continuous bead on thin panels (left) – interrupt the weld often and allow the metal to cool (right)

Typical MIG welding problems and solutions

DEFECT	DEFECT CONDITION	MAIN CAUSE
PORES/PITS		• There is rust or dirt on the base metal. • There is rust or moisture adhering to the wire. • Improper shielding action. (The nozzle is blocked, wind or the gas flow volume is low.) • Weld is cooling off too fast. • Arc length is too long.
UNDERCUT		• Arc length is too long. • Gun angle is improper. • Welding speed is too fast.
OVERLAP		• Welding speed is too slow. • Arc length is too short.
INSUFFICIENT PENETRATION		• Welding current is too low. • Arc length is too long. • The end of the wire is not aligned with the butted portion of the panels.
EXCESS WELD SPATTER		• Arc length is too long. • Rust on the base metal. • Gun angle is too severe.
BEAD NOT UNIFORM		• The contact tip hole is worn or deformed and the wire is oscillating as it comes out of the tip. • The gun is not steady during welding.
BURN THROUGH		• The welding current is too high. • The gap between the metal is too wide. • The speed of the gun is too slow. • The gun to base metal distance is too short.

Oxy-acetylene welding

Oxy-acetylene welding is a type of fusion welding. Acetylene and oxygen are mixed in the torch chamber, ignited at the end of the torch tip and used as a high temperature heat source (approximately 3,000 degrees C or 5,400 degrees F) to melt and join the welding rod and base metal together.

Since it's difficult to concentrate the heat in one area, it affects the surrounding areas and reduces the strength of steel panels. *Because of this fact, vehicle manufacturers don't use oxy-acetylene welding on assembly lines or recommend its use in most body repair procedures.* This welding method is used in various operations where heat is required to repair accident damaged bodies (brazing, flame cutting and removal of paint).

Oxy-acetylene welding equipment
The oxy-acetylene welding outfit consists of a torch, regulators, acetylene tank, oxygen tank and hoses.

A steel tank is filled with oxygen at a pressure of approximately 147 bar (2,133 psi) at 35 degrees C (95 degrees F). The tank is usually painted black to identify it as an oxygen container.

A second steel tank is packed with calcium carbide, charcoal, rock wool or other porous substance that's saturated with acetylene dissolved in acetone and liquefied under a pressure of 15 bar (220 psi) at 15 degrees C (59 degrees F) or less. The tank is painted brown to identify it as containing acetylene gas.

The regulator reduces the pressure coming from the tanks to the desired level and maintains a constant flow rate. The

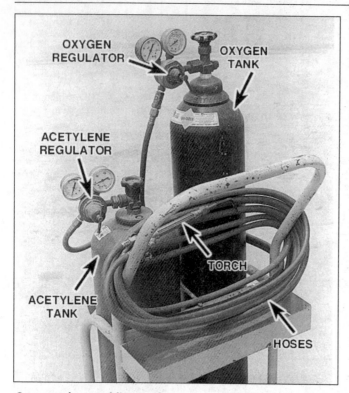

Oxy-acetylene welding outfit

oxygen pressure is usually maintained at 1.0 to 5.0 bar (14 to 71 psi), while the acetylene pressure is normally held in a much lower 0.1 to 0.3 bar (1.4 to 4.3 psi) range.

The torch body mixes the oxygen and acetylene from the tanks in the proper proportions and produces a flame capable of melting steel. There are two main types of torches: **Welding torches** and **cutting torches**.

The welding torch usually consists of a handle, a mixing head and an interchangeable tip, although some manufacturers combine the mixing head and tip in one component. The torch handle has threaded fittings for attaching the oxygen and acetylene hoses and valves for adjusting the flame and turning off the gases entirely. Torches should be handled with care – since they're made of brass, they can easily be damaged. Don't overtighten the valves when shutting off the gas and be very careful when changing tips – don't nick or otherwise damage the mating surfaces where the tip attaches to the mixing chamber or handle.

The cutting torch consists of an oxygen tube and valve for conducting high pressure oxygen attached to a welding torch. The flame outlet has a small oxygen hole located in the centre of the tip, which is surrounded by holes arranged in a spherical pattern. The outer holes are used for pre heating.

Oxy-acetylene flame types

When acetylene and oxygen are mixed and burned in the air, the condition of the flame varies, depending on the volume of oxygen and acetylene. There are three types of oxy-acetylene flames: **Neutral**, **carburising** and **oxidising**. The flame type is determined by the oxygen to acetylene ratio.

Neutral Flame

The standard flame is said to be a 'neutral flame'. Acetylene and oxygen mixed in a one to one ratio by volume produces a neutral flame. This type of flame has a brilliant white core surrounded by a clear blue outer flame. The neutral flame is the most desirable flame for welding most materials.

Carburising Flame

The carburising flame is also called a surplus or reduction flame and is produced by mixing slightly more acetylene than oxygen. This flame differs from the neutral flame in that it has three parts. The core and the outer flames are the same

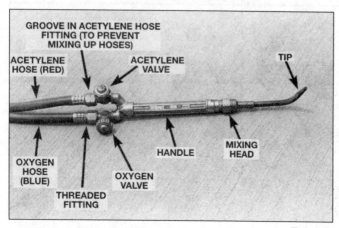

Welding torch components

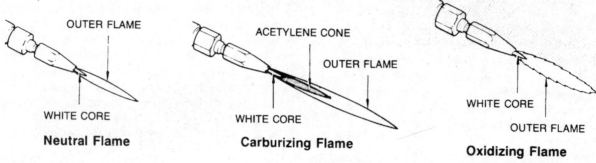

Neutral Flame   **Carburizing Flame**   **Oxidizing Flame**

Oxy-acetylene torch flame characteristics

as the neutral flame, but between them is an intermediate, light coloured acetylene cone enveloping the core. The length of the acetylene cone varies according to the amount of surplus acetylene in the gas mixture. For a double surplus flame, the oxygen-acetylene ratio is about 1 to 1.4 (by volume). A carburising flame is used for welding aluminium, nickel and other alloys.

Oxidising Flame

The oxidising flame is obtained by mixing slightly more oxygen than acetylene. The oxidising flame resembles the neutral flame in appearance, but the acetylene core is shorter and its colour is a little more violet compared to the neutral flame. The outer flame is shorter and fuzzy at the end. Ordinarily, this flame oxidises melted metal, so it's not used for welding.

Welding torch flame adjustment

As stated at the beginning of this Chapter, oxy-acetylene welding isn't used extensively on modern auto bodies, but it is used for burning off paint and the brazing of certain panels at factory brazed seams.

1 Attach the appropriate tip to the end of the torch. Use the standard tip for sheet metal (each torch manufacturer has a different system for measuring the size of the tip orifice).

2 Set the oxygen and acetylene regulators at the recommended pressure (1.0 to 4.9 bar (14 to 71 psi) for oxygen; 0.1 to 0.3 (1.4 to 4.3 psi) for acetylene).

3 Open the acetylene valve about 1/2 turn and ignite the gas. Continue to open the valve until the black smoke disappears and a reddish yellow flame appears. Slowly open the oxygen valve until the center cone becomes sharp and well defined. This type of flame is called a neutral flame and is used for welding steel.

4 If acetylene is added to the flame or oxygen is removed from the flame, a carburising flame will result.

5 If oxygen is added to the flame or acetylene is removed from the flame, an oxidising flame will result.

Note: *Another way to ignite the gas is to open both the oxygen and acetylene valves slightly (about 1/4 turn), then ignite the mixture. A little practice is necessary, but this method generates far less smoke. However, if both the valves are opened without igniting the gas immediately, an explosive sound will occur when the mixture is finally ignited.*

Cutting torch flame adjustment

The cutting torch is sometimes used in body repair to rough cut damaged panels. To adjust the flame . . .

1 Adjust the oxygen and acetylene valves for a neutral flame.

2 Open the pre-heating oxygen valve slowly until an oxidising flame appears. This makes it difficult for melted metal to remain on the surface of the cut panel, allowing for clean edges.

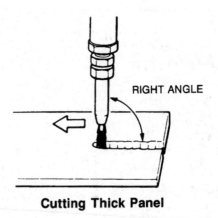

Cutting Thick Panel

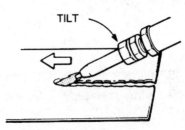

Cutting Thin Panel

Thick panel cutting

3 Heat a portion of the base metal until it's red hot. Just before it melts, open the high pressure oxygen valve and cut the panel. Advance the torch while making sure the panel is melting and being cut apart. This method is also widely used for thin panels, when there are several pieces overlapped together, or for a side member, even when there's an internal reinforcement.

Thin panel cutting

4 Heat a small spot on the base metal until it's red hot. Just before it melts, open the high pressure oxygen valve and incline the torch so it's pointing in the direction it's moving to cut the panel. When cutting thin material, tilting the tip of the torch ensures the cut will be clean and fast (this prevents panel warpage). **Note:** *As soon as the cutting operation is completed, quickly turn off the high pressure oxygen flow used for cutting and pull the torch away from the base metal. This will prevent sparks from entering the tip and igniting the oxygen-acetylene mixture in the torch handle (in extreme cases the ensuing fire could melt the torch handle).*

Flame abnormalities

When changes occur during the welding operation (such as overheating of the tip, adhesion of spatter or fluctuations in the gas pressure), the flame will be affected. Always keep an eye on the condition of the flame. Abnormalities and their causes and cures are shown in the accompanying chart.

Chapter 12

Oxy-acetylene welding flame abnormalities and remedies

SYMPTOM	CAUSE	REMEDY
Flame fluctuations	Moisture in the gas, condensation in the hose. Insufficient acetylene supply.	Remove the moisture from the hose. Adjust the acetylene pressure. Have the tank refilled.
Explosive sound while lighting the torch	Oxygen or acetylene pressure is incorrect. Removal of mixed in gases is incomplete. The tip orifice is too large. The tip orifice is dirty.	Adjust the pressure. Remove the air from inside the torch. Replace the tip. Clean the orifice in the tip.
Flame cut off	Oxygen pressure is too high. The flame outlet is clogged.	Adjust the oxygen pressure. Clean the tip.
Popping noises during operation	The tip is overheated. The tip is clogged. The gas pressure adjustment is incorrect. Metal deposited on the tip.	Cool the flame outlet (while letting a little oxygen flow). Clean the tip.
Oxygen flow is reversed Oxygen is flowing into the path of the acetylene.	The tip is clogged. Oxygen pressure is too high. Torch is defective (the tip or valve is loose). There is contact with the tip and the deposit metal.	Clean the tip. Adjust the oxygen pressure. Repair or replace the torch. Clean the orifice.
Backfire There is a whistling noise and the torch handle grip gets hot. Flame is sucked into the torch.	The tip is clogged or dirty. Oxygen pressure is too low. The tip is overheated. The tip orifice is enlarged or deformed. A spark from the base metal enters the torch causing an ignition of gas inside the torch. Amount of acetylene flowing through the torch is too low.	Clean the tip. Adjust the oxygen pressure. Cool the tip with water (letting a little oxygen flow). Replace the tip. Immediately shut off both torch valves. Let torch cool down. Then re-light the torch. Readjust the flow rate.

Brazing

The term brazing refers to the use of a filler material, with a lower melting point than the base metal, that's melted and flows into the narrow spaces between the pieces of base metal by capillary action. There are two types of brazing – soft brazing (commonly known as soldering) and hard brazing (using brass or nickel filler rods). Ordinarily, the term brazing refers to hard brazing.

Since the pieces of base metal are joined together at a relatively low temperature, where the base metal doesn't melt, there's less distortion and stress (less panel warpage). Brazing metal has excellent flow characteristics, it penetrates well into narrow gaps and is convenient for filling gaps in body seams. Since the base metal doesn't melt, it's possible to join otherwise incompatible metals. However, since there's no penetration, and the base metal is joined only at the surface, it isn't very strong and won't resist repeated loads or an impact. Because of these characteristics, brazing is a relatively easy skill to master.

Vehicle assembly plants sometimes use arc brazing to join the roof and quarter panels together. Arc brazing uses the same principles as MIG welding, however, brazing metal is used instead of welding wire. Since the amount of heat applied to the base metal is low, overheating is minimized and, as mentioned before, there's little distortion or warpage of the base metal.

In order to produce brazing material with good qualities, such as flow characteristics, melting temperature, compatibility with base metals and strength, it's made of two or more metals. There are many types of brazing metals, but brass is generally the most common (copper and zinc are the main ingredients of the brass brazing rods used for body repairs).

Generally speaking, the surface of metal exposed to the air is covered with a film of oxidation, which thickens when heat is applied. A special material called 'flux' is used to remove the oxidation (flux not only removes oxidation, it also prevents the formation of new oxidation and enhances the bond between the base metal and the brazing material).

If brazing material is melted over an oxidized surface, the brazing material won't adequately bond to the base metal and surface tension will cause the brazing material to form into small balls. The oxidation should be removed by applying flux to the surface of the base metal and then heating it until it becomes liquid. After the oxidation has been removed, the brazing material will adhere to the base metal and the braze joint will be much stronger.

Since the strength of the brazing material is lower than the base metal, braze joints must be overlapped as much as possible (joint strength is dependent on the surface area of the pieces being joined). Even when the pieces are made of the same material, the brazed joint surface area must be larger than a welded joint. As a general rule, the overlapping portion must be three or more times wider than the panel thickness.

A typical brazing operation should be carried out as follows . . .

1 Clean the base metal. As mentioned above, if there's oxidation, oil, paint, or dirt on the surface of the base metal, the brazing material won't flow properly. The contaminants, if allowed to remain on the surface, may cause eventual joint failure. Even though flux acts to remove oxidation and most other contaminants, it's not strong enough to completely remove everything, so first clean the surface with a wire brush.

2 After the base metal is clean, apply flux uniformly to the braze joint surface (if a brazing rod with flux in it is used, this step isn't necessary).

3 Heat the joint area of the base metal to a uniform temperature capable of melting the brazing rod material. **Note:** *Adjust the torch to produce a carburising flame.*

4 When the base metal is hot enough, melt the brazing rod onto it, letting it flow naturally. Stop heating the area when the brazing material has flowed into the gaps between the pieces being joined. Since brazing material flows easily over a heated surface, it's important to heat the entire joint area to a uniform temperature. DO NOT melt the brazing material prior to heating the base metal (the brazing material won't adhere to it if you do). If the surface temperature of the base metal gets too high, the flux won't clean the base metal – the result is a poor bond and an inferior joint.

5 Once the brazed joint has cooled, rinse off the remaining flux sediment with water and scrub the surface with a stiff wire brush. Baked and blackened flux can be removed with a sander or a sharp tool.

After the base metal is hot enough to melt the brazing rod material, touch the end of the rod to the metal and allow it to flow into the joint

Notes

Glossary

A

Abrasive
A gritty substance used for sanding, grinding of cutting

Achromatic
'Neutral' colours; eg, whites, greys, beiges

Acrylic
A clear chemical compound used for the production of resins used in 2-pack and enamel paints that provides excellent colour, durability and gloss

Activator
A component of filler or 2-pack paint which reacts chemically with another component to form a hard finish

Additives
Chemicals added to paint in relatively small quantities to impart of improve desirable properties

A-pillar
Windscreen pillar

Atomise
The process of breaking up paint into a fine mist be the spray gun

B

Back masking
A masking technique where rolled masking tape or foam tape is used to avoid hard edges when spraying up to a masked line

Base coat
A solid colour, pearlescent or metallic colour coat over which a clear coat must be sprayed

Base paint
See *Tinter*

Bezel
The frame or rim surrounding a light or opening in the body

Binder
A constituent of paint which is used to hold the pigments together, and provide the medium for the pigments to flow and bond to a surface

Binding agent See *Binder*

Bleeding
A paint fault where the old paint coat 'bleeds' through the new top coat

Glossary

Blistering

A paint fault where small bubbles form in the new paint coat

Blooming

A paint fault where a pale white film forms on the new paint coat

Body filler

A heavy bodied plastic material that dries very hard, used to fill small dents and creases in vehicle bodies

B-pillar

The pillar between the front and rear doors on four/five door vehicles, or at the rear edge of the front door on two/three door models

Bridging

A characteristic of undercoats that occurs when a scratch or other imperfection in the surface isn't completely filled. Usually, due to under reducing the primer or using thinners that are too fast

Build

The thickness of the paint film deposited on the body during spraying

C

Cataphoretic dipping

An electrical process used in a vehicle factory-finishing process, in which body panels are submerged in a tank of paint/electrolyte solution in order to coat them evenly with primer

Catalyst

See *Activator*

Cathodic dipping

See *Cataphoretic dipping*

Cellulose

A paint in which a cellulose-based binder is used

Centreline

A line passing through the centre of a headlight, wheel or the vehicle itself

Chalking

A white surface coat appearing on a painted surface as it weathers

Checking

A paint fault where small, fine lines or cracks appear in the paint top coat

Chromatic

Clearly-defined colours; eg, reds and greens

Clear-coat

A transparent top-coat sprayed over the top of a colour coat

Colour coat

A coloured paint layer sprayed over the top of primer to give a vehicle its colour

Compound

A very fine abrasive, usually in paste or liquid form, used to polish out imperfections in paint

Compounding

Compounding involves 'cutting' the finish with a compounding paste or cream to remove any minor imperfections in the finish before final polishing

Conversion coating

Metal treatment process that improves paint adhesion and corrosion resistance

Coverage

The surface area that a given quantity of paint will cover adequately

C-pillar

The pillar connecting the roof to the rear quarter panel

Cratering

The formation of holes in the paint coat due to surface contaminants

Cross coating

See *Drop coating*

Curing

The final drying process of a paint coat, where it reaches maximum hardness

D

De-nibbing

Light sanding to remove particles of dust or dirt, or possibly small insects, which settle on the paint or lacquer surface during drying

Degrease

Cleaning the grease from a surface that's going to be painted

Door skin

The outer sheet metal panel of a door, available as a replacement part for most vehicles

Drip rail/moulding

The curved metal or plastic moulding around the edge of the roof that directs water away from the side windows

Drop coating

A spraying method used to cover 'striping' in a metallic colour coat. For a drop coat, the air pressure is lowered, and the panel is sprayed in the opposite direction to the previous passes. This method should not be used on highly visible panel areas

Dry spray

A paint fault where the paint pigment isn't being held properly by the binder, or where the binder evaporates before the paint reaches the surface

E

Electrophoresis/Electrophoretic dipping

See *Cataphoretic dipping*

Electrostatic spraying

A paint spraying process where the paint particles are electrostatically-charged, and instead of a conventional spray gun, special jets are used to spray the paint onto the electrostatically-charged body

Enamel

A paint which dries due to a chemical reaction between two or more elements

Etch primer

The purpose of an etch primer is to replicate the galvanising process used to protect vehicle panels against corrosion. Etch primers contain an acid which etches bare metal, ensuring that there is a very strong bond between the primer and the panel surface

Extender

See *High-build primer*

F

Fan

The pattern left by a spray gun

Fanning

The use of air pressure through a spray gun to speed up the drying process. This is not recommended!

Feather edge

To sand the edge of a paint layer so it tapers down to the metal surface, leaving no ridge or edge

Filler

A material used to fill large imperfections in the surface of a panel, which can be sanded level with the surrounding panel surfaces, to provide a smooth surface ready for priming

Fish-eyes

A paint fault where small pits form in the final paint coat, usually caused by an insufficiently clean surface

Flash

The initial drying of the paint coat, where most of the paint solvent evaporates

Flash-off

The 'flash-off time' is the recommended time for which a coat of paint must be left to air dry after spraying, to allow most of the volatile solvent material in the paint to evaporate

Flatting

A process where a mild abrasive is used to 'scuff' the surface of the existing paint (or lacquer) coat, providing a key to enable new paint (or lacquer) to adhere

Fog coat

To spray a fine layer of thinned paint over an old painted surface to provide a better surface for following coats of paint to adhere to

G

Galvanising

Galvanising involves coating a panel with a thin layer of zinc to provide corrosion protection

Gloss

The ability of a paint to shine or reflect light

H

Hard edge

A hard edge is produced when paint is sprayed directly up to an edge such as a piece of trim, or masking tape. The build-up of new paint film produces a step between the new paint and the surrounding original finish, which is highly visible

Hardener

See *Activator*

High-build primer

A primer paint which is sprayed before colour coat is applied, and has three main functions; to provide a relatively thick coating which will fill any small imperfections; to provide an element of stone chip resistance; and to provide a coating which can be sanded to give a smooth, sound base on to which colour coat can be sprayed

Hold out

The ability of a surface to keep the top layer of paint from sinking in or being absorbed

HVLP

High Volume Low Pressure. A method of spraying paint, which uses a low air pressure, and a high volume of paint. This spraying method reduces the level of overspray, and reduces VOC emissions

I

Isolator

A layer applied between the old surface and the new primer to prevent any reaction between the two

Glossary

L

Lacquer

A paint which dries through solvent evaporation or by oxidation of the binder. A term also used to describe a clear-coat

Lap joint

An overlapping joint between two panels, usually filled with solder or lead unless covered by a moulding

Lifting

Surface distortion or shrivelling while the top paint coat is being applied or drying

Lower rear panel

The body sheet metal between the boot lid and the rear bumper

M

Metal conditioner

An acid based metal cleaner that removes rust and corrosion from bare metal, etches it for better adhesion and forms a corrosion resistant film

Metallic paint

Paint that contains both pigment and metallic flakes in suspension

Metamerism

A phenomenon whereby two samples of a colour look the same under a particular colour of light, but are in fact made up from different mixtures of pigments. When the two samples are viewed under a different light source, they appear to be different colours

Mist coat

The final colour coat, sprayed with paint that's been highly thinned with slow evaporating thinners

Mottling

Spotty or striped looking metallic paint caused by the flakes flowing together

O

OEM

Original Equipment Manufacturer

Orange peel

A paint fault where a rough surface is left due to the paint coats failing to flow together

Overlap

The spray pattern which puts each successive layer of paint partially over the previous layer

Overspray

Particles of paint which settle and dry on areas surrounding the repair area during spraying

Oxidation (1)

The combining of oxygen with the paint surface to produce chalking and dullness in the paint finish

Oxidation (2)

The combining of oxygen with the enamel paints, which dries and cures the paint

P

Panel wipe

A solvent-based cleaning fluid which is used to remove grease and contamination from panels during the refinishing process

Peeling

The loss of adhesion between the paint and substrate that results in the paint separating from it

Peroxide

A strong oxidising agent which is used as a hardening agent in body fillers

Phosphatising

A process in which a bare vehicle body shell is submerged in a bath containing a solution of various phosphate salts. Crystalline metal phosphates are deposited on the panels to give corrosion protection, and to provide a good base to enable paint to adhere

Pigment

Very fine particles of solid material, which are used to give a paint its colour and 'body'

Pinholing

Holes that form in the undercoat or paint

Polyurethane

A chemical used in the production of resins for enamel paints

Polyester

A paint in which an polyester-based binder is used. Usually dries matt and finished with a clear-coat

Primer

A paint of neutral colour which is designed to provide a coating which will fill any small imperfections (eg, minor scratches and sanding marks) in the finish underneath, and to provide a coating which can be sanded to give a smooth, sound base on to which colour coat can be sprayed

Primer filler

See *High-build primer*

Primer sealer

An undercoat that improves the adhesion of the paint and seals old painted surfaces that have been sanded

Q

Quarter panel
The sheet metal from the rear door opening to the taillights and from the rear wheel arch to the base of the roof and boot lid/tailgate opening

R

Reducer
The solvent used to thin enamel paints

Regulator
The mechanism used to raise and lower window glass. Also, the device used to adjust the pressure of gas or air leaving a cylinder or compressor

Resin
A substance which is neither volatile, nor solid; eg, the binder in a paint

Respirator
A protective device worn over the mouth and nose to filter out particles and fumes in the air being breathed. May be fed with its own air supply. An air-fed mask

Retarder
A very rich, slow drying solvent type additive that slows the evaporation rate of a paint

Roll masking
See *Back masking*

Rubbing compound
A mild abrasive that smoothes and polishes paints

Runs and sags
Surface imperfections that form after the too heavy application or primer or paint (the most common paints problem encountered)

S

Sand scratch swelling
The swelling of scratches in the undercoat by solvents in the paint coat

Sanding block
A hard, flexible block used t provide a smooth, consistent backing surface for the paper when hand sanding

Sealer
A special undercoat applied between the primer, or old finish and the new paint coat to give maximum adhesion and hold out and to prevent sand scratch swelling

Settling
The pigment particles settling out of the binder in the spray gun cup

Silicones
A very common ingredient in waxes and polishes that makes them smooth; also the primary cause of fish eyes in the paint

Solid colour
A paint in which only solid colour pigments are used; ie, a paint without metallic or pearlescent pigments. Solid colour base coats are available, which give a matt finish, and require a clear-coat to be sprayed over the top

Solids
The pigments and binders which remain on the painted surface after the solvents evaporate

Solvent
A Volatile Organic Compound (VOC), such as acetone, petroleum products, butyl acetate, etc

Solvent-based paint
A paint which contain solvents and thinners consisting of Volatile Organic Compounds (VOCs), such as acetone, petroleum products, and butyl acetate

Solvents
The 'thinners' used to dissolve or dilute another liquid

Solvent popping
Blisters that form on the paint film, caused by trapped solvents

Stopper
A low density body filler

Substrate
A material to which paint is applied; eg, galvanised steel, plastic, aluminium, etc.

Surface dry
A paint imperfection where the top layer of paint dries while the layer underneath remains fluid

Surfacer
See *High-build primer*

T

Tack coat
The first coat of paint dried to the point where it can just be touched without feeling sticky

Tack rag
A rag which comes saturated with a special varnish used to remove dust and sanding particles from a surface before painting

Thinners
A solvent which is added to paint to reduce its viscosity

Glossary

Tinter
A coloured base paint. To mix a specific paint colour, a number of tinters are mixed in the proportions specified in the paint manufacturer's paint formulation

Top-coat
The final layer of paint to be sprayed. Usually either a solid colour coat, or a clear lacquer coat

Two-tone
Two different colours on a single paint job

U

Undercoat
The material applied before the paint is applied (primer, sealer, isolator etc.)

V

Vehicle
The paint components except the pigments

Viscosity
The degree of thickness of a liquid

VOC
Volatile Organic Compound. Chemical substances which rise into the atmosphere and react with nitrous oxides to produce ozone. The most significant source of VOCs is chemical solvents

W

Water-based paint
A paint in which water forms the main constituent of the solvent and thinner (the paint still contains some solvent)

Water-borne paint
See *Water-based paint*

Water spotting
A paint problem caused by the evaporation of water on a paint coat before its completely dry, which results in the dulling of the paint gloss in random spots

Wet spots
Discolouration, where the paint fails to dry and adhere uniformly, caused by grease or finger prints

Wet-on-wet
The application of a paint layer on top of an existing paint layer before the existing paint layer is fully dry

Wrinkling
Surface distortion of the paint coat (shrivelling) that occurs in a thick coat of paint before the layer under it has dried properly

Length (distance)

Inches (in)	x 25.4	= Millimetres (mm)	x 0.0394	=	Inches (in)
Feet (ft)	x 0.305	= Metres (m)	x 3.281	=	Feet (ft)
Miles	x 1.609	= Kilometres (km)	x 0.621	=	Miles

Volume (capacity)

Cubic inches (cu in; in³)	x 16.387	= Cubic centimetres (cc; cm³)	x 0.061	=	Cubic inches (cu in; in³)
Imperial pints (Imp pt)	x 0.568	= Litres (l)	x 1.76	=	Imperial pints (Imp pt)
Imperial quarts (Imp qt)	x 1.137	= Litres (l)	x 0.88	=	Imperial quarts (Imp qt)
Imperial quarts (Imp qt)	x 1.201	= US quarts (US qt)	x 0.833	=	Imperial quarts (Imp qt)
US quarts (US qt)	x 0.946	= Litres (l)	x 1.057	=	US quarts (US qt)
Imperial gallons (Imp gal)	x 4.546	= Litres (l)	x 0.22	=	Imperial gallons (Imp gal)
Imperial gallons (Imp gal)	x 1.201	= US gallons (US gal)	x 0.833	=	Imperial gallons (Imp gal)
US gallons (US gal)	x 3.785	= Litres (l)	x 0.264	=	US gallons (US gal)

Mass (weight)

Ounces (oz)	x 28.35	= Grams (g)	x 0.035	=	Ounces (oz)
Pounds (lb)	x 0.454	= Kilograms (kg)	x 2.205	=	Pounds (lb)

Force

Ounces-force (ozf; oz)	x 0.278	= Newtons (N)	x 3.6	=	Ounces-force (ozf; oz)
Pounds-force (lbf; lb)	x 4.448	= Newtons (N)	x 0.225	=	Pounds-force (lbf; lb)
Newtons (N)	x 0.1	= Kilograms-force (kgf; kg)	x 9.81	=	Newtons (N)

Pressure

Pounds-force per square inch (psi; lbf/in²; lb/in²)	x 0.070	= Kilograms-force per square centimetre (kgf/cm²; kg/cm²)	x 14.223	=	Pounds-force per square inch (psi; lbf/in²; lb/in²)
Pounds-force per square inch (psi; lbf/in²; lb/in²)	x 0.068	= Atmospheres (atm)	x 14.696	=	Pounds-force per square inch (psi; lbf/in²; lb/in²)
Pounds-force per square inch (psi; lbf/in²; lb/in²)	x 0.069	= Bars	x 14.5	=	Pounds-force per square inch (psi; lbf/in²; lb/in²)
Pounds-force per square inch (psi; lbf/in²; lb/in²)	x 6.895	= Kilopascals (kPa)	x 0.145	=	Pounds-force per square inch (psi; lbf/in²; lb/in²)
Kilopascals (kPa)	x 0.01	= Kilograms-force per square centimetre (kgf/cm²; kg/cm²)	x 98.1	=	Kilopascals (kPa)
Millibar (mbar)	x 100	= Pascals (Pa)	x 0.01	=	Millibar (mbar)
Millibar (mbar)	x 0.0145	= Pounds-force per square inch (psi; lbf/in²; lb/in²)	x 68.947	=	Millibar (mbar)
Millibar (mbar)	x 0.75	= Millimetres of mercury (mmHg)	x 1.333	=	Millibar (mbar)
Millibar (mbar)	x 0.401	= Inches of water (inH₂O)	x 2.491	=	Millibar (mbar)
Millimetres of mercury (mmHg)	x 0.535	= Inches of water (inH₂O)	x 1.868	=	Millimetres of mercury (mmHg)
Inches of water (inH₂O)	x 0.036	= Pounds-force per square inch (psi; lbf/in²; lb/in²)	x 27.68	=	Inches of water (inH₂O)

Torque (moment of force)

Pounds-force inches (lbf in; lb in)	x 1.152	= Kilograms-force centimetre (kgf cm; kg cm)	x 0.868	=	Pounds-force inches (lbf in; lb in)
Pounds-force inches (lbf in; lb in)	x 0.113	= Newton metres (Nm)	x 8.85	=	Pounds-force inches (lbf in; lb in)
Pounds-force inches (lbf in; lb in)	x 0.083	= Pounds-force feet (lbf ft; lb ft)	x 12	=	Pounds-force inches (lbf in; lb in)
Pounds-force feet (lbf ft; lb ft)	x 0.138	= Kilograms-force metres (kgf m; kg m)	x 7.233	=	Pounds-force feet (lbf ft; lb ft)
Pounds-force feet (lbf ft; lb ft)	x 1.356	= Newton metres (Nm)	x 0.738	=	Pounds-force feet (lbf ft; lb ft)
Newton metres (Nm)	x 0.102	= Kilograms-force metres (kgf m; kg m)	x 9.804	=	Newton metres (Nm)

Power

Horsepower (hp)	x 745.7	= Watts (W)	x 0.0013	=	Horsepower (hp)

Velocity (speed)

Miles per hour (miles/hr; mph)	x 1.609	= Kilometres per hour (km/hr; kph)	x 0.621	=	Miles per hour (miles/hr; mph)

Fuel consumption*

Miles per gallon, Imperial (mpg)	x 0.354	= Kilometres per litre (km/l)	x 2.825	=	Miles per gallon, Imperial (mpg)
Miles per gallon, US (mpg)	x 0.425	= Kilometres per litre (km/l)	x 2.352	=	Miles per gallon, US (mpg)

Temperature

Degrees Fahrenheit = (°C x 1.8) + 32   Degrees Celsius (Degrees Centigrade; °C) = (°F - 32) x 0.56

It is common practice to convert from miles per gallon (mpg) to litres/100 kilometres (l/100km), where mpg x l/100 km = 282

Notes

Haynes Manuals – The Complete UK Car List

Title	Book No.
ALFA ROMEO Alfasud/Sprint (74 - 88) up to F *	0292
Alfa Romeo Alfetta (73 - 87) up to E *	0531
AUDI 80, 90 & Coupe Petrol (79 - Nov 88) up to F	0605
Audi 80, 90 & Coupe Petrol (Oct 86 - 90) D to H	1491
Audi 100 & 200 Petrol (Oct 82 - 90) up to H	0907
Audi 100 & A6 Petrol & Diesel (May 91 - May 97) H to P	3504
Audi A3 Petrol & Diesel (96 - May 03) P to 03	4253
Audi A4 Petrol & Diesel (95 - 00) M to X	3575
Audi A4 Petrol & Diesel (01 - 04) X to 54	4609
AUSTIN A35 & A40 (56 - 67) up to F *	0118
Austin/MG/Rover Maestro 1.3 & 1.6 Petrol (83 - 95) up to M	0922
Austin/MG Metro (80 - May 90) up to G	0718
Austin/Rover Montego 1.3 & 1.6 Petrol (84 - 94) A to L	1066
Austin/MG/Rover Montego 2.0 Petrol (84 - 95) A to M	1067
Mini (59 - 69) up to H *	0527
Mini (69 - 01) up to X	0646
Austin/Rover 2.0 litre Diesel Engine (86 - 93) C to L	1857
Austin Healey 100/6 & 3000 (56 - 68) up to G *	0049
BEDFORD CF Petrol (69 - 87) up to E	0163
Bedford/Vauxhall Rascal & Suzuki Supercarry (86 - Oct 94) C to M	3015
BMW 316, 320 & 320i (4-cyl) (75 - Feb 83) up to Y *	0276
BMW 320, 320i, 323i & 325i (6-cyl) (Oct 77 - Sept 87) up to E	0815
BMW 3- & 5-Series Petrol (81 - 91) up to J	1948
BMW 3-Series Petrol (Apr 91 - 99) H to V	3210
BMW 3-Series Petrol (Sept 98 - 03) S to 53	4067
BMW 520i & 525e (Oct 81 - June 88) up to E	1560
BMW 525, 528 & 528i (73 - Sept 81) up to X *	0632
BMW 5-Series 6-cyl Petrol (April 96 - Aug 03) N to 03	4151
BMW 1500, 1502, 1600, 1602, 2000 & 2002 (59 - 77) up to S *	0240
CHRYSLER PT Cruiser Petrol (00 - 03) W to 53	4058
CITROËN 2CV, Ami & Dyane (67 - 90) up to H	0196
Citroën AX Petrol & Diesel (87 - 97) D to P	3014
Citroën Berlingo & Peugeot Partner Petrol & Diesel (96 - 05) P to 55	4281
Citroën BX Petrol (83 - 94) A to L	0908
Citroën C15 Van Petrol & Diesel (89 - Oct 98) F to S	3509
Citroën C3 Petrol & Diesel (02 - 05) 51 to 05	4197
Citroen C5 Petrol & Diesel (01-08) Y to 08	4745
Citroën CX Petrol (75 - 88) up to F	0528
Citroën Saxo Petrol & Diesel (96 - 04) N to 54	3506
Citroën Visa Petrol (79 - 88) up to F	0620
Citroën Xantia Petrol & Diesel (93 - 01) K to Y	3082
Citroën XM Petrol & Diesel (89 - 00) G to X	3451
Citroën Xsara Petrol & Diesel (97 - Sept 00) R to W	3751
Citroën Xsara Picasso Petrol & Diesel (00 - 02) W to 52	3944
Citroen Xsara Picasso (03-08)	4784
Citroën ZX Diesel (91 - 98) J to S	1922
Citroën ZX Petrol (91 - 98) H to S	1881
Citroën 1.7 & 1.9 litre Diesel Engine (84 - 96) A to N	1379
FIAT 126 (73 - 87) up to E *	0305
Fiat 500 (57 - 73) up to M *	0090
Fiat Bravo & Brava Petrol (95 - 00) N to W	3572
Fiat Cinquecento (93 - 98) K to R	3501
Fiat Panda (81 - 95) up to M	0793
Fiat Punto Petrol & Diesel (94 - Oct 99) L to V	3251
Fiat Punto Petrol (Oct 99 - July 03) V to 03	4066
Fiat Punto Petrol (03-07) 03 to 07	4746
Fiat Regata Petrol (84 - 88) A to F	1167
Fiat Tipo Petrol (88 - 91) E to J	1625
Fiat Uno Petrol (83 - 95) up to M	0923
Fiat X1/9 (74 - 89) up to G *	0273
FORD Anglia (59 - 68) up to G *	0001

Title	Book No.
Ford Capri II (& III) 1.6 & 2.0 (74 - 87) up to E *	0283
Ford Capri II (& III) 2.8 & 3.0 V6 (74 - 87) up to E	1309
Ford Cortina Mk I & Corsair 1500 ('62 - '66) up to D*	0214
Ford Cortina Mk III 1300 & 1600 (70 - 76) up to P *	0070
Ford Escort Mk I 1100 & 1300 (68 - 74) up to N *	0171
Ford Escort Mk I Mexico, RS 1600 & RS 2000 (70 - 74) up to N *	0139
Ford Escort Mk II Mexico, RS 1800 & RS 2000 (75 - 80) up to W *	0735
Ford Escort (75 - Aug 80) up to V *	0280
Ford Escort Petrol (Sept 80 - Sept 90) up to H	0686
Ford Escort & Orion Petrol (Sept 90 - 00) H to X	1737
Ford Escort & Orion Diesel (Sept 90 - 00) H to X	4081
Ford Fiesta (76 - Aug 83) up to Y	0334
Ford Fiesta Petrol (Aug 83 - Feb 89) A to F	1030
Ford Fiesta Petrol (Feb 89 - Oct 95) F to N	1595
Ford Fiesta Petrol & Diesel (Oct 95 - Mar 02) N to 02	3397
Ford Fiesta Petrol & Diesel (Apr 02 - 07) 02 to 57	4170
Ford Focus Petrol & Diesel (98 - 01) S to Y	3759
Ford Focus Petrol & Diesel (Oct 01 - 05) 51 to 05	4167
Ford Galaxy Petrol & Diesel (95 - Aug 00) M to W	3984
Ford Granada Petrol (Sept 77 - Feb 85) up to B *	0481
Ford Granada & Scorpio Petrol (Mar 85 - 94) B to M	1245
Ford Ka (96 - 02) P to 52	3570
Ford Mondeo Petrol (93 - Sept 00) K to X	1923
Ford Mondeo Petrol & Diesel (Oct 00 - Jul 03) X to 03	3990
Ford Mondeo Petrol & Diesel (July 03 - 07) 03 to 56	4619
Ford Mondeo Diesel (93 - 96) L to N	3465
Ford Orion Petrol (83 - Sept 90) up to H	1009
Ford Sierra 4-cyl Petrol (82 - 93) up to K	0903
Ford Sierra V6 Petrol (82 - 91) up to J	0904
Ford Transit Petrol (Mk 2) (78 - Jan 86) up to C	0719
Ford Transit Petrol (Mk 3) (Feb 86 - 89) C to G	1468
Ford Transit Diesel (Feb 86 - 99) C to T	3019
Ford Transit Diesel (00-06)	4775
Ford 1.6 & 1.8 litre Diesel Engine (84 - 96) A to N	1172
Ford 2.1, 2.3 & 2.5 litre Diesel Engine (77 - 90) up to H	1606
FREIGHT ROVER Sherpa Petrol (74 - 87) up to E	0463
HILLMAN Avenger (70 - 82) up to Y	0037
Hillman Imp (63 - 76) up to R *	0022
HONDA Civic (Feb 84 - Oct 87) A to E	1226
Honda Civic (Nov 91 - 96) J to N	3199
Honda Civic Petrol (Mar 95 - 00) M to X	4050
Honda Civic Petrol & Diesel (01 - 05) X to 55	4611
Honda CR-V Petrol & Diesel (01-06)	4747
Honda Jazz (01 - Feb 08) 51 - 57	4735
HYUNDAI Pony (85 - 94) C to M	3398
JAGUAR E Type (61 - 72) up to L *	0140
Jaguar MkI & II, 240 & 340 (55 - 69) up to H *	0098
Jaguar XJ6, XJ & Sovereign; Daimler Sovereign (68 - Oct 86) up to D	0242
Jaguar XJ6 & Sovereign (Oct 86 - Sept 94) D to M	3261
Jaguar XJ12, XJS & Sovereign; Daimler Double Six (72 - 88) up to F	0478
JEEP Cherokee Petrol (93 - 96) K to N	1943
LADA 1200, 1300, 1500 & 1600 (74 - 91) up to J	0413
Lada Samara (87 - 91) D to J	1610
LAND ROVER 90, 110 & Defender Diesel (83 - 07) up to 56	3017
Land Rover Discovery Petrol & Diesel (89 - 98) G to S	3016
Land Rover Discovery Diesel (Nov 98 - Jul 04) S to 04	4606
Land Rover Freelander Petrol & Diesel (97 - Sept 03) R to 53	3929
Land Rover Freelander Petrol & Diesel (Oct 03 - Oct 06) 53 to 56	4623

Title	Book No.
Land Rover Series IIA & III Diesel (58 - 85) up to C	0529
Land Rover Series II, IIA & III 4-cyl Petrol (58 - 85) up to C	0314
MAZDA 323 (Mar 81 - Oct 89) up to G	1608
Mazda 323 (Oct 89 - 98) G to R	3455
Mazda 626 (May 83 - Sept 87) up to E	0929
Mazda B1600, B1800 & B2000 Pick-up Petrol (72 - 88) up to F	0267
Mazda RX-7 (79 - 85) up to C *	0460
MERCEDES-BENZ 190, 190E & 190D Petrol & Diesel (83 - 93) A to L	3450
Mercedes-Benz 200D, 240D, 240TD, 300D & 300TD 123 Series Diesel (Oct 76 - 85)	1114
Mercedes-Benz 250 & 280 (68 - 72) up to L *	0346
Mercedes-Benz 250 & 280 123 Series Petrol (Oct 76 - 84) up to B *	0677
Mercedes-Benz 124 Series Petrol & Diesel (85 - Aug 93) C to K	3253
Mercedes-Benz A-Class Petrol & Diesel (98-04) S to 54	4748
Mercedes-Benz C-Class Petrol & Diesel (93 - Aug 00) L to W	3511
Mercedes-Benz C-Class (00-06)	4780
MGA (55 - 62) *	0475
MGB (62 - 80) up to W	0111
MG Midget & Austin-Healey Sprite (58 - 80) up to W *	0265
MINI Petrol (July 01 - 05) Y to 05	4273
MITSUBISHI Shogun & L200 Pick-Ups Petrol (83 - 94) up to M	1944
MORRIS Ital 1.3 (80 - 84) up to B	0705
Morris Minor 1000 (56 - 71) up to K	0024
NISSAN Almera Petrol (95 - Feb 00) N to V	4053
Nissan Almera & Tino Petrol (Feb 00 - 07) V to 56	4612
Nissan Bluebird (May 84 - Mar 86) A to C	1223
Nissan Bluebird Petrol (Mar 86 - 90) C to H	1473
Nissan Cherry (Sept 82 - 86) up to D	1031
Nissan Micra (83 - Jan 93) up to K	0931
Nissan Micra (93 - 02) K to 52	3254
Nissan Micra Petrol (03-07) 52 to 57	4734
Nissan Primera Petrol (90 - Aug 99) H to T	1851
Nissan Stanza (82 - 86) up to D	0824
Nissan Sunny Petrol (May 82 - Oct 86) up to D	0895
Nissan Sunny Petrol (Oct 86 - Mar 91) D to H	1378
Nissan Sunny Petrol (Apr 91 - 95) H to N	3219
OPEL Ascona & Manta (B Series) (Sept 75 - 88) up to F *	0316
Opel Ascona Petrol (81 - 88)	3215
Opel Astra Petrol (Oct 91 - Feb 98)	3156
Opel Corsa Petrol (83 - Mar 93)	3160
Opel Corsa Petrol (Mar 93 - 97)	3159
Opel Kadett Petrol (Nov 79 - Oct 84) up to B	0634
Opel Kadett Petrol (Oct 84 - Oct 91)	3196
Opel Omega & Senator Petrol (Nov 86 - 94)	3157
Opel Rekord Petrol (Feb 78 - Oct 86) up to D	0543
Opel Vectra Petrol (Oct 88 - Oct 95)	3158
PEUGEOT 106 Petrol & Diesel (91 - 04) J to 53	1882
Peugeot 205 Petrol (83 - 97) A to P	0932
Peugeot 206 Petrol & Diesel (98 - 01) S to X	3757
Peugeot 206 Petrol & Diesel (02 - 06) 51 to 06	4613
Peugeot 306 Petrol & Diesel (93 - 02) K to 02	3073
Peugeot 307 Petrol & Diesel (01 - 04) Y to 54	4147
Peugeot 309 Petrol (86 - 93) C to K	1266
Peugeot 405 Petrol (88 - 97) E to P	1559
Peugeot 405 Diesel (88 - 97) E to P	3198
Peugeot 406 Petrol & Diesel (96 - Mar 99) N to T	3394
Peugeot 406 Petrol & Diesel (Mar 99 - 02) T to 52	3982

* Classic reprint

* Classic reprint

CL24.08/09

Preserving Our Motoring Heritage

< The Model J Duesenberg
Derham Tourster.
Only eight of these
magnificent cars were
ever built – this is the
only example to be found
outside the United States
of America

Almost every car you've ever loved, loathed or desired is gathered under one roof at the Haynes Motor Museum. Over 300 immaculately presented cars and motorbikes represent every aspect of our motoring heritage, from elegant reminders of bygone days, such as the superb Model J Duesenberg to curiosities like the bug-eyed BMW Isetta. There are also many old friends and flames. Perhaps you remember the 1959 Ford Popular that you did your courting in? The magnificent 'Red Collection' is a spectacle of classic sports cars including AC, Alfa Romeo, Austin Healey, Ferrari, Lamborghini, Maserati, MG, Riley, Porsche and Triumph.

A Perfect Day Out

Each and every vehicle at the Haynes Motor Museum has played its part in the history and culture of Motoring. Today, they make a wonderful spectacle and a great day out for all the family. Bring the kids, bring Mum and Dad, but above all bring your camera to capture those golden memories for ever. You will also find an impressive array of motoring memorabilia, a comfortable 70 seat video cinema and one of the most extensive transport book shops in Britain. The Pit Stop Cafe serves everything from a cup of tea to wholesome, home-made meals or, if you prefer, you can enjoy the large picnic area nestled in the beautiful rural surroundings of Somerset.

John Haynes O.B.E.,
Founder and
Chairman of the
museum at the wheel
of a Haynes Light 12.

< Graham Hill's Lola
Cosworth Formula 1
car next to a 1934
Riley Sports.

The Museum is situated on the A359 Yeovil to Frome road at Sparkford, just off the A303 in Somerset. It is about 40 miles south of Bristol, and 25 minutes drive from the M5 intersection at Taunton.
Open 9.30am - 5.30pm (10.00am - 4.00pm Winter) 7 days a week, *except Christmas Day, Boxing Day and New Years Day*
Special rates available for schools, coach parties and outings Charitable Trust No. 292048